NEW MEXICO

PRIVATE LAND CLAIMS

HOUSE OF REPRESENTATIVES
36ᵀᴴ CONGRESS, 1ˢᵀ SESSION; EX. DOC. NO. 14

HERITAGE BOOKS
2019

HERITAGE BOOKS
AN IMPRINT OF HERITAGE BOOKS, INC.

Books, CDs, and more—Worldwide

For our listing of thousands of titles see our website
at
www.HeritageBooks.com

A Facsimile Reprint
Published 2019 by
HERITAGE BOOKS, INC.
Publishing Division
5810 Ruatan Street
Berwyn Heights, Md. 20740

Originally published 1860

— Publisher's Notice —
In reprints such as this, it is often not possible to remove blemishes from the original. We feel the contents of this book warrant its reissue despite these blemishes and hope you will agree and read it with pleasure.

International Standard Book Numbers
Paperbound: 978-0-7884-2721-3
Clothbound: 978-0-7884-6960-2

36TH CONGRESS, } HOUSE OF REPRESENTATIVES. { Ex. Doc.
1st Session. } { No. 14.

NEW MEXICO—PRIVATE LAND CLAIMS.

LETTER

FROM

THE SECRETARY OF THE INTERIOR,

COMMUNICATING

Documents in relation to private land claims in New Mexico.

FEBRUARY 10, 1860.—Referred to the Committee on Private Land Claims, and ordered to be printed.

DEPARTMENT OF THE INTERIOR,
Washington, February 3, 1860.

SIR: I have the honor herewith to transmit, for the action of Congress under the eighth section of the act approved July 22, 1854, the transcripts of nineteen private land claims in New Mexico, designed for the House of Representatives, as indicated in the letter of the Commissioner of the General Land Office, of the 30th November last, of which a copy is now enclosed.

Similar documents, submitted by the Commissioner in the same letter, for the Senate of the United States, have been this day transmitted to the presiding officer of that body.

Very respectfully, your obedient servant,

J. THOMPSON,
Secretary.

Hon. W. PENNINGTON,
Speaker of the House of Representatives.

GENERAL LAND OFFICE, *November* 30, 1859.

SIR: I have the honor to transmit herewith, in duplicate, the documents in relation to nineteen private land claims, numbers 20 to 38, both inclusive, in New Mexico, with the request that they may be laid before the ensuing Congress for their final action thereon. These claims have been investigated and approved by the surveyor general of New Mexico, with the exception of number 26, which has been rejected by him.

The foregoing documents are put up in two separate packages, marked "U. S. House Reps.," and "U. S. Senate," and each of the nineteen claims is accompanied by a schedule of documents specified in the exhibit " A " herewith.

I have the honor to be, very respectfully, your obedient servant,
S. A. SMITH,
Hon. J. THOMPSON, *Commissioner.*
Secretary of the Interior.

EXHIBIT A.

Private land claims and town site grants in New Mexico, as approved or rejected by the surveyor general of said Territory, submitted for the final confirmation of Congress.

Number of claim.	Names of claimants.	Number of accompanying docum't.	Description of documents composing each claim.
20	Town of Las Vegas and Thos. Baca et als.	9	1. Notice, (Thos. Baca et als;) 2. Grant—Spanish; 3. Grant—translation; 4. Testimony; 5. Notice, (town of Las Vegas;) 6. Grant—Spanish; 7. Grant—translation; 8. Testimony; and 9. Report
21	Town of Tajique............	5	1. Notice; 2. Grant—Spanish; 3. Grant—translation, 4. Testimony; 5. Report.
22	Town of Torreon............	6	1. Notice—Spanish; 2. Notice—translation; 3. Grant—Spanish; 4. Grant—translation; 5. Testimony; 6. Report.
23	Town of Manzano	7	1. Notice; 2. Power of attorney—Spanish; 3. Power of attorney—translation; 4. Grant—Spanish; 5. Grant—translation; 6. Testimony; 7. Report.
24	Town of San Isidro..........	5	1. Notice—Spanish; 2. Notice—translation; 3. Grant—Spanish; 4. Grant—translation; 5. Report.
25	Town of Cañon de San Diego...	6	1. Notice; 2. Notice—translation; 4. Grant—translation; 5. Testimony; 6. Report.
26	Juan B. Vigil et al.............	11	1. Notice; 2. Grant—Spanish; 3. Grant—translation; 4. Order of possession—translation; 5. Resignation of Chacon—translation; 6. Conveyance—Spanish; 7. Conveyance—translation; 8. Proclamation of Gen Kearney; 9. Testimony; 10. Report and notice of appeal.
27	Town of Las Trampas	6	1. Notice—Spanish; 2. Notice—translation; 3. Grant—Spanish; 4. Grant—translation; 5 Testimony; 6. Report.
28	Heirs of Sebastian Martin......	4	1. Notice; 2. Grant—Spanish; 3. Grant—translation; 4. Report.
29	Town of Antonchico	6	1. Notice; 2. Grant—Spanish; 3. Grant—translation; 4. Testimony; 5. Report; 6. Notice of appeal.
30	Indians of Laguna	9	1. Notice; 2. Grant No. 1—Spanish; 3. Grant No 1—translation; 4. Grant No. 2—Spanish; 5. Grant No. 2—translation; 6. Conveyance—Spanish; 7. Conveyance—translation; 8. Testimony; 9. Report. R. Pueblo of Laguna grant—Spanish; R. Pueblo of Laguna grant—translation.
31	Gaspar Ortiz.................	5	1. Notice; 2. Grant—Spanish; 3. Grant—translation; 4. Testimony; 5. Report.
32	Town of Mora................	7	1. Notice; 2. Grant—Spanish; 3. Grant—translation; 4. Receipt for deed—Spanish; 5. Receipt for deed—translation; 6. Testimony; 7. Report.
33	Heirs of P. Armendaris	9	1. Notice; 2. Additional petition; 3. Grant, testimony, &c.—Spanish; 4. Grant—translation; 5. Additional grant—translation; 6. Testimony—translation; 7. Testimony—translation; 8. Testimony; 9. Report.
34	Heirs of Pedro Armendaris.....	6	1. Notice and testimony—Spanish; 3. Grant—translation; 4. Testimony—translation; 5. Testimony; 6. Report.
35	Antonio Sandoval	5	1. Notice; 2. Grant—Spanish; 3. Grant—translation; 4. Testimony; 5. Report.
36	Town of Charnita	5	1. Notice; 2. Grant—original; 3. Grant—translation; 4. Testimony; 5. Report.
37	Town of Tejon	6	1. Notice—Spanish; 2. Notice—translation; 3. Certificate of possession—Spanish; 4. Certificate of possession—translation; 5. Testimony; 6. Report.
38	Ramon Vigil	4	1. Notice; 2. Grant—Spanish; 3. Grant—translation; 4. Report.

Documents composing claim No. 20.

1. Notice, Thomas Baca et al.
2. Grant, Spanish, Thomas Baca et al.
3. Grant, translation, Thomas Baca et al.
4. Testimony, Thomas Baca et al.
5. Notice, town of Las Vegas.
6. Grant, Spanish, town of Las Vegas.
7. Grant, translation, town of Las Vegas.
8. Testimony, town of Las Vegas.
9. Report.

CLAIM NO. 20.

TOWN OF LAS VEGAS.—THOMAS BACA et al.

NOTICE.

Territory of New Mexico,
County of Santa Fé.

To the Hon. William Pelham, surveyor general of the Territory of New Mexico, under the act of Congress approved July 22, A. D. 1854:

Your petitioners, the surviving heirs-at-law of one Luis Cabeza de Baca, deceased, would respectfully state that, on the 16th day of January, 1821, the provincial deputation of the State of Durango granted to the ancestor of your petitioners, Luis Cabeza de Baca, a tract of land called the "Las Vegas Grandes," and which said grant was afterwards ratified by the provincial deputation of New Mexico, and which said grant has for its boundaries the following landmarks, to wit: On the north the Chapellote river; on the south the boundary of San Miguel del Bado; on the east the Aguage de la Llegua and the boundary of Antonio Ortiz, and on the west the summit of the Pecos mountains, all of which will more fully appear by reference to the said grant, now on file in the office of the surveyor general, No. 137, and the grant to Antonio Ortiz, No. 727, and the grant to San Miguel del Bado, No. 125, to all of which reference is hereby made. Your petitioners further state that said lands, marks, and boundaries are well known and easily discovered, but inasmuch as no survey of said lands has as yet ever been made, the quantity of land included within said boundaries is unknown to your petitioners. Your petitioners further state that it will appear by reference to said grant that it was made to the said Luis Cabeza de Baca and his male children, and invested him and his male children with an absolute title to said lands.

Your petitioners further state that the said Luis Cabeza de Baca and his male children took possession of said lands under said grant, built a ranch upon said lands, and with their servants and stock, consisting of about six hundred mules and horses, continued to use, occupy, and possess the lands aforesaid, and after several years' peaceable and quiet occupancy of said lands they were driven away from them by the hostilities of the Indians, and the said six hundred mules and horses, of the value of thirty-six thousand dollars, were taken away by the said hostile Indians. Your petitioners further state that hostilities continued to exist upon the part of the Indians, so that said lands could not be occupied by them until about the year 1835, at which time a grant was made by the provincial deputation of New Mexico to Juan de Dios Maese, Miguel Archuleta, Manuel Duran, and twenty-five others, extending to any others desiring to settle within the grant to the lands of your petitioners, as will more fully appear by reference to said grant, now on file in the office of the surveyor general, and No. 12 on the docket book. Your petitioners further state that at the time said grant was made by the provincial deputation of New Mexico to the said Juan de Dios Maese and others, the said deputation, and said Juan de Dios and other grantees, well knew that said lands of right belonged to and were the lands of your petitioners under the previous grant of the State of Durango, confirmed and ratified by the provincial deputation of New Mexico, by means whereof the said grant is fraudulent and void, and the said Juan de Dios Maese and others acquired no title to said lands under said grant, and the said lands still rightfully belong to your petitioners.

Your petitioners further state that said lands are situated in the county of San Miguel, in the Territory of New Mexico. Your petitioners further state that said Luis Cabeza de Baca has long since departed this life, and the only male children of the said Luis Cabeza de Baca, now living, are the following, to wit: Luis Baca, Prudencio Baca, Jesus Baca the 1st, Felipe Baca, Jesus Baca the 2d, Domingo Baca, and Manuel Baca. Your petitioners further state that the following sons of Luis Cabeza de Baca are dead, to wit: Juan Antonio Baca, José Baca, José Miguel Baca, Ramon Baca, and Matio Baca; and, at the time of their decease, they left the following children and heirs-at-law then surviving, to wit: Juan Antonio Baca left him surviving the following children: Jesus Maria Baca, Francisco Tomas Baca, Incarnacion Baca, José Baca, Josefa Baca, Guadalupe Baca, Altagracia Baca, Nicolas Baca, Tomas Baca, and Trinidad Baca. José Baca left him surviving the following children: Antonio Baca, Felipe Baca, José Maria Baca, Francisco Baca, Fernando Baca, and Polonio Baca. José Miguel Baca left him surviving the following children, to wit: Diego Baca, Quirina Baca, Romaldo Baca, Guadalupe Baca, Paulina Baca, and Martina Baca. Ramon Baca left him surviving the following child, to wit: Ygnacio Baca. Mateo Baca left him surviving the following children, to wit: Luis Baca, Alejandro Baca, Juan de Dios Baca, and Martin Baca. Your petitioners further state that the foregoing list contains all the surviving heirs of the said Luis Cabeza de Baca, deceased, known to your petitioners, and they are all residents of the Territory of New Mexico. Your petitioners further state that the infancy of many of said heirs, the internal revolutions of the republic of Mexico, the war with the United States, and the acquisition of this Territory by the United

States, have hitherto prevented them from regaining possession of said lands thus wrongfully taken from them. Your petitioners therefore ask that their title be investigated, and that such steps be taken in the premises as will secure to them the benefits of said grant, and a legal title to the same under the said act of Congress of July 22, 1854. All of which is respectfully submitted.

JOHN S. WATTS,
Attorney for Petitioners.

SURVEYOR GENERAL'S OFFICE,
Santa Fé, New Mexico, August 31, 1859.

The above is a true copy of the original on file in this office.

WM. PELHAM,
Surveyor General.

GRANT—SPANISH.

EXELENTISIMO SEÑOR: El ciudadano Juan Antonio Cabeza de Baca á nombre de su padre Don Luis Maria por la mejor via y en la nas bastante forma á V. E. hace presente que en el 16 de Enero de 1821, elevó mi citado padre ante la Exma. Diputacion, proval de Durango la representacion que devidamente acompaño y en su consecuencia se dispuso lo que el actual Señor Gefe Politico transcribe al Alcalde del Bado en el oficio que de la misma manera acompaño.

Estos legales pasos pintos con lo que el Señor Gefe Politico en su citado oficio mando al Alcalde del Bado han hecho creer á mi padre que el terreno llamado comunmente Las Vegas Grandes es propiamente suyo y por, lo mismo no deve ser donado deviendo advertir á V. E. que dicho terreno ha estado ocupado con nuestros bienes, y de consiguiente se ha llamado mi padre poseedor de él, mas si acaso la falta de no tener mi padre el documento de posesion es motivo para que no reconozca á nosotros el terreno referido, suplico á V. E. tenga la bondad de tomar en consideracion que esta falta no es calpa de mi padre, pues jamas ha dejado de reclamar, y antes si creo es preferente á cualesquiera otro tanto por el tiempo que ha poseido aquel terreno como por los pasos que ha dado para lograr con plenitud su solicitud. Por tanto á V. E. pido y suplico se sirva mandar se estienda en favor de mi citado padre el respectivo documento con los requisitos necesarios por ser asi de justicia.

SANTA FÉ, 15 *de Febrero de* 1825.

JUAN ANTONIO CABEZA DE BACA.

Se presentó esta solicitud en la sesion del dia 16 de Febrero de 1826, y en la misma quedó despachada en favor de la parte á cuyo nombre representó D. Juan Antonio Cabeza de Baca.

[Rubric.]

Don Luis Maria Cabeza de Baca, vecino en la provincia del Nuevo Mexico, por si y diez y siete hijos varones se presenta ante el supremo tribunal de la diputacion de provincia correspondiente á la del Nuevo Mexico, á quien corresponde la demarcacion y reparto de terrenos valdios y sin dominio y dice que hallandose en los terminos indicados un sitio propio para labor y pasteos nombrandose Las Vegas Grandes en el rio de las Gallinas jurisdiccion del Bado y no gozar de ninguna amplitud y si mucha estreches en el que ruido de lo que resulta graves perjuicios, por tales motivos suplico se me haga gracia y adjudique el referido sitio para los fines que refiere y con desaogo cultivar sas campos adelantar por este medio la agricultura pastear los animales que la providencia se ha servido darme y proporcionar por este medio el sociego y tranquilidad que solicito.

Esta misma solicitud hize á el gobierno de esta provincia y en decreto de 18 del proximo, pasado Febrero se me adjudica en compañia de ocho vecinos del Bado, estos tenicado propiedad de tierras donadas no les interesa para lo que solo con el numero de mis citados hijos hago la nueva solicitud amparado de las savias y beneficas desposiciones de las soberanas cortes. Por tanto suplico al supremo tribunal á quien privativamente compete esta gracia se digne concedermela con sus respectivos linderos, y son por el norte el rio del Chapellote, por el sur el lindero del Bado, por el pomente la cumbre de la sierra del Pecos, y por el Oriente el Aguage de la Llegua y el lindero de Don Antonio Ortiz, gracia que espero de la benignidad del referido supremo tribunal.

Nuevo Mexico, *y* 16 *de Enero de* 1821.

LUIS MARIA CABEZA DE BACA.

Por representacion de Don Luis Maria Cabeza de Baca dirigida á la Exma. Diputacion Provincial de Durango en 16 de Enero de 1821, estando sageta esta provincia á aquella ilustre corporacion é informe hecho por el Señor Gobernador Coronel Don Facundo Melgares, sobre el contenido de la referida representacion la su consecuencia tuvo á bien poner la orden que á la letra es como signe:

" Supuesto que los socios de Don Luis Maria Cabeza de Baca tienen otros terrenos en que poder mantener sus ganados ha determinado esta diputacion que se adjudique al segundo el llamado comanmente Las Vegas Grandes siempre que aguellos no hayan fabricado casas alli ó emprendido otros gastos á no ser que voluntariamente se contengan en que se lo reintegre Baca asignandoles en la parte que digevon ellos mismos igual porcion á la que disputaban en las Vegas. Lo que participo á V. para su cumplimiento y á fin de que la porga en noticia de los interesados. Dios guarde á V. muchos años. Durango, 29 de Mayo, de 1821. Diego Garcia Condé, Miguel de Zubirria, Señor Gobernador de Nuevo Mexico."

Y lo inserto á V. para que en cumplimiento de lo dispuesto pase al espresado sitio á mercenar al referido D. Luis Maria Cabeza de Baca, en los terminos que espresa sa representacion que se acompaña á este respecto de no haber emprendido ningun trabajo los ocho vecinos del Bado que en sa primer instancia lo habian acompañado formando V. á continuacion de la referida representacion el espediente correspondiente que vendra á este archivo de donde se le dará testimonio de hijuela al interesado. Dios gñe á V. muchos Años.

Santa Fé, 17 *de Octubre de* 1823.

BARTOLOMÉ BACA.

Sr. Alcalde del Bado, D. Manuel Antonio Baca.

Sesion publica del dia 16 de Febrero de 1825, Libro 2° de las Actas de las sesiones de sa excelencia á fojas 40 parafo 3 le leyó una solicitud de D. Juan Antonio Cabeza de Baca referiendose á la concesion de terrenos que le hizo en 1821, la Exma. Diputacion Proval. de Durango á cuya corporacion en aquella fecha correspondia al Nuevo Mexico. Se resolvió se le estienda la correspondiente diligencia dandose legitimo testimonio de ella al interesado y corroborandose la merced dada por fha. corporacion en la fha. ya citado cuyo documento será presentado como corresponde al Alcalde Territorial del Bado, para que con presencia de la merced dada á D. Salvador Montoya se le ponga al referido Don Luis Maria Cabeza de Baca é hijos varones en posesion del referido terreno con arreglo á lo que sobre la materia se ha acordado y á la parte sin perjuicio do tercero se le ha concedido. Antonio Ortiz, presidente; Pedro Garcia, José Francisco Baca, José José Francisco Ortiz, Pedro Bautista Pino, Matias Ortis; Juan Bautista Vigil, secretario.

Por mandado de su ex.,

JUAN BAUTISTA VIGIL, *Srio.*

SAN MIGUEL DEL BADO, 26 *de Dic. de* 1829.

Sin embargo de haber ocurrido Don Miguel Baca y Don Mateo Baca, el 2° en la tarde del dia sobre que reïntegrará la posesion que la Exma. Diputacion adjudico á D. Luis Maria Cabeza de Baca é hijos y no pudiendo verificarlo por haber publicado vando á los ciudadanos de mi cargo para el 21 para dar principio á la eleccion de mi subsesor y ayuntamiento y al 2° dia de la eleccion me enfermé de tal modo de que suspendi la eleccion hasta 3° que concluí, al 5° me resultó mi enfermedad pues hasta me confesé como constará por los enviados de D. Luis Maria Cabeza de Baca, y estos han sido los motivos de no haber dado cumplimiento al orden

TOMAS SENA, *Alcalde Constitucional.*

SANTA FÉ, *Enero* 13 *de* 1826.

Proceda el alcalde constitucional del Bado á dar la posesion concedida.

NORBONA.

Sor. Comte. Gral. y Gob. de este Territorio:

El ciudadano Luis Maria Cabeza de Baca, con la mayor sumision y respecto anto V. S. parece y dice que con motivo de tener hechos repetidos reclamos á los Señores Alcaldes del Bado sobre que se me valla á posesionar en el parage que comunmente llaman Las Vegas que tengo donado por la Exma. Diputacion Provincial de Durango, desde el año de 1821, y acuerdo de la Exma. Diputacion de este Territorio, como consta por los documentos que acompañan á esta mi presentacion que constan de cinco fojas utiles y un manifiesto del Señor

Alcalde D. Tomas Sena, los que impondrān á V. S. para su resolucion—por lo que suplico á V. S. si me asistiere alguna justicia se sirva pasar orden al alcalde del partido del Bado, pase á cumplir lo dispuesto.

Santa Fé, 13 de Enero de 1826.
LUIS MARIA CABEZA DE BACA,
Perseguido.

Surveyor General's Office,
Santa Fé, N. M., (*Translator's Department,*)
August 25, 1859.

The foregoing is a true copy of the original now on file in this office.
DAVID V. WHITING,
Translator.

GRANT—TRANSLATION.

Secretary's office of the
Most Excellent Territorial Deputation of New Mexico.

I, the undersigned, secretary of the most excellent territorial deputation of Santa Fé, New Mexico, certify that in the book in which are recorded the proceedings of said most excellent deputation, on the fortieth page of said book, is to be found the action taken on a petition presented by Don Juan Antonio Cabeza de Baca, in the following words literally taken therefrom, viz:

Most excellent sir: The citizen Juan Antonio Cabeza de Baca, in the name of his father, Don Luis Maria, in the best form and most approved manner represents to your excellency that on the 16th day of January, 1821, my said father presented to the most excellent provincial deputation of Durango the petition herewith presented, and it was therefore ordered by that body that the communication addressed by the present political chief to the justice of the peace of El Bado, which is herewith presented, be concurred in.

These legal steps, together with those taken by the political chief in his communication addressed to the justice of El Bado, have caused my father to believe that the lands commonly called Las Vegas Grandes are his property, and consequently should not be granted away, at the same time calling your excellency's attention to the fact that said lands have been occupied with our stock, and my father has consequently been considered its proper owner; further, if the fact of my father not being able to produce the documents of possession will be any cause for not recognizing said land as his, I pray your excellency to take into consideration that my father is not to be blamed in this matter, as he has never ceased to present his claim; on the contrary, it should be preferred to all others, not only on account of the length of time which he has held it, but also for having taken the steps necessary to complete his perfect title thereto. Therefore I pray your excellency to cause the proper title deed to be issued in favor of my aforesaid father, with all the necessary requisites, being in justice due to him.

Santa Fé, *February* 16, 1825.
JUAN ANTONIO CABEZA DE BACA.

Don Luis Maria Cabeza de Baca, resident of the province of New Mexico, for himself and in the name of seventeen male children, appears before the supreme tribunal of the deputation of the province of New Mexico, to whom corresponds the distribution and marking out of the unclaimed public lands, and states that a certain tract of land suitable for cultivation and pasturage, called the Vegas Grandes, on the Gallinas river, in the jurisdiction of El Bado, being in the above condition, and not having sufficient room, and being very much confined, I suffer a great many injuries: therefore I pray that the aforesaid tract of land be granted to me for the purposes above mentioned, in order that I may with convenience cultivate the soil and advance the interests of agriculture, pasture the animals Providence has been pleased to favor me with, and live in the quietude and repose I aspire to.

This same petition was presented to the government of this province, and in a decree of the 18th of February last the grant was made to me in company with eight citizens of El Bado. These persons having other grants take no interest in this grant. I therefore, with my said children, renew my application under the protection of the wise and beneficent laws of the sovereign cortes. I therefore pray the supreme tribunal, to whose jurisdiction belongs the conferring of this grant, to donate it to me, with the following boundaries, which are: on the north the Chapellote river; on the south the boundary of El Bado; on the west the summit of the Pecos mountain; on the east the Aguage de la Llegua and the boundary of Don Antonio Cortiz—a benefaction which I expect from the liberality of the aforesaid supreme tribunal.

NEW MEXICO, *January* 16, 1821.
LUIS MARIA CABEZA DE BACA. [Rubric.]

In view of the petition presented by Don Luis Maria Cabeza de Baca to the most excellent provincial deputation of Durango on the 16th day of January, 1821, this province being subordinate to that corporation, and the report made by his excellency the governor Colonel Facundo Melgares, touching the contents of said petition, therefore they saw proper to issue an order which is literally as follows: Supposing that the partners of Don Luis Maria Cabeza de Baca have other lands where they can pasture their stock, this deputation has determined to grant unto the second the land commonly called the Vegas Grandes, provided the others have erected no buildings on said lands or incurred other expenses, unless they shall agree that the amounts disbursed be refunded to them by the aforesaid Baca, assigning to them a portion equal to that held by them in the Vegas Grandes, in the place to be designated by themselves, of which you are hereby informed, so that you may cause the same to be complied with and the parties interested be informed thereof. God preserve you many years. Durango, May 29, 1821. Signed, Diego Garcia Conde. Signed, Miguel de Zubirria. To his excellency the governor of New Mexico. And I enclose the same to you in order that, in compliance with what has been ordered, you proceed to place the

aforesaid Luis Maria Cabeza de Baca in possession, according to the terms set forth in his petition, which is herewith enclosed, the eight citizens included in his first petition having placed no improvements on the aforesaid land, placing immediately after his petition the proceedings had by you in the premises, which will be returned to these archives, from whence a certified copy will be given to the party interested. God preserve you many years. Santa Fé, October 17, 1823.
BARTOLOMÉ BACA.
Don MANUEL ANTONIO BACA, *Justice of El Bado.*

Public session of the 16th day of February, 1825, book second of the proceedings of said body, page 40, section 3.

A petition from Don Juan Antonio Cabeza de Baca was read, referring to the grant of land made to him in one thousand eight hundred and twenty-one by the most excellent provincial deputation of Durango, to which corporation New Mexico was subject at that period. It was resolved that the proper writ be issued, giving a copy thereof to the party interested, and confirming the grant made by said corporation on the date aforesaid; which documents will be presented, as required, to the territorial justice of El Bado, who, having then there the grant made to Don Salvador Montoya, will place the aforesaid Don Luis Maria Cabeza de Baca and male children in possession of the aforesaid land according to the action had in the premises, and which has been granted to the party without injury to any third party.

ANTONIO ORTIZ, *President.*
PEDRO GARCIA.
JOSE FRANCISCO BACA.
JOSE FRANCISCO ORTIZ.
PEDRO BAUTISTA PINO.
MATIAS ORTIZ.
JUAN BAUTISTA VIGIL, *Secretary.*

SANTA FÉ, *February* 27, 1825.
A correct copy of the original deposited in the archives of this most excellent deputation of New Mexico, under my charge.
JUAN BAUTISTA VIGIL, *Secretary.*

Fees for the present copy, twenty hard dollars.
VIGIL.

SAN MIGUEL DE BADO, *December* 26, 1825.
Although Don Miguel Baca and Don Mateo Baca appeared before me on the 20th, in the afternoon, asking the restoration of the land granted to Don Luis Maria Cabeza de Baca and children by the most excellent deputation, and not being able to do so on account of having promulgated an order to the citizens of my jurisdiction to commence on the 21st an election for my successor and members of the corporation, and having been so much indisposed on the second day of the election that I suspended said election until the 3d, and which I terminated on the 5th, my disease having reached its crisis, and was

obliged to confess, as will be proven by the messengers of Don Luis Maria Cabeza de Baca, and these have been the reasons for not having complied with the order.

THOMAS SENA, *Constitutional Justice.*
Santa Fé, *January* 13, 1826.

Let it proceed to the constitutional justice of El Bado, to give the possession granted.

NARBONA.

To his excellency the Commanding General and Governor of this Territory:

The citizen Luis Maria Cabeza de Baca with the greatest submission and respect appears before you and states: That having applied several times to the justices of El Bado to place me in possession of the tract commonly called Las Vegas Grandes, granted to me by the provincial deputation of Durango in the year 1821, and confirmed by the most excellent deputation of this Territory, as will appear by the documents accompanying this my petition, and contained in five written pages, and the statement of the justice Don Thomas Sena, which will give you the information you may require in your decision, I therefore pray your excellency that, if I have any right, you will be pleased to direct the justice of the precinct of El Bado to fulfil what has been rd ered.

LUIS MARIA CABEZA DE BACA, *persecuted.*
Santa Fé, *January* 13, 1826.

Surveyor General's Office, Translator's Department,
Santa Fé, New Mexico, July 31, 1859.

The foregoing is a correct translation from the original Spanish on file in this office.

DAVID V. WHITING, *Translator.*

Surveyor General's Office,
Santa Fé, New Mexico, September 17, 1859.

The foregoing is a true copy from the original now on file in this office.

WM. PELHAM, *Surveyor General.*

TESTIMONY.

Evidence on the part of defendants.

Donaciano Vigil sworn:

Question. Have you any interest in this claim?

Answer. I have no interest in this claim; I live beyond the limits of the grant.

Question. Did you know Ramon Obren in the year 1835, and what office did he hold?

Answer. I did; he was secretary of the provincial deputation.

Question. Is his signature to all the documents pertaining to the grant of Las Vegas genuine?

Answer. It is; I know his signature, having seen him write.

Question. Do you know the signature of Francisco Saricino; have you seen him write; and what office did he hold in 1835?

Answer. I know his signature. The one appended to the document shown me is genuine; I have seen him write; I believe he was political chief in 1835.

Question. Do you know the grant of Las Vegas, and do you know when it was settled, and who were the first settlers?

Answer. I do not; I believe it was settled between the years 1833 and 1835. Manuel Duran and Juan de Dios Maese were the first settlers that I knew.

Question. What was the custom of granting lands in 1819, and what power had the government of Durango to make grants in this Territory at that time?

Answer. Under the Spanish government the power to grant lands was vested in the governors. The department of Durango ought not to have had any power to grant lands in this Territory, as it had a civil government of its own, and the governor had authority to make grants. At that time the government of Mexico was divided into three military departments, to whom all civil suits were appealed. The local and economical governments of the different towns was confided to the governors of the provinces, and especially the granting of lands.

Question. How old are you, and what offices have you held under the governments of Mexico and the United States?

Answer. I am 56 years old. Under the Mexican government I had charge of the secretary's office of the military department from 1824 to 1836. After that period I had charge of the secretary's office under the civil authorities at different times. Under that of the United States I was secretary of state from 1846 to 1851.

Question. After the establishment of the Mexican government, in whom was vested the power to grant land?

Answer. After the change of government the laws remained the same until the power was afterwards vested in the provincial deputation, although this step was not necessary, as the power was always vested in the governors. After 1836 the power to grant lands was extended to the prefects of the districts.

DONACIANO VIGIL.

Sworn and subscribed before me this 6th day of April, 1858.
WM. PELHAM,
Surveyor General.

Testimony for defendants.

José Miguel Sanchez sworn:

Question. Have you any interest in this claim, and where do you reside?

Answer. I have not; I reside at Tecolote.

Question. Do you know the grant to Las Vegas made to Juan de Dios Maese, Manuel Duran, and others?
Answer. I do.
Question. Is your own signature and that of José Ulibarri to the deed of possession to petitioners to Las Vegas grant genuine?
Answer. They are.
Question. What office did you and José Ulibarri hold at the time that document was signed?
Answer. José Ulibarri was justice of the peace at that time, and I was his clerk.
Question. Were the lands divided out between the individuals contained in the list attached to the grant at that time?
Answer. They were.
Question. Was there any other settlement upon any portion of the Vegas grant when these lands were distributed?
Answer. There was none that I knew of.
Question. Did you receive any notice from Luis Maria Baca, or any other person, of any adverse claim to the lands distributed?
Answer. We did not.
Question. How long have you lived in the county of San Miguel?
Answer. Since 1816.
Question. Was there any settlement there at any time prior to the parties being placed in possession by you; and if so, what was the nature of the settlement, and by whom was it settled?
Answer. I knew of none up to the time the parties were placed in possession by us.
Question. Do you know of any persons pasturing cattle there previous to this purchase, and who were they?
Answer. I do not.
Question. Had you been often upon the land before these parties were placed in possession?
Answer. I had not.

JOSÉ MIGUEL SANCHEZ.

Sworn and subscribed before me this 7th day of April, 1858.
WM. PELHAM,
Surveyor General.

JOSÉ DE JESUS ULIBARRI sworn:

Question. Have you any interest in this grant, and where do you reside?
Answer. I reside at Las Vegas.
Witness excused.

JOSÉ ANTONIO CASADOS sworn:

Question. Have you any interest in this claim, and where do you reside?
Answer. I have not; I live at Las Vegas.
Question. How old are you?
Answer. Seventy years of age.

Question. Do you know the Vegas grant; and when was it first settled, to your knowledge?

Answer. I do; it was first settled in the year 1831. Manuel Duran, Miguel Martinez, Miguel Archuleta, Juan de Dios Maese, Juan José Martinez, Rafael Rodriguez, Sebastian Duran, and Juan Pedro Archuleta were among the first settlers. I was a shepherd at that time, and with them several times.

Question. Were there any settlements of any kind previous to that time, within your knowledge?

Answer There were none.

Question. What was your opportunity of knowing there was none?

Answer. Because I was over the entire country with the stock under my charge.

Question. Whose stock did you have charge of; and was there any other stock pastured there, and to whom did it belong?

Answer. It belonged to Don Antonio Ortiz, of Santa Fé. Cattle of José Antonio Ulibarri and Esteban Lopez, and others, pastured there at the same time. There was a small body of troops stationed there at the time.

Question. Where was the body of troops stationed, and in what year?

Answer. On the opposite side of the river, where the town of Las Vegas is now situated. The troops were there from 1829.

Question. Did you know those lands in 1819, 1820, and 1821?

Answer. I was there for the first time in 1829.

Question. How long have you lived in San Miguel, and where did you live previous to your removal to San Miguel?

Answer. I have lived there since 1820; I lived in Santa Fé before my removal there

Question. Did you know Luis Maria Baca; and where did he live up to the time of his death, and where have his children lived since?

Answer. I did. He and his children lived at Peña Blanca.

JOSÉ ANTONIO CASADOS.

Sworn and subscribed before me this 7th day of April, 1858.
WM. PELHAM,
Surveyor General.

Testimony for defendant.

MIGUEL SENA Y QUINTANA sworn:

Question. Where do you live? Have you any interest in the claim of Tomas Baca, or the town of Vegas?

Answer. I reside at San Miguel. I have no interest in either.

Question. Do you know the grant of Las Vegas, and when was it first settled, and by whom?

Answer. I know the town of Vegas, but I do not know its boundaries; I believe it was some time between 1830 and 1834; it was settled by several persons from San Miguel, among whom were Juan de Dios Maese, Manuel Duran, Miguel Martin, and others.

Question. How long have you lived at San Miguel?
Answer. Since 1820.
Question. Were there any settlements on the Vegas lands from that time until it was settled by Juan de Dios Maese and others?
Answer. I did not know of any settlement made there; I live about eight or nine leagues from Las Vegas.
Question. Did you know of any grant made to Luis Maria Baca to the Vegas land, or did you know of his having a ranch or stock upon the land?
Answer. I did not know that he had any grant then; he pastured his stock on the Vegas lands, but I do not know by what authority.
MIGUEL SENA Y QUINTANA.

Sworn and subscribed before me this 6th day of April, 1858.
WM. PELHAM,
Surveyor General.

Testimony for defendants.

DOMINGO GUTIERREZ sworn:

Question. Have you any interest in this claim, and where do you reside?
Answer. I have none; I reside in San Miguel.
Question. How old are you, and how long have you lived in San Miguel?
Answer. I am 64 years old; I have lived in San Miguel 22 years.
Question. Do you know the Vegas grant?
Answer. I have known the grant since it has been settled up to this time.
Question. Who were the first settlers upon it?
Answer. Miguel Martinez, Manuel Duran, Rafael Rodriguez, Juan de Dios Maese; I saw them when they commenced building.
Question. By whom were they placed in possession?
Answer. By José Ulibarri, who was a justice of the peace at that time.
Question. Did you know of any settlement previous to that time?
Answer. I did not.
Question. Were you upon the land before the grant was made?
Answer. I was not.
Question. How many persons do you believe are upon the grant at the present time?
Answer. I do not know; there are a great many; I know the two towns of Vegas, the upper and the lower one.
DOMINGO GUTIERREZ.

Sworn and subscribed before me this 7th day of April, 1858.
WM. PELHAM,
Surveyor General.

For defendants.

DAVID V. WHITING sworn:

Question. Have you ever seen any grant made by the department of Durango, or any of the departments of Mexico, to lands lying in the Territory of New Mexico?
Answer. I have not.
Question. What office do you now hold, and what opportunities have you had of examining the archives?
Answer. I hold the office of chief clerk of the land office in this Territory. The archives of the office are under my charge, and a greater portion of the land titles now in the office were selected by me from the archives of the Territory.
Question. By whom were the other grants in the Territory made in the year 1819, if you know of any?
Answer. I do not recollect if there are any others on file. If there are, I cannot remember them now.

DAVID V. WHITING.

Sworn and subscribed before me this 19th of April, 1858.
WM. PELHAM,
Surveyor General.

SURVEYOR GENERAL'S OFFICE,
Santa Fé, New Mexico, August 20, 1859.

The above is a true copy of the original on file in this office.
WM. PELHAM,
Surveyor General.

NOTICE.

UNITED STATES OF AMERICA, }
Territory of New Mexico. }

To the Hon. William Pelham, Surveyor General of the Territory of New Mexico:

Francisco Lopez and Henry Connelly and Hilario Gonzales, on behalf of themselves and a large number of citizens of the United States, residents of the town of Las Vegas and its vicinity, in the county of San Miguel, Territory of New Mexico, represent to your honor that they and the citizens they represent are the claimants and legal owners of a certain tract of land lying and being situate in the county of San Miguel, in the Territory of New Mexico, which said land was granted by the provincial deputation of said Territory in the year A. D. 1835, to Juan de Dios Maese, Miguel Archuleta, Manuel Duran, and José Antonio Casados, in their own behalf and that of twenty-five other inhabitants of said county, which said grant is now filed with this petition, (with leave to refer thereto as often as may be necessary,) and the boundaries of said grant are as follows, to wit: Bounded on the north by the Sapello river, on the south by the boundary grant of Don Antonio Ortiz, on the east the Aguage de la Llegua, and on the west the grant of San Miguel del Bado; and the said claimants claim under and by virtue of settlements made under said original grant, and in conformity with the terms of said grant. Your petitioners refer to the laws, usages and customs of Mexico in force at the time of the making of said grant, to the Spanish laws and regulations which were declared and recognized by the government of Mexico to be in force and effect. For which power and authority, see Collection of the Decrees and Orders of the Cortes of Spain, published by Mariano Galvan in 1829, page 56, and from page 91 to 101; see also Decrees of Mexico of June 4 and September 18, 1823, pages 123 and 180, 2 vol. Collection of Decrees; see, also, Ordenanzas de Tierras y Aguas, page 8; Peters' Reports, 436; 1 Howard, 24; 15th Peters, 130; 6th Peters, 621; Holcomb's U. S. Digest, pages 358 to 363.

The said claimants cannot show the quantity of land embraced in said grant, except as the same are set forth in the boundaries of said grant, nor can they furnish a plat of survey of said grant, as no survey of the land has ever been executed.

Your petitioners, the claimants, are also informed and believe that Thomas Cabeza de Baca, for himself and others, are claimants, also, for the lands embraced in said grant and now claimed by your petitioners. Your petitioners pray that their claim and title to said lands be examined as required by law, and that said grant be confirmed to them; and, as in duty bound, will ever pray, &c.

SMITH, HOUGHTON & ASHURST,
For Petitioners.

SURVEYOR GENERAL'S OFFICE,
Santa Fé, New Mexico, August 20, 1859.

The above is a true copy of the original on file in this office.

WM. PELHAM,
Surveyor General.

GRANT—SPANISH.

Sello Tercero. [SELLO.] Dos Reales.

Para los años de mil ochocientos veinte y seis y ochocientos veinte y siete.

YLUSTRE AYUNTAMIENTO: Los ciudadanos Juan de Dios Maese, Miguel Archuleta, Manuel Durán, y José Antonio Casaos, por si y á nombre de veinte y cinco hombres ante V. S. en la mejor y bastante, forma y con arreglo á derecho parecemos y decimos, que teniendo registrado un terreno valdio é inculto conocido comunmente con el nombre de Las Begas, situado en el Rio de las Gallinas, distante de esta poblacion como cinco leguas cuyo terreno solicitamos para formar una regulas sementera teniendo esto los ejidos correspondientes para pastos y abrevaderos, siendo sus linderos por el norte con el Rio del Sapelló, por el sur con el lindero de la merced de Don Antonio Ortiz, por el oriente con el Aguage de la Yegua, por el poniente con el lindero de la merced de San Miguel del Bado, cuya solicitud le haremos sin perjuicio de tercero ni del Nacional * * * * comprometiendonos á recibir la posesion, que pedimos á nombre de la Federacion y cumplir con las condiciones razonables y equitatibas que V. S. en huso de sus atribuciones se sirva poner para la concepcion del terreno sirbiendose pasar esta nuestra instancia al conocimiento de la Exma. Diputacion Territorial prebio el informe de estilo que segun las Leges está encomendado á V. S. para que sa Exa. se sirva mandar se nos dé la referida posesion en la cual se interesa el fomento de la agricultura y bienestar de barias familias desacomodadas, y en cuya virtud: A V. S. pedimos y suplicamos que habiendonos por presentados se sirva deferir á nuestra solicitud en la cual juramos no proceder de malicia y en lo necesario &a.

JUAN DE DIOS MAESE.
MIGUEL ARCHULETA.
MANUEL DURÁN.
JOSÉ ANTONIO CASAOS.

SAN MIGUEL DEL BADO, *Marzo* 20 *de* 1835.

SANTA FÉ, *Marzo* 24, 1835.

Con esta fha. se previene al Alcalde del Bado que proceda en conformidad con lo dispuesto pr. S. E. la Diputacion y este Gobierno.

SARRACINO.

SAN MIGUEL DEL BADO EN LA SALA CONSISTORIAL,
Marzo de 20 *de* 1835.

Por havida la antecedente solicitud por los que los subscriben, esta corporacion deseosa de protejer el aumento de la agricultura y acomodo en tanta familia desacomodada ser cierto ser un terreno valdio el indicado terreno de que se solicit * * * * * juicio de tercero ni del * * * * haber y deseoso de sus man * * * * osos pase esta instancia á la * * * Diputacion Territorial para que * * S. E. habien lo tubiere digne proveerles el terreno solicitado que con ansia se aspiro su vinculacion.

JOSÉ ULIBARRI,
Presidente.

FRANCISCO SENA, Regidor 1º.
GERONIMO GONZALES, Regidor 2º.
JOSÉ CANDELARIO FLORES, Regidor 3º.
LORENZO LUCERO, Regidor 4º.
TOMAS ARAGÓN, Procurador Sind'o.
Ante mí.

JOSÉ ANTONIO CASAOS,
Srio. de Ayuntamiento.

Quaderno 1ro. fo. 6.

Secretaria de la E. Diputacion de Nuebo Mejico, Santa Fé, 23 de Marzo, de 1835.

En acuerdo de hoy ha resuelto S. E. lo que signe :

"Se consede posesion de terreno dentro de los linderos espresados en esta instancia no solamente á los que solicitan ni á los vecinos del Bado, sino generalmente á todo el que se haya desprovisto de tierras pa. lavor con advertencia de que la merced de estos terrenos es sin perjuicio de pastos y abrevaderos comunes, para todo lo cual el Sr. Gefe Político reciverá los solicitudes que se hagan y las mandará proveer conforme lo dispuesto."

En consecuencia de lo dispuesto pase esta Instancia original al Sr. Gefe, Politico para que se sirba ejecutar el mandado por esta E. Diputacion de cuya orden pongo el presente.

R. ABREU, *Srio.*

En representacion de los vecinos * * * Juan de Dios Maese, Miguel Archuleta, Manuel Durán y José Antonio Casaos por si y á nombre de veinte y cinco individuos mas fha. 20 del corriente en qe. solicitan terreno en las Begas ha acordado S. E. la Diputacion Territorial como propio de su resorte lo siguiente:

"Quaderno 1º, folio 6. Sria. de la Exma. Diputacion de Nuebo Mexico, Santa Fé, 23 de Marzo de 1835. En acuerdo de hoy ha resuelto S. E. lo que signe. Se concede posesion de terreno dentro de los linderos espresados en esta instancia no solamente á los qe. solicitan ni á los vecinos del Bado sino generalmente á todo él que se haye desprovisto de tierras para labor con advertencia de qe. la merced de estos terrenos es sin perjuicio de pastos y abrebaderos comunes pa. todo lo cual el Sor. Gefe Político reciverá las solicitudes que se hagan y lasmandará proveer co * * * lo dispuesto. En consecuencia de * * * pase esta Instancia original al Señor Gefe Político pa. qe. se sirva ejecutar lo mandado por esta E. Diputacion de cuya orden pongo el presente.

"RAMON ABREU, *Secretario.*"

Y lo comunico á V. para su mas amplida observancia advirtiendole que las donaciones que haga serán con arreglo á las proporciones de cada uno de los solicitantes á fin de que no dejen sin cultura el terreno que se les señale siendo muy combeniente tambien decir á V. que debe señelarles á los posesionados un parage para una plaza que deverá formar sus habitaciones con todo lo demas que V. crea combeniente para la seguridad de los vecinos quienes por la misma razon de situarse en él parage indicado corresponden á su jurisdiccion, y por lo mismo dispondrá V. todo aquello mas arreglado á las leyes.

Recoja V. la presentacion del asunto que se devuelve á los * * * pues esta deve servir de * * * á lo que V. practique y de cuya operacion dará cuenta á esta gobierno tan luego como esté en estado de hacerlo.

Dios y Libertad!
SANTA FÉ, *Marzo* 24, 1835.

F. SARRACINO.

Señor ALCL., *Constitucional del Bado.*

No ay á la fecha en esta oficina * * * papel del Seyo 3º.
é, 8bre 15, 1835.

SARRACINO.

En N. Señora de los Dolores de las Vegas á seis del mes de Abril del año de mil ochocientos treinta y cinco jurisdiccion de San Miguel del Bado, Yo, el ciudadano José de Jesus Ulibarri y Durán, Alcalde Constitucional, unico de esta jurisdiccion é pasado á esta dicha poblacion hacer el reparto de tierras al numero de veinte y cinco individuos que se espresan en la presentacion fha., 20 de Marzo de 1835, y en gral á los que se hayen improvisto de ella, no solo á los de esta jurisdiccion sino a quantos desacomodados se me presenten, y habiendome hecho á cargo de dicha tierra tomé la medida del norte al sur y luego fué haciendo el reparto con arreglo á la Ley de Colonizacion que habla sobre concesiones de terrenos valdios observando escrupulosamente quanto dispone la Exma. Diputacion Territorial de Nuevo Mexico, en su decreto 23 de Marzo de 1835, y decreto del Señor Gefe Político ciudadano, Francisco Sarracino, fha. 24 del mismo mes reciviendose cada individuo de una gratitua suerta de tierra segua las proporciones de cada uno siempre con la prevencion de que no quedase inculta á todos los que constan en la lista que á este acompaño hasta haber formalizado el arreglo con los mejores * * * que á mí y á los intersados nos pareció conbeniente paraque todos quedasen conformes con sus pertenencias anotandosele á cada uno las varas que les tocó como asi mismo en la predicha lista consta el numero de individuos que havitan esa nueva poblacion y despues de hecho el reparto procedi á notificarles la presentacion que á la cabeza de este documento se haya: asignandole por linderos los mismos que en sa instancia se solicitan quedando advertidos que las aguas y postos son comunes y que las obras de mancomunidad se ejecuten por sus mismos individuos sin contradiccion ninguna y que la plaza señalada la pader del cuadro en contorno de afuera se hagalutre todos y despues de verificada esta obra se le dará conocimiento al Juez para que les señale por igual á cada uno lo que corresponda asi mismo cada uno de por si debe estar bien equipado de armas cayo ciudado se encargará al Tenienta de Policia de aguel Barrio para que este cada ocho dias pase revista de armas y las faltas que advierta dé cuenta á este Jusgado como cabezera de ese Barrio para proveer lo conveniente asi mismo quedan advertidos el que ninguno vendiese su tierra hasta no adquerir el Dro. que las leges los otorga á todo colonizado. Y pava su constancia en lo presente como en lo futuro coloco originales en el archivo de mi cargo firmandolo con tres testigos de asistencia por falta de * * * * * no lo hay en los terminos que * * * * * el Dro. de que doy fee.

JOSÉ DE JESUS ULIBARRI.

De assa.,
    JOSÉ MIGUEL SANCHES.
De assa.,
    ANTONIO NIETO.
Assa.,
    MANUEL DURÁN.

AUTO.—Se colocan los originales que constan insertos en estas diligencias en el archivo de mi cargo constandose de 8 fxs. útiles. Asi lo provei mande y firmé en dicho dia mes y año y la firmó con los de mi asistencia de que doy fee.

JOSÉ DE JESUS ULIBARRI.

De assa.,
MANUEL DURÁN.
De assa.,
ANTONIO NIETO.

Lista en donde consta el numero de Yndebidaos que ocupan en la n'va poblacion titulada Nuestra Señora de los Dolores de las Vegas, y se comprehende el numero de varas de tierra que lo tocó á cada uno, y es como signe, á saber:

C. Asencio Baca - - - - - -	175
C. Simon Bléa - - - - - -	100
C. José de Jesus Ulibarri - - - - -	150
C. Santiago Ortega—escogio en Balindoe - -	100—150
C. Juan de Dios Maese - - - - -	150
Don Antonio Benaoides, con - - - - -	80
Salió Casane y entró Tomas Baca - - - -	100
Salió Sarracino y entró poseandola Juan Maria Griego	200
C. Juan José Baca - - - - - -	200
C. Francisco Lopez - - - - - -	100
C. Tomas Baca - - - - - -	225

Para Guertas por la parte del norte 125 varas y 25 para cameno, abrevadero de una y otra banda y por la parte del sur 75 para guertas, y de aqui signe el reparto entre los individuos que se van anotando advertiendo que el numero estipulado aqui de guertas y camino es enfrente de la plaza que señale de una y otra banda deje este No. de varas para los habitantes de alli repartiendose por igual todos.

C. José Guadalupe Baca—cambió con Don Juan de Dios Maese	150
C. Miguel Rendon - - - - - -	150
C. Rafael Rendon - - - - - -	100
C. Cruz Rendon - - - - - -	150
C. José Lucero - - - - - -	200
C. Toribio Crespin - - - - - -	100
C. Juan Crespin - - - - - -	100
C. Pablo Ulibarri - - - - - -	150
C. Antonio Ulibarri - - - - - -	185
C. Juan Pedro Archuleta - - - - -	150
C. Eulogio Segura, ese dió al c. Tomas Ulibarri - -	100
C. Faustin Ulibarri - - - - - -	100
C. Teodosio Quintana, Salió Quintana y entró Elogio Segura	200
C. Felipe Tafoya - - - - - -	250
C. José de Jesus Durán - - - - -	100
C. José Maria Durán - - - - - -	100
C. Manuel Durán - - - - - -	175
C. Antonio Romo - - - - - -	200
C. Simon Romo - - - - - -	100
C. José Maria Martin - - - - - -	100
C. Miguel Martin - - - - - -	200

C. José Martin - - - - - - 200
C. Antonio Martin - - - - - - 200
C. Juan Nepo. Martin - - - - - 100
C. Miguel Martin 2d - - - - - - 100
C. Juan José Martin - - - - - 100

NOTA.—Que desde José de Jesus Durán para abajo notificados constan posesionados en el ancon de la otra banda del Rio por la parte oriental como asi mismo entre José Maria Martin y Miguel Martin 1°, consta las varas de tierra de guertas y camino abrebadero en la misma banda dicha y para que asi conste firmo este hoy 6 de Abril de 1835. Agregandose á esta lista de reparto los yndividuos que desde esta fha. ocuran á posesionarse.—José de Jesus Ulibarri.

C. Vitorino Baca - - - - - - 150
C. Ylario Gonzales - - - - - - 455
C. Antonio Gallego - - - - - - 200
C. José Antonio Ulibarri 1°, Salió Ulibarri y entró posean do
   Juan Miguel Garcia - - - - - 125
C. Rufino Gonzales - - - - - - 100
C. Ambrosio Gonzales - - - - - 100
C. Santos Gonzales - - - - - - 100
C. Francisco Sanches - - - - - 355
C. Rafael Rodriguez - - - - - 166
C. Julian Ulibarri - - - - - - 225
C. Manuel Tafoya lo sobrante del ancon.
C. Mariano Gonzales, 2°, lo sobrante de otro ancon.
C. Mariano Gonzales, 1° - - - - - 150
C. Manuel Garcia - - - - - - 250
C. Desiderio Maese - - - - - - 100
C. Santiago Ulibarri - - - - - 600
C. Rafael Durán - - - - - - 200
C. José Antonio Flores - - - - - 200
C. José Leon Romero - - - - - 200
C. Vicente Romero - - - - - - 200
C. Rafael Romero - - - - - - 200
C. Miguel Romero - - - - - - 200
C. Juan Christobal Armijo - - - - 220
C. José Miguel Sanchez - - - - 200
C. Francisco Maese - - - - - - 112
C. Franco. Lucero - - - - - - 112
C. Miguel Carrio - - - - - - 150
C. Rafael Castiyo - - - - - - 100
C. José Fernandez Gallego - - - - 100
C. José Dolores Sena - - - - - 185
C. José Ramon Sena - - - - - 125
C. Francisco Sena - - - - - - 200
C. Vicente Villanueba - - - - - 100
C. José Pablo Baca - - - - - - 100
C. Ramon Baca - - - - - - 100
C. Toribio Archuleta - - - - - 100
C. Fernando Chavez—salió charez y entro poseondo Ramon
   Peña - - - - - - - 100

PRIVATE LAND CLAIMS IN NEW MEXICO. 23

C. Toribio Martin	- - - - - -	100
C. Miguel Montaño	- - - - - -	100
C. Jesus Pando	- - - - - -	100
C. Juan Felipe Sanchez	- - - - -	100
C. Maria Encarnacion Armijo	- - - -	100
C. José Flores	- - - - - -	75
C. Cruz Martin, de una banda y dos anconsitos	- -	100
C. Polonio Herrera	- - - - - -	100
C. Jerrel Herrera	- - - - - -	50
C. Fabian Archuleta	- - - - -	100
C. Simon Romo	- - - - - -	100
C. Ramon Vigil, y sele recargo lo sobrante	- - -	100
C. Anastacio Roival	- - - - - -	175
C. Francisco Sanchez, y mas un anconsito	- - -	150
C. Pedro Barela	- - - - - -	100
C. Julian Jimenes	- - - - - -	100
C. Ramon Benavides	- - - - - -	100
C. Antonio Garcia	- - - - - -	100
C. Rafael Rodriguez	- - - - - -	100
C. Pedro Gonzales	- - - - - -	200
C. Andres Truqueque	- - - - -	100
C. Gabriela Crespin	- - - - -	100
C. Ascencio Baca	- - - - - -	100
C. Miguel Archuleta	- - - - - -	1,067
C. José Maria Tafoya	- - - - -	500
C. José Miguel Carrigo	- - - - -	100
C. Cristoval Vaca	- - - - - -	500
C. Miguel Martin	- - - - - -	125
C. Martin Romero	- - - - 100 vs. mas	50 vs.
C. Domingo Gusman	- - - - 100 mas	50 vs.
C. Santiago Sandoval	- - - - - -	50

Nombre de Cañada de los Pecos desde el camino dibisorio de Lo de Mor hasta el arroyo de lo Pecos:

C. Jesus Maria Montoya	- - - - varas	200
C. Santiago Montoya	- - - - - varas	100
C. Antonio José Sais—salió Antonio José Sais y entró Pedro Ortiz	- - - - - - -	100
C. Asensio Saenz	- - - - - -	100
C. Antonio Saenz	- - - - - -	100
C. Tomas Ulibarri	- - - - - -	100
C. Rafael Rodriguez—salió Rodriguez y entró Antonio Saenz por compra	- - - - - - -	100
C. Domingo Peña	- - - - -	200
C Nerio Montoya—salió y entró Anastacio Gonzales	- -	150
C. Luis Maria Gonzales—salió Luis Ma. y entravon Gillono y Vlarico con 75 vs. cada uno	- - - - -	175
C. Patricio Benabides, 150 vs. en el valle de arriba del baranco del rio.		
C. Cristobal Baca	- - - - - -	280
C. Pablo Pando	- - - - - -	100

C. Jesus Pando	100
C. Pedro Garcia	100
C. Sencion Garcia	100
C. Esquipula Baca	100
C. Fabian Archuleta	100
C. Sebastian Durán	200
C. Salbador Martin	200
C. Rafael Martin	200
C. Rafael Niaso	200
C Andres Trujeque	100
C. José Flores	100
C. Franco. Sanches—dejando cincuenta varas para pisos comunes en la banda del lado de la plaza para abajo en donde deben quedar dhas. 50 varas	400

J. Pedro Barela dos anconsitos en los ojos.

Lista de los ciudadanos posesionados en el Puertecito y se hagrega á la lista general de repartos—este es el Puertecito de abajo:

C. Roman Sisneros—no consta por vs.
C. José Pablo Maese—no consta por varas.

C. Juan Sais	varas 350
C. Antonio Sais	varas 250
C. Felipe Tafoya	125
C. José Dolores Durán	100
C. José Durán	126
C. Rafael Castigo	100
C. Rafael Garcia	125

C. Antonio Romo.

C. Francisco Antonio Sanchez, Pasa al Puertecito de arriba	150

C. Juan Martin, para el y su padre del lindero de Mariano Gonzales hasta el Camino.

C. Mariano Gonzales 2º	100
Doña Lorenza Baca	100
Ana Maria Chama	100
C. Augustin Quintana, y un anconsito en el rio que no se midió	100

C. Juan José Martin, del lindera de Augustin al Camino.
C. Juan Gayego, en la puerta del cañoncito de la agua sarca de una barda del arroyo de un peñasco questa en medio del ancon hasta los peñascos de abajo.

Sebastian Durán	varas 100
Jesus Durán	100

En los remanientos de la agua sarca se le posesiona á D. Gregorio Vigil sin variar el terreno y se le señala el desemboque del cañoncito de la agua sarca por el poniente arroyo abajo por el oriente una loma pinabetosa junta á el ereston por el norte y sur dros. comunes respectando las tierras donadas.

Por solicitud de algunos C. C. para que se les diera un pedazo de tierra para huerta en las chorreras de esta plaza admito en dar á cada uno 25 varas de ancho y 50 de largo con previa condicion de que se deben cercar dichas huertas pues á no aserlo asi no tendran dro. á cobrar daños los individuos son los siguientes.

C. Franco. Sanchez - - - - - - 25
C. Antonio Saenz - - - - - - - 25
C. Simon Gallego - - - - - - - 25

En este reparto corta la tierra qe. dado en el llano qe. queda debajo de la acequia qe. se sacó sobre la plaza para segia el templo culla tierra es la que qe. la sobrante al llano desde las comitas limites borar antes de planear el alto á la Vega es ser divisoria unas mojoneras de piedra que ban qe. dando al desconbear el llano para el lado del norte debe qe. dar el camino real vegas.

Junio 11 de 1841.

Reparto.

C. Felipe Tafoya - - - - - - - 150
C. Franco. Antonio Sanches - - - - - 100
C. Miguel Tafoya - - - - - - 100
C. Prudencio Griego - - - - - - 150
C. José Samora - - - - - - - 100

Terreno repartido en la acequia que se sacó nueba para la construccion de su plaza de arriba.

C. Juan Ma. Martin - - - - - - vs. 150
C. José Manuel Angel - - - - - 100
C. Pedro Bustos - - - - - - 200
C. Jesus Castiyo - - - - - - 100
C. José Flores - - - - - - 100
C. Manuel Archuleta - - - - - 100
C. Crisantos Salas - - - - - - 100
C. Felipe Martin - - - - - - 100
C. Antonio José Sais - - - - - - 50

En los ojos los estrangeros Julian y Antonio Donalson.

José Manuel Angel una rinconada que está en el serrito sin variarse.

Don Ramon Aragon un ancon en la otra banda del arroyo de los pesos desde el camino de los carros á unas lomas asules sin variar.

En el puesto de las Vegas á los 25 dias del mes de Novembre de 1846 á solicitud y por concesion oficial que el Señor Juez de Primera Instancia hizo de terreno para labor á los c. c. que alcalse del presente se contienen pase acompañado de los testigos de mi asistencia á hacer el reparto en dicho terreno, y tomando las medidas por parte del norte se comensaron á esto con los individuos que lo solicitaron cuyo reparto es al tenor siguiente.

C. Miguel Antonio Padiya - - - - - vs. 200
C. Gertrudis Zalasar - - - - - - 200
C. Juan Jaramiyo - - - - - - 200
C. Martin Romero - - - - - - 200
C. Jose Ma. Garcia - - - - - - 200
C. Bicente Segura - - - - - - 200
C. Juan José Montoya - - - - - 200
C. José Ma. Maese - - - - - - 200
C. Rafael Durán - - - - - - 200
C. Miguel Martin 2° - - - - - - 200

Aniceto Quintara del lindero de Miguel Martin al camino sin variar.

Los anotados en el presente reparto quedan recividos del numero de varas que á cada uno se le anotan y entendido de que las aguas deben conducirse por el rio en caso de escaces sin tener derecho á tomarlas por ser la labor de abajo de mas preferencia * * * * guia en ningun tiempo * * * * derecho en las aguas * * * * el presente que firmo con los testigos de asistencia con quienes actuo por Receptoria y al que se agregará el oficio original en que se les concedió el terreno debiendo incluirse el presente á la merced general deste mismo de Las Vegas para su constancia y seguridad en todo tiempo de que doy fee.

JUAN DE DIOS MAESE.

Assa. ANTONIO SAENZ.
Assa. FRANCO BUSTAMARA.

* * * 1a. Insa. Del Dist. del Centro:

Ympuesto de la nota de V. fecha de hoy relativa á los pedidos de terrenos de algunos individuos de ese lugar y en contestacion le digo á V. que bien puede posesionarlos del citado terreno en los terminos que se trató hayer.

Con respecto á lo que V. me encargo de que averiguará sobre las declaraciones dadas por el Juez de Barrio es efectivo y en cuya virtud le suplico relebe del mando y encargue Franco. Martin relebando y eximiendo á este de todo servicio.

Dios y Libertad. Balles de San Agustin, Nove. 20 de 1846.

TRINIDAD BARCELÓ.

Señor Juez de Paz, Don JUAN DE DIOS MAESE.

Puesto de Las Vegas á los 17 dias * * * * á solicitud de 7 individuos que han solicitado un terreno valdio aunque á el espacio de tres ó mas años que se donó á otros sujelos que á la fecha no le an puesto mano viendo el poco interes y abandaro de las antes posesionados en el espresado terreno pase yo el C. Hilario Gonzales acompañado de los impetrantes y reconocida la tierra y vista justa su solicitud por ser hombres laboriosos y de industria en materia de agricultura tube á bien posesionarles con el numero de varas que cada uno segun sus facultades puedan darle cultivo demandandoles conocer los requisitos que prebienen las leyes de colonozacion el en que dentro de diez y ocho meses deban poner toda solicitud en sus tierras y de no quedara perdido el derecho y se puedan donar las tierras á otros que no sean parserosos en cultivarlas.

Los individuos son los siguientes que se anotan en el presente reparto que se agregnen á la merced general.

Juan Pedro Archuleta	-	-	-	-	-	50 varas.
Jesus Gayego	-	-	-	-	-	50 "
José Candelario Garcia	-	-	-	-	-	50 "
Rafael Rodriguez	-	-	-	-	-	50 "
José Martin	-	-	-	-	-	50 "
Eulogio Gonzales	-	-	-	-	-	50 "

El presente auto y lista * * * * eto agrégnese al

espresion   *   *   *   *   general para la constancia
  *   *   *   *   del tiempo cui lo firmo con los de mi asistencia de que doi fee.

HILARIO GONZALES.

Assa. Antonio Saenz.
Assa. Ramon Garcia.

Surveyor General's Office, Translator's Department,
Santa Fé, New Mexico, August 25, 1859.

The foregoing is a true copy of the original now on file in this office.

DAVID V. WHITING,
Translator.

GRANT—TRANSLATION.

Seal Third. [seal.] Two Rials.

For the years one thousand eight hundred and twenty-six and eight hundred and twenty-seven.

Most respectful corporation: The citizens Juan de Dios Maese, Miguel Archuleta, Manuel Duran, and Jose Antonio Casaos, for themselves and in the name of twenty-five men, appear before your honorable body in the best and most approved manner, and according to law, and state that having registered a vacant and uncultivated piece of land, commonly known by the name of Las Vegas, on the Gallinas river, about five leagues distant from this settlement, which land we solicit for the purpose of planting a moderate crop, to have also the necessary land for pasture and watering places, and having the following boundaries: on the north the Sapello river, on the south the boundary of the grant made to Don Antonio Ortiz, on the east the Aguage de la Zegua, and on the west the boundary of the grant to San Miguel del Bado, which grant we pray for without injury to any third party, binding ourselves to receive possession in the name of the federation, and to comply with the reasonable and equitable conditions which your excellency, by virtue of the authority conferred upon you, may be pleased to establish for the grant of the land, being pleased to lay this our petition before the most excellent territorial deputation, having first obtained the customary report which by law is intrusted to your excellency, in order that that most excellent body may order the aforesaid grant to be made to us, in which the advancement of agriculture and the well being of several families without occupation are interested. Therefore, we request and pray your excellency that considering us as having presented ourselves, to yield to our petition, which we swear not to be done in malice; and in whatever may be necessary, &c.

JUAN DE DIOS MAESE. (Rubric.)
MANUEL DURAN. (Rubric.)
MIGUEL ARCHULETA. (Rubric.)
JOSÉ ANTONIO CASAOS. (Rubric.)

San Miguel del Bado, *March* 20, 1835.

SANTA FÉ, *March* 24, 1835.

On this date the justice of El Bado is notified to proceed according to the directions of the most excellent deputation and this government.
SARRACINO. (Rubric.)

SAN MIGUEL DEL BADO,
In the Town House, on the 20*th day of March,* 1835.

The foregoing petition, signed by the subscribers thereto, is received. This corporation, desirous of encouraging the advancement of agriculture, and the location of so many families without occupation, and being true that the land solicited as above is public land, and without injury to any third party nor of (torn) * * * let this petition proceed to the most excellent territorial deputation, in order that its excellency, if it sees proper, may provide them with the land prayed for, the entailment of which is earnestly aspired to.

JOSÉ ULIBARRI, *President*. (Rubric.)
FRANCISCO SENA,
First Justice. (Rubric.)
LEONIOS LUCERO,
Fourth Justice. (Rubric.)
GERONIMO GONZALES,
Second Justice. (Rubric.)
THOMAS ARAGON,
Attorney. (Rubric.)
JOSÉ CANDELARIA FLORES,
Third Justice. (Rubric.)

Before me,
JOSÉ ANTONIO CASAOS,
Secretary of Corporation. (Rubric.)

(Book 1st, page 6.)

OFFICE OF THE MOST EXCELLENT DEPUTATION OF NEW MEXICO,
Santa Fé, March 23, 1835.

In consultation of to-day, its excellency has resolved as follows:

The land contained within the boundaries expressed in this petition is granted not only to the petitioners and the residents of El Bado, but also generally to all who may be destitute of lands to cultivate, provided "that the grant to these lands is made on condition that the pasture and watering places are free to all. In view of all which, the political chief will receive the petition which may be made, and shall cause them to be provided for agreeably to what has been ordered."

In compliance with instructions, let these original proceedings be forwarded to the political chief, who will be pleased to execute what is therein ordered by this deputation, by whose order the foregoing is done.

R. ABREU, *Secretary*. (Rubric.)

In reference to a petition made by the President's (torn) * * * Juan de Dios Maese, Miguel Archuleta, Manuel Duran, and José Antonio Casaos, for themselves and in the name of twenty-five other individuals, dated the 20th inst., in which they solicited land in Las Vegas, its excellency the provincial deputation has resolved the following in reference to the matter:

(Book 1st, page 6.)

OFFICE OF THE SECRETARY OF THE MOST EXCELLENT
DEPUTATION OF NEW MEXICO,
Santa Fé, March 23, 1835.

In consultation of to-day its excellency has resolved as follows:

The land contained within the boundaries expressed in this petition is granted not only to the petitioners and the residents of El Bado, but also generally to all who may be destitute of lands to cultivate, provided "that the grant to these lands is made on condition that the pasture and watering places are free to all. In view of all which, the political chief will receive the petitions which may be made, and shall cause them to be provided for, agreeably to what has been ordered."

In compliance with instructions, let these original proceedings be forwarded to the political chief, who will be pleased to execute what is therein ordered by this deputation, by whose order the foregoing is done.

R. ABREU, *Secretary.* (Rubric.)

And I communicate it to you for the entire compliance therewith, taking into consideration that the grants are to be made according to the means of each one of the petitioners, in order that they may not leave any land which may be given to them without cultivation. It is also convenient to suggest that you should select a site for a town to be built by the inhabitants, together with such other steps as you may deem proper for the security of the inhabitants, who, on account of settling on the land indicated, will be included in your jurisdiction; you will therefore adopt such measures as will be most conformable to the laws.

You will retain the petition relative to the matter, and return (torn) as this should be (torn) of the proceedings had by you; of all which you will inform this government so soon as it is in condition to do so.

God and Liberty.

F. SARRACINO. (Rubric.)

SANTA FÉ, *March* 24, 1835.

To the Constitutional Justice of El Bado:

At this time there is no paper with the third seal in this office.
SARRACINO.

At Nuestra Señora de los Dolores de Las Vegas, on the sixth day of the month of April, in the year one thousand eight hundred and thirty-five, jurisdiction of San Miguel del Bado, I, the citizen José de Jesus Ulibarri y Duran, constitutional justice, the only one in this jurisdiction, proceeded to this town for the purpose of distributing the lands to twenty-five individuals, mentioned in the petition dated March 28, 1835, and in general to those who are without lands, not only those within this jurisdiction, but also any one who may present himself to me who has no occupation; and having examined the land, I took the measures from north to south, after which I made the distribution according to that portion of the colonization law which refers to grants of the public lands, complying with the greatest care with the directions of the most excellent territorial deputation of New Mexico, contained in its decree of the 23d of March, 1835, and the decree of his excellency the political chief, citizen Francisco Sarracino, dated the 24th of the same month; each individual received a gratuitous piece of land according to his means, with the understanding that of the lands given to the persons contained in the accompanying list none should remain uncultivated. The whole matter was concluded with the best measures which myself and the parties interested considered the most convenient, in order that each party should be satisfied with his share, setting opposite to each one's name the number of varas he received. The aforementioned list also contains the number of individuals who resided in the new settlement, and, after having made the distribution, I proceeded to make known to them the petition found at the commencement of this document, assigning them the same boundaries as are set forth in the petition. I also informed them that the water and pasture were free to all, and that the joint labor should be done by themselves without any dispute, and that the wall surrounding the town marked out should be made by them all, which being done, that they notify the justice, in order that he may mark out to each one equally the portion he is entitled to. Also, that each one be well provided with arms, the care of which is intrusted to the lieutenant of police of that ward, who shall inspect the arms every eight days, and, should he observe any infraction, to inform this court, as the head of the ward, thereof, so as to provide the necessary measures. They were also informed that no one should sell his lands until he acquired the title prescribed by law to all colonists, and, in order that it may so appear at the present time and in the future, placed the originals in the archives under my charge, signing the same with three attending witnesses, in the absence of (torn), there being none in the terms (torn) law, to which I certify.

JOSÉ JESUS ULIBARRI. (Rubric.)

Attending,
    JOSÉ MIGUEL SANCHEZ. (Rubric.)
Attending,
    ANTONIO NIETO. (Rubric.)
Attending,
    MANUEL DURAN. (Rubric.)

DECREE.—The originals annexed to these proceedings, containing eight written pages, are deposited in the archives under my charge. I have so provided, ordered, and signed on said day, month, and year, and I sign with those in my attendance, to which I certify.

JOSÉ DE JESUS ULIBARRI, (Rubric.)

Attending,
    MANUEL DURAN. (Rubric.)
Attending,
    ANTONIO NIETO. (Rubric.)

List showing the number of individuals who occupy the new settlement entitled "Nuestra Señora de los Dolores de Las Vegas," and showing the number of yards of land each one has received; which is as follows, to wit:

Citizen Acensio Baca	175
Citizen Simon Blea	100
Citizen José de Jesus Ulibarri	150
Citizen Santiago Ortega, selected in Balendre, 150 yards of land,	150
Citizen Juan de Dios Maese	250
Citizen Juan José Baca	200
Citizen Francisco Lopez	100
Citizen Tomas Baca	225

For gardens, 125 varas towards the north, and 25 for a road to the watering place, one each side, and towards the south 750 varas for gardens, from whence the distribution continues, to the individuals contained in the list, noting that the number of yards herein stipulated for gardens and roads is opposite to the square plaza which I marked out on either side. I left this number of yards for the inhabitants of the place, to be divided equally between them:

Citizen José Gaudalupe Baca	150
Citizen Miguel Rendon	150
Citizen Rafael Rendon	100
Citizen Cruz Rendon	150
Citizen José Lucero	200
Citizen Foribio Crespin	100
Citizen Pablo Ulibarri	150
Citizen Antonio Ulibarri	185
Citizen Juan Pedro Archuleta	150
Citizen Eulogia Segma	100
Citizen Ramon Ulibarri	100
Citizen Teodocio Quintana	200
Citizen Felipe Tafallo	250
Citizen José de Jesus Duran	100
Citizen Manuel Duran	175
Citizen Antonio Romo	200
Citizen Simon Romo	100
Citizen José Maria Martin	200
Citizen Miguel Martin	200
Citizen Antonio Martin	200
Citizen Juan Nepomuceno Martin	100
Citizen Miguel Martin, jr.	100
Citizen Juan José Martin	100

NOTE.—That from José de Jesus Duran to the end of the above list the land is situated in a valley on the opposite side of the river, towards the east, also the number of varas set apart for gardens and road to watering place, lie between José Maria Martin and Miguel Martin, sr., on the side above mentioned; and, in order that it may so appear, I have signed this 6th day of April, 1835, attaching to this list of distribution the names of such individuals as may apply for lands after this date.

JOSÉ ULIBARRI.

Citizen Victorine Baca - - - - - 150
Citizen Hilario Gonzalez - - - - - 455
Citizen Antonio Gallego - - - - - 200
Citizen José Antonio Ulibarri, sr., (José Miguel Garcia took the place of Jose Antonio Ulibarri, sr., and entered upon his lands) - - - - - 125
Citizen Rufino Gonzalez - - - - - 100
Citizen Ambrocio Gonzalez - - - - - 100
Citizen Santos Gonzalez - - - - - 100
Citizen Francisco Sanchez - - - - - 355
Citizen Rafael Rodriguez - - - - - 166
Citizen Julian Ulibarri - - - - - 225
Citizen Manuel Tafolla received a portion in the valley.
Citizen Mariano Gonzalez received a portion in another valley.
Citizen Mariano Gonzalez, sr. - - - - 150
Citizen Manuel Garcia - - - - - 250
Citizen Desiderio Maese - - - - - 100
Citizen Rafael Duran - - - - - 200
Citizen Vicente Romero - - - - - 200
Citizen Santiago Ulibarri - - - - - 600
Citizen José Leon Romero - - - - - 200
Citizen José Antonio Flores - - - - - 200
Citizen Rafael Duran - - - - - 200
Citizen Rafael Romero - - - - - 200
Citizen Miguel Romero - - - - - 200
Citizen Juan Christobal Armijo - - - - 220
Citizen José Miguel Sanchez - - - - 200
Citizen Francisco Maese - - - - - 111
Citizen Francisco Lucero - - - - - 112
Citizen Miguel Caerio - - - - - 150
Citizen Rafael Cestillo - - - - - 100
Citizen José Fernando Gallego - - - - 100
Citizen José Dolores Sena - - - - - 185
Citizen José Ramon Sena - - - - - 125
Citizen Francisco Sena - - - - - 200
Citizen Vicente Villanueva - - - - - 100
Citizen José Pablo Baca - - - - - 100
Citizen Ramon Baca - - - - - 100
Citizen Feribio Archuleta - - - - - 100
Citizen Fernando Chaves, (Ramon Pena took his land, the other having left) - - - - - 100
Citizen Foribio Martin - - - - - 100
Citizen Miguel Montaño - - - - - 100
Citizen Jesus Pando - - - - - 100
Citizen Juan Felipe Sanchez - - - - 100
Citizen Maria Encarnacion Armijo - - - - 100
Citizen José Flores - - - - - 75
Citizen Cruz Martin, on the opposite side of the river and two little valleys - - - - - 100
Citizen Polonio Herrera - - - - - 100
Citizen Ferrer Herrera - - - - - 50

PRIVATE LAND CLAIMS IN NEW MEXICO. 33

Citizen Fabian Archuleta	100
Citizen Simon Romo	100
Citizen Ramon Vigil	100
The remainder was given to Juan José Vigil	170
Citizen Anastacio Roibal	175
Citizen Francisco Sanchez, also a little valley	150
Citizen Pedro Barela	100
Citizen Julian Jimenez	100
Citizen Ramon Benavides	100
Citizen Antonio Garcia	100
Citizen Rafael Rodriguez	100
Citizen Pedro Gonzalez	200
Citizen Andres Truqueque	100
Citizen Gabriel Crispin	100
Citizen Ascensio Baca	100
Citizen Miguel Archuleta	1,067
Citizen José Maria Tafoya	700
Citizen José Miguel Carrello	100
Citizen Christobal Baca	500
Citizen Miguel Martin	125
Citizen Martin Romero, 50 more	100
Citizen Domingo Gama, 50 more	100
Citizen Santiago Sandoval	50

Names of those in the cañada of Pecos from the road dividing Lodemora to the arroyo of Pecos:

Citizen Jesus Maria Montoya	varas 200
Citizen Santiago Montoya	100
Citizen Antonio José Suiz	100
Citizen Asensio Sanez	100
Citizen Tomas Ulibarri	100
Citizen Rafael Rodriguez, (Antonio Saenz takes the place of Rodriguez by purchase)	100
Citizen Domingo Peña	200
Citizen Nerio Montoya, (Anastacia Gonzalez takes his place)	150
Citizen Luis Maria Gonzalez	170
Citizen Patricio Benavides, (Guillermo and Valeriano take his place, with 75 varas each in the valley above the ravine on the river)	150
Citizen Christobal Baca	250
Citizen Pablo Pando	100
Citizen Jesus Pando	100
Citizen Pedro Garcia	100
Citizen Acensio Garcia	100
Citizen Esquipula Baca	100
Citizen Julian Archuleta	100
Citizen Sebastian Duran	200
Citizen Salvador Martin	200
Citizen Rafael Niaso	200
Citizen Andres Fruqueque	100

Citizen Francisco Lucero	340
Citizen José Flores	100
Citizen Francisco Sanchez	400

Leaving 50 varas for a public road on the bank below where the plaza is situated, where 50 varas are to be left. Pedro Barela, two little valleys at the springs.

Names of citizens placed in possession of lands at the Puerticito, which is attached to the general list of distribution; that is, the the lower Puerticito:

Citizen Ramon Cisneros, no varas designated.
Citizen José Pablo Maese, no varas designated.

Citizen Juan Sais	varas 350
Citizen Antonio Sais	varas 250
Citizen Felipe Tafoya	125
Citizen José Dolores Duran	100
Citizen José Duran	126
Citizen Rafael Cistillo	100
Citizen Rafael Garcia	125
Citizen Francisco Antonio Sanchez, (Upper Puerticito)	150

Citizen Juan Martin, for himself and father, from the boundary of Mariano Gonzales to the road.

Citizen Mariano Gonzales, jr.	100
Citizen Don Lorenzo Baca	100
Citizen Ana Maria Chama	100
Citizen Augustin Quintana	100

(And a small valley in the river, not measured.)
Citizen Juan José Martin, from the boundary of Augustin to the road.
Citizen Juan Gallego, at the mouth of the cañon of the Aqua Sarca, on one side of the arroyo, from a rock in the middle of the valley to the lower rock.

Citizen Sebastian Duran	100
Citizen Jesus Duran	100

One hundred varas of land were given to Gregorio Vigil of the remaining lands of the Aqua Sarca, designating as boundaries, on the west the little cañon of the Aqua Sarca; on the east the arroyo Abayo; on the north a hill near the creston, and on the south the common boundary, respecting the tracts already donated.

At the request of several citizens asking for lands, composing the drippings of the plaza, for gardens, I have given to each one twenty-five varas in length, with the precise condition that they should fence them in; and in case of not doing so, they cannot claim damages. The individuals are as follows:

Francisco Sanchez	25
Antonio Saenz	25
Simona Gallegos	25

In this respect the quantity of land which I have distributed, and which is watered by the ditch (Acequia) which was constructed across the square for the purpose of finishing the temple, is the remainder of the plain from the little hills, amounting to twenty varas, before descending to the meadow, which is divided by certain mounds of stone on the northern side before descending to the plain where the public road is to run.

VEGAS, *June* 11, 1841.

Distribution.

Felipe Tafoya	150
Francisco Antonio Sanchez	100
Miguel Tafoya	100
Prudencio Griego	150
José Zamora	100

Land distributed on the new ditch (acequia) which was opened for the construction of the upper town:

Juan Manuel Martin	varas 150
José Manuel Angel	100
Pedro Bastos	200
Jesus Castillo	100
José Flores	100
Manuel Archuleta	100
Crisantos Salas	100
Felipe Martin	100
Antonio José Sais	50

At the springs, the foreigners William and Anthony Donaldson; José Manuel Angel, a little corner in the cerrito, not measured; Don Ramon Vigil, a valley on the other side of the arroyo of the Pecos, from the wagon road to the blue hills, not measured.

In the town of Las Vegas, on the 25th day of November, 1846, at the request and by the official grant of land for cultivation made by the senior justice to the citizens contained in the present list, I proceeded with my attending witnesses to distribute said lands, and taking the measurement on the northern side, the individuals soliciting the same were located in the following manner:

	Varas.
Miguel Antonio Fadrique	200
Gertrudis Salazar	200
Juan Jarmillo	200
Martin Romero	200
José Maria Garcia	200
Vicente Segma	200
Juan José Montoya	200
Jesus Maria Maese	200
Rafael Duran	200
Miguel Martin, jr.	200

Anisteo Quintana, from the boundary of Miguel Martin to the road, without measurement.

The persons whose names appear on the foregoing list received the number of varas set opposite their names, it being understood that the water shall run on the bed of the river in case of a scarcity, (not legible) by appointment, and to which shall be attached the original communication granting the land; the present document to be attached to the general grant made to Las Vegas, in order that it may so appear, and for security in all time to come. To which I certify.

JUAN DE DIOS MAESE. [Rubric.]
Attending,
  ANTONIO SAENZ. [Rubric.]
Attending,
  FRANCISCO BUSTAMENTE. [Rubric.]

OFFICE OF THE SEÑOR JUSTICE OF THE DISTRICT OF THE CENTRE.

Informed of the contents of your note of to-day, touching petitions for lands made by certain individuals of that place. In reply, I have to state that you are authorized to place them in possession of said land on the conditions referred to yesterday.

In reference to what you requested me to investigate, touching the evidence given by the police officer, I reply that it is true; therefore you are requested to remove him from office, and appoint Francisco Martin, relieving him and exonerating him from all duty.

God and liberty.

TRINIDAD BARCELO.
VALLEYS OF SAN AUGUSTIN, *November* 20, 1846.

To the Justice of the Peace, Don Juan de Dios Maese:

Las Vegas, on the 17th day, (torn,) at the request of seven individuals who have registered a tract of public land, although the aforesaid land was given over three years since to another individual, who has not placed his hand on it; and seeing the neglect and little interest taken by the former possessor of the land, I, the citizen Hilario Gonzalez, accompanied by the petitioners, having examined the land, and considered their petition just, both being laborers and industrious in matters of agriculture, I saw proper to place them in possession of the number of varas of land which each one can cultivate; with the further provision, besides those provided in the colonization laws, that within eighteen months they shall use every effort to prevent their land from lying idle, and thereby lose their title thereto, and be given to others who will cultivate them.

The following are the individuals to whom lands were distributed, which list shall be attached to the general grant:

Juan Pedro Archuleta	50 varas.
Jesus Gallego	50 "
José Candalaria Garcia	50 "
Rafael Rodriguez	50 "
José Martin	50 "
Eujogio Gonzalez	50 "

HILARIO GONZALEZ. [Rubric.]
Attending,
  ANTONIO SAENS. [Rubric.]
Attending,
  RAMON GARCIA. [Rubric.]

SURVEYOR GENERAL'S OFFICE,
Translator's Department, Santa Fé, N. M., July 10, 1857.

The above is a correct translation of the original on file in this office.

DAVID V. WHITING,
Translator.

SURVEYOR GENERAL'S OFFICE,
Santa Fé, New Mexico, August 20, 1859.

The above is a true copy of the original on file in this office.

WM. PELHAM,
Surveyor General.

TESTIMONY.

JOSÉ FRANCISCO SALAS sworn:

Question. Where do you reside? Are you in any way related to the claimants, or have you any interest in the claim?

Answer. I live at Peña Blanca. I am not related to any of the claimants, neither have I any interest in the claim.

Question. Did you know Luis Maria Cabeza during his lifetime?

Answer. I did.

Question. When did he die?

Answer. I saw him die, and was present when he was buried, but do not recollect exactly how long ago it was, but think it has been twenty-five years ago, more or less.

Question. How did he die?

Answer. He was killed by a soldier under the Mexican government. I was informed that he was killed on account of having some contraband property in his possession, belonging to an American, which he refused to deliver up.

Question. Do you know Luis Baca, Prudencio Baca, Jesus Baca, senior, Felipe Baca, Jesus Baca, junior, Domingo Baca, and Manuel Baca?

Answer. I know them all.

Question. Whose children are they?

Answer. They are sons of Don Luis Baca.

Question. Are these the only living sons of Luis Maria Cabeza de Baca?

Answer. They are.

Question. Were you acquainted with Juan Antonio Baca, José Baca, José Miguel Baca, Ramon Baca, and Mateo Baca?

Answer. I did know them; they are all dead. They were sons of Don Luis Baca.

Question. Did Juan Antonio Baca leave any children at his death?

Answer. He did; they were Jesus Maria Baca, Francisco Thomas Baca, Encarnacion Baca, José Baca, Josefa Baca, Guadalupe Baca, Attagracia Baca, Nicolas Baca, Tomas Baca, and Trinidad Baca.

Question. Did José Baca leave any children at his death?

Answer. He did not.

Question. Did José Miguel Baca leave any children at his death?

Answer. He did; they were Diego Baca, Quirina Baca, Romnaldo Baca, Guadalupe Baca, Paulina Baca, and Martina Baca.

Question. Did Ramon Baca leave any children at his death?

Answer. He did; they are Ygnacio Baca, and no other.

Question. Did Mateo Baca leave any children at his death?

Answer. He did; they are Luis Baca, Alexandro Baca, Juan de Dios Baca, and Martin Baca.

Question. Whose children are Antonio Baca, Felipe Baca, José Maria Baca, Francisco Baca, Fernando Baca, and Polonia Baca?

Answer. They are the children of José Baca.

Question. Are the above mentioned all the children and grandchildren of Luis Maria Cabeza de Baca?

Answer. They are.

Question. Do you know the place situated in this Territory and known as "Las Vegas Grandes?"

Answer. I do.

Question. Do you know of its having been in the possession of Don Luis Maria Cabeza de Baca; and if so, for how long?

Answer. They were in his possession. I had cattle there, belonging to Don Antonio Baca, for sixteen years; we were driven off, and returned again when the Indians became quiet. Don Luis Maria resided there for the space of ten years.

Question. What improvements did he make upon the place?

Answer. He had a hut built at the Loma Montosa, where himself and the cattle remained for a greater portion of the time; I did not see any other improvements; I had charge of the sheep herd, and sometimes would come to the hut, but the greater portion of the time I was in another direction with the sheep.

Question. When did you go there for the first time?

Answer. It must have been between the years 1822 and 1823.

Question. Was any other person in possession, or had any other person made any improvements on the land when you went there, except Don Luis and his sons?

Answer. I saw no other person there, or any other improvements made.

Question. What was the cause of the place being abandoned or left?

Answer. Because the Indians drove us away.

Question. What amount of stock was there when you were driven away?

Answer. I had 3,000 sheep; I do not know how much horned cattle was there; the men had cows there that they milked.

Question. Did they cultivate any of the land?

Answer. They did not.

Question. Were there any horses or mares kept there?

Answer. They had a great many there.

Question. In what year were they driven away by the Indians?

Answer. I do not remember in what year.

Question. Are not some of the heirs above mentioned still under twenty-one years of age?

Answer. They are all over twenty-one years of age.

Question. How old is the youngest one of the heirs?
Answer. There are many of the grandchildren under age yet.

Cross-examined.

Question. Were there not some houses built, or land cultivated, on the Vegas Grandes tract before you left?
Answer. There were no houses built or land cultivated before I left.
Question. Do any of the heirs live at Las Vegas Grandes?
Answer. They do; Francisco Baca and one of his brothers and Fernando Baca reside there; Polonia Baca also resides there.
Question. Do these persons hold their titles under the original grant to Luis Maria Cabeza de Baca?
Answer. They hold their lands under the grant made to Luis Baca.
Question. How do you know it?
Answer. They are all children of José Baca, who was one of the heirs, and I believe they hold the land under him.
Question. How long did you remain on the land?
Answer. About ten years.
Question. Was there any other improvement on the land except the jacal mentioned?
Answer. There was not.
Question. When you left the Vegas Grandes was there any person there cultivating the soil?
Answer. There was no one cultivating it then.
Question. Are any of the heirs you mentioned above cultivating the land now?
Answer. I believe they are. I have not seen them cultivating the land, but suppose, as they are hard-working men, that they work to support themselves.
Question. Do you know whether they occupy the land as heirs of Luis Baca, or do they hold the land under the present possessors and holders of the Vegas Grandes?
Answer. I cannot say.
Question. How were you run off by the Indians?
Answer. They took all the horses and mares, and were returning constantly to the ranch. We then left it and came in to the settlements.
Question. How many persons were on the ranch at that time?
Answer. Six men, more or less.
Question. Did the Indians kill any one, or do anything besides run off the stock?
Answer. They did not. The Pawnees were always said to be the Indians who ran off the stock.

his
JOSÉ FRANCISCO × SALAS,
mark.

Sworn and subscribed before me this 27th day of January, 1858.
WILLIAM PELHAM,
Surveyor General.

Manuel Antonio Baca, sworn:

Question. Have you any interest in this claim?

Answer. I have none.

Question. Do you bear any relationship to the heirs of Luis Maria Cabeza de Baca?

Answer. I am their second cousin.

Question. Were you an alcalde in the precinct of San Miguel del Bado in the year 1826?

Answer. I have been a justice of the peace for many years. I do not remember if I was one in that year; the documents will show that fact.

Question. Do you know the handwriting and signature of Juan Bautista Vigil, and if so, how do you know it?

Answer. I do not.

Question. Were you acquainted with Luis Maria Cabeza de Baca during his lifetime, and the sitio of Las Vegas Grandes?

Answer. I did know him. I also knew the sitio of Las Vegas Grandes.

Question. Did you receive an order to place Luis Maria Cabeza de Baca in possession of said sitio?

Answer. I do not remember what order I received when I placed him in possession. I believe it was public land, and he asked for it.

Question. When did you place him in possession?

Answer. I do not remember; it was many years ago.

Question. Were you an alcalde of the precinct of El Bado when you placed him in possession?

Answer. I do not remember. I must certainly have been one when I placed him in possession, but I am not certain of the fact.

Question. How long did Luis Maria Cabeza de Baca remain in possession?

Answer. I do not know; but I do remember that I divided out a portion of the Vegas lands

Question. Was any other person in possession of the place when you placed Baca in possession, or was it unoccupied?

Answer. There was no other person in possession at the time; it was entirely uncultivated and unoccupied.

Question. Did you have the title conceded to Luis Baca when you put him in possession?

Answer. I must have had it in my hands, but do not remember. I believe, but am not certain, that the land was granted to Mr. Baca for pasturing purposes, and not for cultivation.

Question. Did you make a report in writing of the fact of having placed him in possession?

Answer. I ought to have done so. The documents will show. I do not remember.

Question. According to the best of your recollection, at what time did you place him in possession?

Answer. I do not remember. I have been a justice of the peace in San Miguel for many years, but do not recollect the year I placed him in possession. The documents will show the year.

Question. Can you identify the documents now presented to you as the ones you had at the time?

Answer. They are the documents that were in his hands.

MANUEL ANTONIO BACA.

Sworn and subscribed this 28th day of January, 1858.
WM. PELHAM,
Surveyor General.

JOAB HOUGHTON sworn:

Question. Do you know the handwriting and signature of Juan Bautista Vigil, and how do you know it?

Answer. I do; I have seen him write, and know the signature on the documents No. 137 and letter A to be his genuine signature and rubric; I do not know from my own knowledge that he was secretary to the deputation, but have seen his name attached to several documents in that capacity.

J. HOUGHTON.

Sworn and subscribed before me this 28th day of January, 1858.
WM. PELHAM,
Surveyor General.

JOSÉ MARIA MONTOYA sworn:

Question. Have you any interest in this claim?
Answer. I have none.
Question. Are you related to any of the claimants?
Answer. I do not know.
Question. Do you know the place called Las Vegas Grandes, in San Miguel county?
Answer. I do.
Question. Do you know if Luis Maria Cabeza de Baca was ever in possession of it; and if so, when and for how long?
Answer. I do not know.
Question. Was that tract occupied previous to the establishment of the town of Las Vegas?
Answer. I do not know.
Question. Where do you live?
Answer. At the town of Tecolote.
Question. When was Tecolote first settled?
Answer. I do not know.

JOSÉ MARIA MONTOYA.

Sworn and subscribed before me this 28th day of January, 1858.
WM. PELHAM,
Surveyor General.

REMIGIO RIVERA sworn:

Question. Have you any interest in this claim?
Answer. I have no interest in the claim; neither am I related to the claimants.

Question. After the death of Don Luis Maria Cabeza de Baca which of his children managed his affairs?

Answer. Juan Antonio Baca, the father of Thomas Baca, managed the affairs of the estate; I did not know Don Luis Baca.

Question. Do you know when Don Juan Antonio Baca died?

Answer. On the 20th February, 1835; he was killed by the Navajo Indians.

Question. Who then and now managed the business of the heirs?

Answer. Don Thomas Baca.

Question. Do you know anything about a certain petition addressed by Thomas Baca to Governor Armijo, objecting to the settlement of persons on the Vegas Grandes; and if so, state what you know?

Answer. In the year 1848, as Don Thomas Baca was on his way to Abiquin with his family, (I was his clerk at that time,) he left a petition with me, addressed to General Armijo, (it was dated September 20, 1837,) in reference to certain persons who intended settling on the Vegas Grandes, to which said Baca objected, as the land belonged to the heirs of Luis Maria Cabeza de Baca.

Question. What was done with the petition?

Answer. The petition was delivered, in my presence, by Thomas Baca to Mr. Skinner.

Question. Were there other title papers placed at the same time in Mr. Skinner's possession?

Answer. I do not know; I only saw the petition delivered.

Question. Was there anything on the petition to show at what time it had been presented to Governor Armijo?

Answer. On the 20th day of September, 1837.

REMIGIO RIVERA.

Sworn and subscribed before me this 1st of February, 1858.
WM. PELHAM,
Surveyor General.

SURVEYOR GENERAL'S OFFICE,
Santa Fé, New Mexico, September —, 1859.

I certify that the above is a true copy of the original on file in this office.
WM. PELHAM,
Surveyor General.

REPORT.

The heirs of Luis Maria Baca and the town of Las Vegas.

The first of the above-mentioned cases was filed in this office on the 19th of June, 1855, and the second on the 11th of September of the same year.

These cases were set for trial at different periods, but owing to the absence of counsel and witnesses were not brought to a final close until the 10th of December, 1858.

The claim of the heirs of Luis Maria Baca is based on the following facts, as set forth in the original papers filed in the office by the claimants:

On the 16th of January, 1821, Luis Maria Cabeza de Baca, in his own name and that of seventeen male children, petitioned the provincial deputation of the State of Durango, under whose jurisdiction he avers the province of New Mexico then was, for a tract of public land suitable for cultivation and pasture, called the Vegas Grandes, on the Gallinas river, in the jurisdiction of El Bado. In this petition he states that a like petition had been made to the authorities of the province of New Mexico, and that by a decree of the 18th of February, 1820, the land was granted to him and eight other persons; but as these persons already possessed land elsewhere, they took no interest in its cultivation, and prays that the grant be made to himself and his aforementioned children, with the following boundaries, to wit: On the north the Chapellote river, on the south the boundary of El Bado, on the west the summit of the Pecos mountain, and on the east the Aguage de la Llegua and the boundary of Don Antonio Ortiz. On the 29th of May, Diego Garcia Conde and Miguel de Zubiria, president and secretary of the provincial deputation of Durango, informed Facando Melgares, the governor of New Mexico, that on the supposition that the companions of Don Luis Maria Cabeza de Baca had other lands whereon to pasture their cattle, that deputation had determined to confer upon the said Baca the land commonly called Vegas Grandes, provided the other parties had erected no buildings on the land or made any other improvements, unless it was voluntarily agreed between the parties that Baca should reimburse them for any improvements they might have made, and that an equal quantity of land should be assigned to them wherever they would select it, in place of those donated to Baca; and the governor of New Mexico was requested to inform the parties of what had been done.

On the 17th day of October, 1823, Bartolomé Baca, political chief of New Mexico, directed the alcalde of El Bado to place Luis Maria Cabeza de Baca in possession of the land called for in his petition, as the eight individuals who accompanied him in his first petition had placed no improvements on the land; and the alcalde was required to certify at the foot of the order the proceedings had by him in the premises.

On the 27th day of February, 1825, Juan Bautista Vigil, the secretary of the most excellent deputation of New Mexico, certified that at the session of the 16th of the same month a petition of Don Juan Antonio Cabeza de Baca, son of Luis Maria C. de Baca, and one of the grantees, was read, in which he refers to the grant made in the year 1821 by the provincial deputation of Darango, *to which corporation New Mexico at that time belonged*, and it was resolved that a record of the proceedings in the case be made and a true copy thereof given to the petitioner, and ratifying the grant made by the corporation of Durango on the date aforementioned. The petitioner was required to present himself before the territorial justice of El Bado with the copy above referred to, who, having then there the grant made to Salvador Montoya, was required to place the aforesaid Luis

Maria Baca and male children in possession of the aforesaid land, in accordance with the proceedings had in the premises and without injury to any third party.

On the 26th of December, 1825, Tomas Sena, the constitutional justice of El Bado, assigned as a reason for not placing the parties in possession of the land, as he had been ordered to do, that a proclamation had been issued for the election of his successor, at which he was compelled to attend, and that on the second day after the election had commenced he was taken violently ill, and was compelled to postpone the election, as was well known to the messengers of Don Luis Maria Cabeza de Baca.

On the 13th of January, 1826, Governor Narbona again ordered the constitutional justice to place the parties in possession of the land granted.

The testimony of Manuel Antonio Baca shows that the parties were placed in possession of the land, although there is no documentary evidence of the fact.

The claim of Las Vegas is based on the following proceedings:

On the 20th day of March, 1835, Juan de Dios Maese, Miguel Archuleta, Manuel Duran, and José Antonio Casaos, for themselves and in the name of twenty-five others, petitioned the corporation of El Bado for a tract of land for cultivation and pasture situated in the county of El Bado and bounded as follows: on the north by the Sapello river, on the south by the boundary of the grant of Don Antonio Ortiz, on the east by the Aguage de la Llegua, and on the west by the boundary of the town of El Bado.

On the same day the corporation of El Bado transmitted the petition to the territorial deputation, with the recommendation that the petition be granted.

On the 23d of March of the same year the grant was made by the territorial deputation with the boundaries asked for, with the further provision that persons who owned no lands were to be allowed the same privilege of settling upon the grant as those who petitioned for it.

On the 24th of the same month and year Francisco Sarracino, the acting governor or political chief, directed the constitutional justice of El Bado to place the parties in possession, which was done on the 6th day of April of the same year.

It is not supposed that Congress intended, upon the establishment of the office of the surveyor general of New Mexico, that he should be required to determine questions of right between parties, but simply to ascertain whether the claims presented to him were of such a nature as to separate the land embraced within the boundaries set forth in them from the public domain, and that conflicting claims between parties should be adjudicated before the proper tribunals of the country having jurisdiction in the premises.

Under this view of the case it will not be necessary to refer to any other points made by counsel than those touching the sufficiency of the titles given and under which the respective parties claim.

It is contended by the last grantees that the concession made to Baca by the provincial deputation of Durango was void for want of power in the tribunal that assumed to make it.

At the time the grant was made to Baca the country was in a state of confusion, arising from the severance of Mexico from the parent country. Many of the States had not yet given their adhesion to the new order of things, and in some places, as remote in the interior as New Mexico, were not even aware that a new order of things had been established; therefore the several authorities of the country exercised the power intrusted to them by the King of Spain or his lawful authorities, and as it is not disavowed that the State of Durango held jurisdiction over the province of New Mexico, it is supposed, even in the absence of any positive proof, that the deputation of that State acted within the scope of its authority when it made the grant to Baca; but in the confirmation of the grant by the territorial deputation of New Mexico in 1825, it is conceded that the province of New Mexico was under the jurisdiction of that State, and that any grant made by its legally constituted authorities was a good and valid one. In the case under consideration, no condition was attached; the grant was an absolute one. It has been held by our courts that where no conditions were attached they could not be raised by implication. So satisfied was Governor Melgares that the deputation of Durango had a right to make the concession, that he ordered the grantees to be placed in immediate possession, which he would not have done had he doubted in the least that the authorities of that State had exceeded their powers in granting lands in the province over which he presided as governor.

But supposing the grant made to Baca by the deputation of Durango to have been null and void, its confirmation by the territorial deputation of New Mexico in 1825, at which period, it is not denied, it had the power to grant lands, would be equivalent to a new grant; and, as it is complete in itself so far as the severance of the land granted is concerned, to separate it from the public domain, it is a matter of very little importance whether the former grant by the deputation of Durango was valid or not. This grant is therefore deemed to be a good and valid one.

The grant made to Juan de Dios Maese and others is not contested on the ground of any want of formality in the proceedings, but, as far as the documentary evidence shows, is made in strict conformity with the laws and usages of the country at the time.

Testimony is introduced to show that the heirs of Baca protested in 1837 against the occupancy of the land by the claimants under the latter grant, and that they went upon the land knowing the existence of a prior grant; but as these matters are not deemed to be pertinent to the case so far as this office is concerned, it is not necessary to comment upon them.

It is firmly believed that the land embraced in either of the two grants is lawfully separated from the public domain and entirely beyond the disposal of the general government, and that in the absence of the one the other would be a good and valid grant; but as this office has no power to decide between conflicting parties, they are referred to the proper tribunals of the country for the adjudication of their respective claims, and the case is hereby respectfully referred to Congress through the proper channel for its action in the premises.

WM. PELHAM, *Surveyor General.*

SURVEYOR GENERAL'S OFFICE,
Santa Fé, New Mexico, December 18, 1858.

SURVEYOR GENERAL'S OFFICE,
Santa Fé, New Mexico, August 31, 1859.
The foregoing is a correct copy of the original on file in this office.
WM. PELHAM,
Surveyor General.

CLAIM NO. 21.

TOWN OF TAJIQUE.

Schedule of documents composing claim No. 21.

1. Notice.
2. Grant, Spanish.
3. Grant, translation.
4. Testimony.
5. Report.

NOTICE.

THE TERRITORY OF NEW MEXICO,}
County of Santa Fé.

To the Hon. William Pelham, surveyor general of New Mexico:

The petition of the people of the town and settlement of Tajique, of the county of Valencia and Territory of New Mexico, respectfully represents: That they are the present owners and occupants of a certain sitio or tract of land known as the sitio of the town of Tajique, situated in the county of Valencia, east of the mountain of Manzano, being one square league, and bounded as follows, to wit: On the south reaching to a large cedar tree, which is in the cañada (or glen) called the Cañada de Los Pinos, a little above; on the north to the Cañada de Los Migas; on the west to the Mesita de la Cueva; and on the east to "El Pino Solo," (lone pine.) Petitioner refers to the title herewith filed as an exhibit (A) for the names of the original claimants or grantees, of whom the present claimants are the heirs, legatees, and assignees, many of whom are at this time working, and too numerous to be mentioned in this petition. The title to said land in said town of Tajique is perfect, bearing date the 17th of March, 1834, and given or derived from Francisco Saricino, political chief and acting governor, acting under authority of the laws of Mexico in force and bearing date from the year 1813 to the year 1837, being the colonization laws from time to time passed in the republic of Mexico. Your petitioners know of no claim conflicting with the claim aforesaid, and therefore they pray that the same may be confirmed, and they will ever pray, &c.

S. M. BAIRD,
Attorney for claimants.

SURVEYOR GENERAL'S OFFICE,
Santa Fé, New Mexico, August 23, 1859.

The above is a true copy of the original on file in this office.

WM. PELHAM,
Surveyor General.

GRANT—SPANISH.

Exmo. Sor. : Manuel Sanchez por si y á nombre de diez y nueve individuos, todos vecinos de Valencia á V. E. hacen presente : Que haviendo descubierto un terreno propio para elaborar en el punto de Tagique, yermo y del que por lo mismo no resulta peyuicio de tercero, y antes si a los solicitantes mejora de situacion por la escases en que se encuentran de tierras para sembrar, se ha de server V. E. en obsequio de las leyes que recomiendan el ramo de agricola, mandar se les done el espresado terreno que se compone de media legua, en circumferencia, potestanto en esta parte las costas buena fé, &c. Valencia, Marzo 9 de 1834. Manuel Sanchez.

Santa Fe, Marzo 17, de 1834. El alcalde constitucional de Valencia á cuya jurisdiccion corresponde Tagique segun estoy informado, hara el reparto que se solicita dentro del lindero que piden, con tal que de ello no resulte perjuicio a tercero, entendiendose que cuando la Exma. Diputacion se reuna confirmará la posesion, que ahora aprueba provisio nalmente este gobierno, en obsequio de que el tiempo de las siembras no se retarde. Sarracino.

En este puesto de Tagique á los nueve dias del mes de Abril de mil ochocientos treinta y cuatro, en cumplimiéntode la ordero provisional del Senor Gefe politico sobre que se posesionaran para que no perdieran sus siembras los individuos que pidieron se les mercenará dicho punto con media legua en contorno, á cuyo objeto pase yo el cuidadano Vicente Otero, alcalde constitucional del partido de Valencia con dos testigos de asistencia por corresponder á aquella alcaldia, dando principio á medir el contorno de la media legua, haviendo señalado primeramente ciento sesenta y dos varas en el terreno mas á proposito para que formaran su plaza, y del centro de esta se tiraron las medidas de la media legua para los cuatro rumbos en estos terminos. La primera al sur que alcanzó á un cedro grueso que esta en la cañada que se nombra de los Pinos poco arriba. La segunda al Norte hasta la cañada de las migas donde se señaló un pino con una cruz. La tercera al poniente hasta la mesita de la cueva, donde se señaló otro pino con una cruz. La cuarta al oriente hasta el pino solo, concluidas que fueron dichas medidas en presencia de doce de los agraciados, se omitio repartirles la tierra de labor que correspondiera á cada uno, por no haber ocurrido siete de los alistados, en el acto ordenando á los presentes fueran haciendo sus siembras, entendidos de que con oportunidad volveria a verificari la reparticion de dicha tierra, sugetandose á no quedar ninguno con derecho de lo que rompa y si á lo que les toque por la suerte, con solo la obligacion de romper les otra tanta de tierra en lo que les toque por el que posesione en la roba ; y para la devida constancia y fines consiguientes, firmo este documento yo el espresado alcalde con los de mi asistencia de que doy fe. Vicènte Otero. De asistencia, Jacinto Sanchez. De asistencia, José Manuel Maldonado. En este puesto de Tagique a los viente y cuatro dias del mes de Diciembre de mil ochocientos trienta y cuatro. Yo el C. Vicente Otero, alcalde constitucional de la jurisdiccion de Valencia, en cumplimiento del antecedente documento, por ante los testigos de mi asistencia hize comparecer á los vecinos agraciados en este punto, á quienes presentes los impuse de la operacion que îba á hacer segun lo tratado en el citado antecedente documento á lo cual se ofrecieron gustosos a recivir lo que á cada uno justamente correspondiera de tierra de labor, y en su consecuencia hecho el calculo, comenze a hechar las medidas de poniente a oriente, de ciento doce varas á cada uno haviendo dejado primero doce varas de chorreras á la plaza, quedando posesionados en los terminos siguientes. 1°. Medida á Maria Gertrudis Chavez, que conlinda con la tierra de Antonio Otero. 2°. Antonio Otero, conlinda con las de Maria Gertrudis Chavez, y las de Manuel Garcia. 3. Manuel Garcia, conlinda con las de Antonio Otero, y las de José Lorenzo Otero. 4. José Lorenzo Otero, conlinda con las de Manuel Garcia, y las de Matias Sanchez. 5. Matias Sanchez, conlinda con las de José Lorenzo Otero, y las de José Antonio Samora. 6. José Antonio Samora, conlinda con las de Matias Sanchez, y las de Rafael Sanchez. 7. Rafael Sanchez, conlinda con las de José Antonio Samora, y las de Francisco Moya. 8. Francisco Moya, conlinda con las de Rafael Sanchez, y las de José Manuel Maldonado. 9. José Manuel Maldonado, conlinda con las de Francisco Moya, y las de Cristobal Samora. 10. Cristobal Samora, conlinda con las de Jose Manuel Maldonado, y las de Lazaro Ramirez. 11. Lazaro Ramirez, conlinda con las de Cristobal Samora, y las de Mateo Anaya. 12. Mateo Anaya, conlinda con las de Lazaro Ramirez, y las de Ygnacio Sedillo. 13. Ygnacio Sedillo, conlinda con las de Mateo Anaya, y las de Roman Samora. 14. Roman Samora, conlinda con las de Ygnacio Sedillo, y las de Domingo Samora. 15. Domingo Samora, conlinda con las de Roman Samora, y las de José Chavez. 16. José Chavez, conlinda con las de Domingo Samora, y las de Antonio Sanchez. 17. Antonio Sanchez, conlinda con las de José Chavez. José Sanchez del temploal poniente. Dioinicio Vigil del templo al poniente, quedand) todos con derecho de rompar de Norte a Sur, por la linea de su tierra lo que necesiten, sin salir de la media legua que se les mercenó, siendo advertencia que á todos los que les ha tocado tierra rota en su merced que otros rompieron, para Abril proximo de 1835, les han de romper otra tanta en la que ler ioco iriaza, y de no verificarlo asi, sembraran en tierra rota hasta que se les rompa, quedando todos conformes en esto y demas reparto ; y para que las gozen en quieta y pacifica posesion, por si sus heroderes y sucesores, y cumplido el tiempo que señalan las leyes de la materia en iguales gracias, para que puedan venderlas ó cambiarlas á la persona que fuere su voluntad. Eyo el espresado alcalde àye que autorizaba este documento, como lo autorizo en toda forma de derecho y con arreglo á las facultades que me son conferidas, firmandolo con los de mi asistencia de que doy fe. Vicente Otero. De asistencia José Antonio Maldonado. De asistencia.

Es copia fiel y legalmente sacada de su original á que me remito, pedida por los interesados.

Tagique, 25 de Diciembre, de 1834.

VICÈNTE OTERO.

Surveyor General's Office, Translator's Department,
Santa Fé, New Mexico, August 23, 1859.

The above is a true copy of the original on file in this office.

DAVID V. WHITING,
Translator.

GRANT—TRANSLATION.

Valencia, *March* 9, 1834.

Most Excellent Sir: Manuel Sanchez, for himself and in the name of nineteen individuals, all residents of Valencia, represents to your excellency that having discovered a tract of land suitable for cultivation at the point of Tajique, which is vacant, and consequently will not be to the injury of any third party, on the contrary, the condition of the petitioners will be bettered on account of the limited amount of land which they can now cultivate, and that your excellency, in compliance with the law which recommends the encouragement of agriculture, be pleased to direct that the above-mentioned land, containing one-half of a league in circumference, be donated to them, protesting to pay all costs in good faith, &c.

MANUEL SANCHEZ.

Santa Fé, *March* 17, 1834.

The constitutional justice of Valencia, to which jurisdiction Tajique belongs, as I am informed, will make the division asked for, within the boundaries they set forth, provided no injury will result to any third party, the grant temporarily made by the government, to avoid delay in planting their crops, being subject to the confirmation of the most excellent deputation when it shall meet.

SARRACINO.

At this point of Tajique, on the ninth day of April, one thousand eight hundred and thirty-four, in compliance with the provisional order of the political chief to place the parties in possession, in order that the individuals who asked for a grant to said land, containing one-half league in circumference, should not lose their crops, I, Citizen Vicente Otero, constitutional justice of the township of Valencia, proceeded to the place for that purpose, with two attending witnesses, which said office is entitled to, commencing by measuring the one-half league in circumference, having in the first place set aside one hundred and seventy-two varas in the most convenient place for a town site, and from the centre thereof the one-half league in the direction of the four cardinal points of the compass was measured in the following manner: the first towards the south, which reached to a thick cedar a little above the cañon called "De los Pinos;" the second towards the north, to the cañon De Las Migas, where a pine tree was marked with a cross; the third towards the west, to the little table lands of the Cueva, where another pine tree was marked with a cross; the fourth towards the east to the lone pine, said measurements having been made in the presence of twelve of the grantees. The subdivision of the arable land to which each one was entitled to was omitted, on account of the absence of seven of those contained in the granting act, directing the persons present to commence planting their crops, with the understanding that when the proper time arrived I would return to subdivide the land, informing them that no one acquired any right to the land he cultivated excepting those to whom it should fall by lot, with the condition that whosoever received the land which was broken up should break up a like quantity for the first occupant; and for the purpose of placing this on record and other proper objects, I, the aforesaid justice, signed this document, with my attending witnesses, to which I certify.

VICENTE OTERO.

Attending:
JACINTO SANCHEZ.
JOSÉ MANUEL MALDONADO.

At this place of Tajique, on the twenty-fourth day of December, one thousand eight hundred and thirty-four, I, Citizen Vicente Otero, constitutional justice of the jurisdiction of Valencia, in fulfilment of the foregoing document, and in the presence of my attending witnesses, I caused to appear before me the persons to whom this place was granted, who, being present, I informed them of the operation to be performed, as set forth in the foregoing document, and they willingly consented to receive whatever titleable land each one was justly entitled to; whereupon, the calculation being made, I commenced measuring from west to east one hundred and twelve varas to each one; leaving out, in the first place, twelve varas as outlets to the town, having placed them in possession in the following order: 1st. Measured to Maria Gertrudis Chaves, who is bounded by the lands of Antonio Otero. 2d. Antonio Otero, who is bounded by the lands of Maria Gertrudis Chaves and those of Manuel Garcia. 3d. Manuel Garcia, who is bounded by Antonio Otero and José Lorenzo Otero. 4th. José Lorenzo Otero, bounded by Manuel Garcia and Matias Sanchez. 5th. Matias Sanchez, bounded by José Lorenzo Otero and José Antonio Zamora. 6th. José Antonio Zamora, bounded by Matias Sanchez and Rafael Sanchez. 7th. Rafael Sanchez, bounded by José Antonio Zamora and Francisco Moya. 8th. Francisco Moya, bounded by Rafael Sanchez and José Maria Maldonado. 9th. José Maria Maldonado, bounded by Francisco Moya and Cristobal Zamora. 10th. Cristobal Zamora, bounded by José Maria Maldonado and Lazaro Ramirez. 11th. Lazaro Ramirez, bounded by Cristobal Zamora and Mateo Anaya. 12th. Mateo Anaya, bounded by Lazaro Ramirez and Ignacio Cedillo. 13th. Ignacio Cedillo, bounded by Mateo Anaya and Roman Zamora. 14th. Roman Zamora, bounded by Ignacio Cedillo and Domingo Zamora. 15th. Domingo Zamora, bounded by Roman Zamora and José Chavez. 16th. José Chavez, bounded by Domingo Zamora and Antonio Sanchez. 17th. Antonio Sanchez, bounded by José Chavez; José Sanchez to the west of the temple; Divinsio Vigil to the west of the temple; giving to all the privilege of breaking up such land as they may want, on a line with their own, without going beyond the half league granted to them; it being understood that those having received land which has been broken up by others, within their lot, shall break up an equal quantity for the person entitled to it on unbroken land, by the month of April, 1835; and if said condition is not complied with, they will continue using the land they have broken up originally until other land is broken for them. All having expressed their satisfaction at this and all other matters connected with the division of the land, and in order that they, their heirs and successors, may enjoy the same peaceably and quietly, and in order that they may barter their land or dispose of it to whomsoever they may see proper at the expiration of the period prescribed by law for such grants, I, the aforesaid justice, said I would authorize this document, as I did authorize it, in due form of law, and by virtue of the powers in me vested, signing with those in my attendance, to which I certify.

VICENTE OTERO.

Attending:
JOSÉ ANTONIO MALDONADO.

The above is a true and faithful copy of the original to which reference is made, asked for by the parties interested.

VICENTE OTERO.

TAJIQUE, *December* 25, 1834.

SURVEYOR GENERAL'S OFFICE,
Santa Fé, New Mexico, May 1, 1859.

The foregoing is a correct translation of the original on file in this office.

DAVID V. WHITING,
Translator.

The foregoing is a true copy of the original on file in this office.
WM. PELHAM,
Surveyor General, Santa Fé, New Mexico.

TESTIMONY.

PEDRO CANDELARIA and JOSÉ MARIA LUCERO sworn:
Question. Have you any interest in this case?
Answer. We have not.
Question. How long has the town been settled?
Answer. We have both known it to have been settled before 1842, and it was in existence when the United States took possession of the country in 1846.
Question. What is the present population of the town?
Answer. About 420 souls.

PEDRO CANDELARIA.
JOSÉ M. LUCERO.

Sworn and subscribed before me this 6th day of May, 1859.
WM. PELHAM, *Surveyor General.*

SURVEYOR GENERAL'S OFFICE,
Santa Fé, New Mexico, August 23, 1859.
The above is a true copy of the original on file in this office.
WM. PELHAM,
Surveyor General.

REPORT.

This case was set for trial on the 6th day of May, 1859.

The parties claim a perfect title to the lands embraced within the limits of said town by virtue of a grant made to Manuel Sanchez and nineteen other individuals, on the 17th day of March, 1834, by Francisco Sarracino, the political chief or acting governor of New Mexico at that time; and judicial possession given to the parties by Vicente Otero, the constitutional justice of the precinct of Valencia, on the 24th December, 1834, by order of the political chief.

The document presented as the basis of their claim is a certified copy of all the proceedings had in the case, made by the justice of the peace who placed them in possession.

Testimony has also been produced to prove that the town was in existence in the year 1846.

The title being complete, and the existence of the town having been duly proven, the grant to the town of Tajique is approved and ordered to be transmitted to Congress for its action in the premises.

WM. PELHAM,
Surveyor General.

SURVEYOR GENERAL'S OFFICE,
Santa Fé, New Mexico, May 10, 1859.

SURVEYOR GENERAL'S OFFICE,
Santa Fé, New Mexico, July 21, 1859.
The foregoing is a true copy of the original on file in this office.
WM. PELHAM,
Surveyor General.

Documents composing claim No. 22.

1. Notice—Spanish.
2. Notice—translation.
3. Grant—Spanish.
4. Grant—translation.
5. Testimony.
6. Report.

CLAIM NO. 22.

TOWN OF TORREON.

NOTICE—SPANISH.

Aviso.—Al agrimensor general del Nuevo Mejico se le avisa por el presente que bajo las prevenciones de la 8ª seccion del decreto del Congreso aprobado el dia 22 de Julio de 1854, titulado "Un acto para crear los destinos de agrimensor general del Nuevo Mejico, Kansas y Nebraska, para conceder donaciones á los pobladores actuales, y para otros fines."

Yo Nerio Antonio Montoya (y en comun con otros) vecino del condado de Valencia en el Territorio de Nuevo Mejico, reclamo la donacion de un sitio de plaza y labor, conocido con el nombre del Torreon en dicho condado, y el dicho recamante es el original, ha estado en posesion continua desde la consecion del titulo y terreno hasta la fecha y desde entonces hasta la presente se halla poblado. El titulo adjunto al presente aviso es completo pues en el este la peticion hecha al H. Antonio Sandobal prefecto por el govierno de Mejico y el dicho prefecto en uso de sus facultades por la ley de 4 de Enero de 1813 y 20 de Marzo de 1837, y otros sobre la materia decretó la solicitud en favor del reclamante para que en comun con otros personas y familias fuera poblado el dicho sitio, para lo cual el Juez de Paz ordenado por el Prefecto Sandobal y en uso de sus atribuciones consedio al reclamante la posesion judicial que consta el en titulo que se acompaña á este aviso, en la cual consta que desde el dia 10 de Marzo de 1841, este en posecion el reclamante del dicho sitio de plaza y labor, la cantidad de varas reclamadas son de norte á sur cinco mil varas, y de oriente á poniente una y media leguas, todo dentro de los limites de los linderos espresados en el titulo. El espresado terreno esta dentro del condado de Valencia en el precinto nombrado el Torreon y Tagique.

SANTA FÉ, *Enero* 8 *de* 1856.

NERIO ANTONIO MONTOYA.

SURVEYOR GENERAL'S OFFICE, TRANSLATOR'S DEPARTMENT,
Santa Fé, New Mexico, September 10, 1859.

The above is a true copy of the original on file in this office.

DAVID V. WHITING,
Translator.

NOTICE—TRANSLATION.

The surveyor general of New Mexico is hereby informed that under the provisions of the eighth section of the act of Congress approved July 22, 1854, entitled "An act to establish the office of surveyor general of New Mexico, Kansas, and Nebraska, to grant donations to actual settlers therein, and for other purposes," I, Nerio Antonio

Montoya, (and in common with others,) resident of the county of Valencia, in the Territory of New Mexico, claim the donation of a site for a town and for cultivation, known by the name of El Torreon, in said county, and the said claimant has had continued possession from the date the said site was granted up to the present date, and that it has been occupied during that period. The title accompanying this petition is perfect, as it contains the petition made to the Hon. Antonio Sandoval, a prefect under the government of Mexico; and the said prefect by virtue of the authority vested in him by the laws of January 4, 1813, and March 20, 1837, and others appertaining to the case, decreed in favor of the claimant that in common with other persons and families they should settle said site, whereupon the justice of the peace, directed by the prefect, Sandoval, and by virtue of the authority in him vested, placed the parties in judicial possession, as will appear by the deed herewith accompanying, by which it appears that the claimant has been in possession of said town site and lands for cultivation from the 10th of March. The quantity claimed is from north to south five thousand varas, and from east to west one and one-half league, all within the boundaries expressed in the deed. The aforementioned land is situated in the county of Valencia, in the precinct called Torreon and Tajique.

NERIO ANTONIO MONTOYA.

Santa Fé, *January* 8, 1856.

Surveyor General's Office, Translator's Department,
Santa Fé, New Mexico, June 15, 1859.

The foregoing is a correct translation of the original on file in this office.

DAVID V. WHITING,
Translator.

Surveyor General's Office,
Santa Fé, New Mexico, August 27, 1859.

The above is a true copy of the original on file in this office.

WM. PELHAM,
Surveyor General.

GRANT—SPANISH.

Sello Tercero. [sello.] Dos Reales.

Para los años de mil ochocientos cuarenta y mil ochoerentos cuarenta yuna.

En esta jurisdicion de Valencia á los quinso dias del mes de Febrero de mil ochocientos cuarenta y uno, ante mi el C. Vicente Otero Juez de Paz suplente de dicha jurisdicion, y los testigos de mi asistencia, comparecieron veinte y siete individuos de esta misma jurisdicion diciendo que en virtud de no tener terreno en que poder cultivar tierra para poder mantener sus familias estan propuestos á pedir el punto del Torreon, y que á cuyo fin, confieren por este, todo su poder y amplio, á Don Nerio Antonio Montoya para que á su nombre y representacion de sus propias personas derecho y acciones, solicite la merced del espresado punto del Torreon, á donde corresponde, y para los fines que son consiguientes, estiendo el presente poder firmandolo con los testigos de mi asistencia de que doy fee.

VICENTE OTERO.

De asistencia: JOAQUIN ALARIA.
De asistencia: JUAN SANCHES.

Admito el antecedente poder.

NEREO ANTO. MONTOYA.

Señor Prefecto D. Antonio Sandobal:

El C. Nereo Antonio Montoya vecino de Valencia por se y á nombre de los individuos que cita el adjunto poder ante V. S. con el devido respecto paresco y digo; que viendome escaso tanto yo como mis poderdantes, de terreno de labor para la manutencion de nuestras familias y hallandose libre sin perjuicio de tercero el ojo del Torreon, cuya veracidad de las tierras que este baña prometen una esperanza muy ventajosa en la agricultura cosa muy bien recomendable por nuetras sabias leyes, bajo estos principios paso vendidamente á suplicar á V.S. se sirva en nombre de la nacion concedernos el goce de dicho terreno en los terminos siquientes; que del ojo ya citado para el Norte con las tierras de Tajique que habra cosa de ochocientas varas para el sur una legua, para el oriente hasta donde alcanza la agua y por el poniente hasta el rancho do mi pertenencia que habra cosa de quinientas varas, por lo espuesto.

H. V.S. pido y suplico se me conceda lo que pido, para que se nos estienda la merced de estilo sin perjuicio de los derechos judiciales con lo que reciviremos merced.

Alburquerque, Febrero 16 de 1841.

NEREO ANTONIO MONTOYA.

BARELAS, *Febrero* 23 *de* 1841.

Pasa esta instancia al Juez de Paz de Tome para que informe circumstanciadamente tanto sobre si los licitantes tienen terrenos de que subsistir, como si el que solicitan es baldio y no pertenece á alguna persona y la naturaleza del terreno.

SANDOBAL.

FRANCISCO SARRACINO, *Secretario.*

TOME, *Marzo* 3 *de* 1841.

En cumplimiento al Decrets del Sov. Prefecto Don Antonio Sandobal fecha 23 del proximo Febrero, digo que los individuos anotados en la adjunta lista me he informado no tienen tierras suficientes en que subsistir y el terreno solicitado ofrece las ventagas que el presentante espone en su antecedente presentacion, no es perjuicio de terceros y esta baldio. So tachado no vale.

JUAN DE JESUS CHAVEZ.

BARELAS, *Marzo 3 de* 1841.

Por lo que resulta del anterior informe parece no haber obstaculo para conceder á los licitantes la gracia que solicitan, en tal virtua pase esta instancia al Juez de Paz de Tome D. Juan Chavez para que pase á dar la posesion que por esta Prefectura se les concede nacional y personalmente en el nominado terreno cuya posesion formalozara el dicho Juez á nombre de la Nacion Mejicana (Q. D. G.) con todas las solemnidades de estilo y sin perjucio de tercero, dejandro libres los pastos, leñaderos, cortes de madera, y caminos acustombrados, solo para labor plaza corrales y demas usos comunes y necesarios señalandoles el terreno suficiente para uno y otro sopena de nulidad si incurrieren en alguna falta, y en la misma incurriran si no cultivan la tierra dentro del termino prevenido por las leyes ; á cuyo efecto el predicho juez formara el espediente correspondiente, y con el dara cuenta á esta Prefectura para que quede archivado en sus registros.

ANTONIO SANDOBAL.

FRANCISCO SARRACINO, *Secretario.*

En esta jurisdicion de Tome á los diez dias del meo de Marzo del año de mil ochocientos cuarenta y uno yo el juez de Paz de dicha jurisdiccion C. Juan de Jesus Chavez, en virtua de la comision que me es conferida por el Sov. Prefecto del Segundo Distrito D. Antonio Sandobal por el anterior decreto de tres del corriente, y en cumplimiento de dicho decreto pase el puesto del Torreon y hallandome en el citado parago con situacion de Don Nerio Antonio Montoya y los demas pobladores que constan en la adjunta lista á quienes les hise saber la merced que antecede y no haviendo resultado contradicion de partes, pase con dos testigos de asistencia que al efecto nombre á reconocer el terreno, y tirando las medidas de Norte á Sur una legua de oriente á poniente legua y media, y les puse por linderos de Norte á sur el lindero de Tajique por el Norte, sur el serro del cuerbo, oriente en donde junta la cañada del Torreon con la del Cuerbo, Poniente el lindero del rancho del sitado Don Nereo Antonio Montoya dentro de estas medidas les medi á cada poblador cien varas de tierra para lavor tirados de oriente á poniente, á mas de las cien varas en donde les señale la plaza para corra les y demas usos comunes les di á cada poblador un pedaso de tierra para huertas inmediatas á la misma plaza pues asi me parecio de justicia y que los mismos pobladores asi me pidieron lo que les concedi como queda dicho, á Don Nerio Antonio Montoya le di á mas de las cien varas que tiene senaladas el ancon que esta al Norte del mismo serro del Torreon, á Mauricio Sanches le di por suerte el anconsisto del Rancho del finado Don Bartolome Baca al sur hasta el camino acostumbrado del cañon de los Comanches oriente hasta el camino de Tajique, Norte el Rio, Poniente á donde nace el ojo que les concedi para que las go sen por si sur hijos herederos y subsesores, cultivadas dichas tierras en el termino de la ley todo lo que les concedi nacional y personalmente á nombre del Supremo Gobierno de la Nacion Mejicana (Q. D. G.) á cuya masa pertenecemos quedandos advertidos los dichos pobladores del sitado decreto del Sov. Prefecto y en cuya los cogi de la mano los pasie poriachas tiaras tiranon piedras arrancaron sacates dieron voces diciendo todos á una vos viva viva el Supreme Gobierno de la Nacion Mejicana (Q. D. G.) y en señal de verdadera posesion la que les di y aprendieron quieta y pacifica sin contradicion, y para que conste lo puse por diligencia que firme con los de mi asistencia con quenes antuo á falta de escribanos que no los hay en este Departmento en dicho dia mes y año de que doy fee como dicho es. So entre renglon C. Juan de Jesus Chavez, vale.

JUAN DE JESUS CHAVES.

Asistencia :
    Juan Luera,
Asistencia:
    Antonio Barela.

Otro si por no haber citado los linderos de las tierras de labor que les señale lo pongo en este auto, y son de Norte a Sur desde la Mecita que esta á el otro lado del Rio, sur le asequia madre en donde quedan dose varas libres para que transiten y saquen sus cosechas los referidos pobladores doy fe fecha.

JUAN DE JESUS CHAVEZ.

Asistencia:
    Juan Luera.
Asistencia:
    Antonio Barela.

SURVEYOR GENERAL'S OFFICE, TRANSLATOR'S DEPARTMENT,
Santa Fé, New Mexico, September 10, 1859.

The above is a true copy of the original on file in this office.

DAVID V. WHITING, *Translator*.

GRANT—TRANSLATION.

Seal third. [SEAL.] Two reals.

For the years one thousand eight hundred and forty and one thousand eight hundred and forty-one.

In this jurisdiction of Valencia, on the fifteenth day of February, in the year one thousand eight hundred and forty-one, before me, Citizen Vicente Otero, substitute justice of the peace of said jurisdiction, and my attending witnesses, appeared twenty-seven individuals of this same jurisdiction, who stated that, having no land to cultivate to procure the means of supporting their families, they have determined to ask for the site called Torreon, and for that purpose they hereby confer ample authority upon Don Nerio Antonio Montoya, in their name and representing their persons, rights, and interests, to solicit a grant to the aforementioned site of Torreon from the proper authority, and for the benefit of whom it may concern I have executed this power of attorney, signing the same with my attending witnesses, to which I certify.

Attending :
    Joaquin Alarid.
    Juan Sanches.

VICENTE OTERO.

I accept the foregoing trust.

NERIO ANTONIO MONTOYA.

Seal third. [SEAL.] Two reals.
For the years one thousand eight hundred and forty and one thousand eight hundred and forty-one.

To the honorable prefect, Don Antonio Sandoval:

Citizen Nerio Antonio Montoya, a resident of Valencia, for himself and in the name of the individuals contained in the accompanying power of attorney, appears before your honor with all due respect and states, that myself as well as my clients being short of tillable land for the support of our families, and the Torreon spring being unoccupied, and the fertility of the soil it waters being such that it promises to yield a bountiful crop and be a benefit to agriculture, a purpose so much recommended by our wise law ; for these reasons I humbly pray your honor to grant us, without injury to third parties, the above-mentioned lands in the name of the nation, with the following boundaries : From the spring above mentioned towards the north with the lands of Tajique, a distance of about eight hundred varas ; to the south one league ; on the east as far as the water reaches, and on the west to the farm belonging to me, being a distance of about five hundred varas. In view of all which I pray and request your honor to grant our petition in order that the customary title deed may be executed without injury to judicial rights, by which we will receive grace.

NERIO ANTONIO MONTOYA.

ALBUQUERQUE, *February* 16, 1841.

BARELAS, *February* 23, 1841.

This petition is referred to the justice of Tomé to report fully if the petitioners have any lands from which to obtain their subsistence, and also if the land they ask for is vacant and belongs to no one, and what is the nature of the land.

SANDOVAL.

FRANCISCO SARRACINO, *Secretary.*

TOMÉ, *March* 1, 1841.

In compliance with the decree of the prefect, Don Antonio Sandoval, dated on the 23d day of February last past, I have to report that I have ascertained that the persons contained in the accompanying list have not lands sufficient to subsist on, and that the land solicited offers all the advantages the petitioner claims for it. It will not injure any third party and is unoccupied. What has been erased is void.

JUAN DE JESUS CHAVES.

BARELAS, *March* 3, 1841.

From the foregoing report it appears that there is no obstacle in granting the request of the petitioners ; therefore these proceedings are referred to Don Juan Chaves, justice of the peace of Tomé, in order that he may proceed to give them the national and personal possession of the land granted by this prefecture, which possession will be formally made in the name of the Mexican nation, (which may God preserve,) with all the customary solemnities, and without injury to third parties, leaving pastures, wood, timber, and customary roads free, excepting lands for cultivation, town site, enclosures, and for other necessary and common uses, giving a sufficient amount of land to each one, under penalty of forfeiture if they commit any crime or if they fail to cultivate the land within the time prescribed by law; for which purpose the aforesaid justice will take such steps as may be necessary, reporting the same to this prefecture in order that it may be filed in its archives.

ANTONIO SANDOVAL.

FRANCISCO SARRACINO, *Secretary*.

In this jurisdiction of Tomé, on the 10th day of March, one thousand eight hundred and forty-one, I, Citizen Juan de Jesus Chaves, justice of the peace of said jurisdiction, by virtue of the commission entrusted to me by Don Antonio Sandoval, prefect of the second district, in the foregoing decree of the third instant, and in compliance with said decree I proceeded to the site of El Torreon, and being then there, having summoned Don Nerio Montoya and the other settlers whose names appear on the accompanying list, to whom I made known the foregoing grant, and no question having arisen, I proceeded, with two attending witnesses whom I appointed for the purpose, to examine the land, and measuring the same from north to south one league, and from east to west one and a half league, I gave them from north to south, as their northern boundary, the boundary of Tajique; on the south the Cuero mountains; east, the junction of the Torreon cañon with that of the Cuero; west, the boundary of the farm of Don Nerio Montoya. Within these boundaries I gave to each settler one hundred varas of land for cultivation, measured from east to west. In addition to the one hundred varas I assigned to them for building the town, enclosures, and other common purposes, I gave to each settler a piece of land immediately adjoining the town for gardens, considering the same to be just, and having been requested to do so by the settlers, which request I complied with, as aforestated. In addition to the hundred varas above mentioned, I gave to Don Nerio Montoya the valley which is north of the Torreon mountain. I gave to Mauricio Sanchez, for his share, the little valley of the farm of the late Bartolomé Baca, to the common road of the cañon de Los Camanches, towards the south; on the east to the Tajique road; on the north the river, and on the west to the source of the spring, which I gave them to hold for themselves, their children, heirs, and successors, said lands to be cultivated within the period prescribed by law; all of which was granted rationally and personally in the name of the Mexican nation, (which may God preserve,) to which they belong. The settlers being notified of the aforementioned petition of the honorable prefect, I took them by the hand, walked with them over the land; they threw stones, pulled up grass, and all at one time cried long life, long life, to the supreme government of the Mexican nation, (which may God preserve;) and in testimony of legal possession, which I gave them, and they received quietly and peaceably, without opposition; and in order that it may so appear, I placed it on record, signing the same with my attending witnesses, with whom I act in the absence of notaries, there being none in this territory on said day, month, and year, to which I certify as above stated. Citizen Juan de Jesus Chaves interlined is valid.

JUAN DE JESUS CHAVES.

Attending:
JUAN LUERA.
ANTONIO BARELA.

Addenda.—Not having mentioned the boundaries of the tillable lands I measured out for them, I state them in this decree, and they are, from north to south, from the little table land on the opposite side of the river, south to the main ditch, (Acequia Madre,) where twelve varas are left free for a road and to allow the said settlers to transport their crops. I certify date *ut supra.*

JUAN DE JESUS CHAVES.

Attending:
JUAN LUERA.
ANTONIO BARELA.

SURVEYOR GENERAL'S OFFICE, TRANSLATOR'S DEPARTMENT,
Santa Fé, New Mexico, June 15, 1859.

The foregoing is a correct translation of the original on file in this office.

DAVID V. WHITING,
Translator.

SURVEYOR GENERAL'S OFFICE,
Santa Fé, New Mexico, August 30, 1859.

The above is a true copy of the original on file in this office.

WM. PELHAM,
Surveyor General.

TESTIMONY.

JOSÉ MARIA LUCERO sworn:
Question. Have you any interest in this claim?
Answer. I have not.
Question. How long have you resided in the Territory, and what have been your opportunities for knowing the town of Torreon?
Answer. I have resided in the Territory for forty years; I reside near the town and pass through it nearly every day.
Question. Was the town in existence in 1846, when the United States took possession in 1846?
Answer. It was.
Question. What is the actual population of the town?
Answer. About eighty families.

JOSÉ MARIA LUCERO.

Sworn and subscribed before me this 6th day of May, 1859.
                    WM. PELHAM,
                        Surveyor General.

                SURVEYOR GENERAL'S OFFICE,
            Santa Fé, New Mexico, August 26, 1859.
The above is a true copy of the original on file in this office.
                    WM. PELHAM,
                        Surveyor General.

PEDRO CANDELARIA sworn:
Question. Have you any interest in this case?
Answer. I have not.
Question. How long have you resided in the Territory, and what have been your opportunities for knowing the town of Torreon?
Answer. I have resided in the Territory for thirty-eight years; I have always lived near the town, and have passed through it several times.
Question. Was the town in existence in 1846 when the United States took possession of the country?
Answer. It was.
Question. What is the actual population of the town?
Answer. About 550 inhabitants.
                    PEDRO CANDELARIA.

Sworn and subscribed before me this 6th day of May, 1859.
                    WM. PELHAM,
                        Surveyor General.

                SURVEYOR GENERAL'S OFFICE,
            Santa Fé, New Mexico, August 26, 1859.
The above is a true copy of the original on file in this office.
                    WM. PELHAM,
                        Surveyor General.

REPORT.

This case was set for trial on the 6th day of May, 1859.
On the 16th day of February, 1841, Nerio Antonio Montoya, authorized and empowered by twenty-seven individuals of the jurisdiction of Valencia, made application to Antonio Sandoval, prefect of the central district of New Mexico, for a tract of land at the Torreon spring, with the boundaries therein mentioned. On the 23d of the same month the prefect, Sandoval, referred the petition to the justice of the peace, requiring him to report upon the condition of the petitioners as well as upon the nature of the land asked for. Juan de Jesus Chavez, the justice, having on the 1st March reported favorably upon the application, he was ordered by Sandoval, the prefect, on the 3d March, 1841, to place the parties in possession, which was done on the 10th of the same month.

Testimony has been introduced by the claimants proving the town to have been in existence in the year 1846. The papers acted upon in the case are original and believed to be genuine. The claimants in their notice refer to the laws of January 4, 1813, and March 20, 1837, for the authority vested in the granting officer to make the grant. The first of these references has no bearing on the case whatever. Owing to the absence of the necessary Mexican statistics, which have not been furinshed and cannot be procured here, this office cannot ascertain if the law referred to gives to the granting officer the authority claimed to have been given to him under that law.

The testimony in the case proves the town to have been in existence in the year 1846, when possession was taken of the country by the United States; and as the instructions to this office concede that the proof of its existence in 1846 is presumptive evidence of a grant having been made, and as no evidence has been produced to prove that the Mexican government disapproved of the action of the prefect, it is believed that the land claimed was considered by the Mexican government to have been severed from the public domain, and as it is the duty of the government of the United States by treaty stipulations to act in the premises in the same manner as the former government would have acted, the claim is hereby approved and ordered to be transmitted to Congress for its action in the premises.

WM. PELHAM,
Surveyor General.

SURVEYOR GENERAL'S OFFICE,
Santa Fé, New Mexico, May 12, 1859.

SURVEYOR GENERAL'S OFFICE,
Santa Fé, New Mexico, August 25, 1859.

The above is a true copy of the original on file in this office.

WM. PELHAM,
Surveyor General.

Schedule of documents comprising claim No 23.

1. Notice.
2. Power of attorney—Spanish.
3. Power of attorney—translation.
4. Grant—Spanish.
5. Grant—translation.
6. Testimony.
7. Report.

CLAIM No. 23.

TOWN OF MANZANO.

NOTICE.

Territory of New Mexico, }
County of Valencia.

To the Hon. *William Pelham, surveyor general of the Territory of New Mexico:*

Your petitioner, Ramon Cisneros, on behalf of himself and his associates, citizens and residents of the town of Manzano, in the county of Valencia, in the Territory of New Mexico, showeth unto your honor: That in the year A. D. 1829, as will appear by document herewith filed, marked exhibit A, a certain tract or parcel of land was ceded to your petitioner and his associates by the then territorial department of New Mexico, as will appear by reference to said document, for the purpose of settlement, and that upon said tract of land a settlement of a town was made called and known as the town of Manzano. The limits and boundaries of said cession are as follows: bounded from north to south from the Torreon to the old Mission of Abo, and from east to west from the table lands of Jumanes to the mountains. That by virtue of said session your petitioner and his associates settled upon and put in cultivation much of the lands thus ceded. That they know of no adverse claim to said land, and prays your honor to grant to him and his associates, whose names appear upon said document, a patent right and certificate to said lands, and that the same may be set apart to them from the public lands of this Territory; and, as in duty bound, will ever pray, &c.

RAMON CISNEROS.

Surveyor General's Office,
Santa Fé, New Mexico, August 10, 1859.
The above is a true copy of the original on file in this office.
WM. PELHAM,
Surveyor General.

POWER OF ATTORNEY TO RAMON CISNEROS—SPANISH.

Territorio de N. M., *Condado de Balencia:*

Juan Luera juez du paz del precinto del Manzano, condado de Balencia, Territorio de N. M., certifico que habiendose funtado en junta dicho pueble ante mi todos los pobladores de la mersed del Manzano, y nombran á Don Ramon Cisneros comisionado, para que haga un aviso escrito y entregar el aviso en manos del agrimensor general, para que haga cualesquier aviso necesario, para asegurar la confirmacion de la mersed al Manzano, solo para el uso de los residentes de la mersed segun las condiciones de dicha mersed.

Y en testimonio de lo mismo pongo mi mano y sello en mi oficina
delante dos testigos Santiago Cumenness y Nepo. Luera este dia
[L. S.] 28 de Diciembre de 1855.

JUAN LUERA,
Juez de Paz.

Testigos:
JAMES CUMMING.
NEPO. LUERA.

SURVEYOR GENERAL'S OFFICE, TRANSLATOR'S DEPARTMENT,
Santa Fé, New Mexico, August 23, 1859.

The above is a true copy of the original on file in this office.

DAVID V. WHITING,
Translator.

POWER OF ATTORNEY TO RAMON CISNEROS—TRANSLATION.

TERRITORY OF NEW MEXICO, *County of Valencia:*

I, Juan Luera, justice of the peace for the precinct of Manzano, county of Valencia, Territory of New Mexico, do hereby certify that the people of said town, composing the settlers under the grant to Manzano, convened before in a public meeting, and appointed Don Ramon Cisneros a commissioner to make a written notice and file the same before the surveyor general, and to do whatever may be necessary to secure the confirmation of the grant to Manzano for the benefit of the residents under the grant, according to the conditions of the same.

In testimony whereof, I have hereunto set my hand and seal, at my
[L. S.] office, before James Cummings and Nepomucino Luera, as witnesses, this 28th day of December, 1855.

JUAN LUERA,
Justice of the Peace.

Witnesses:
JAMES CUMMINGS.
NEPO. LUERA.

SURVEYOR GENERAL'S OFFICE,
Santa Fé, New Mexico, May 18, 1859.

The foregoing is a correct translation of the original on file in this office.

DAVID V. WHITING,
Translator.

SURVEYOR GENERAL'S OFFICE,
Santa Fé, New Mexico, August 12, 1859.

The above is a true copy of the original on file in this office.

WM. PELHAM,
Surveyor General.

GRANT—SPANISH.

M. Ylustre Ayuntamiento de Tomé:

El cuidadano José Manuel Trujillo por si y á nombre de los pobladores del Manzano, que constan anotados en el margen, con el devido respecto hacen presente á V. S. el que caresiendo del titulo de posesion de dicho punto que han poblado, y ser conosido el tal sitio por ningun dueño, se ha de servir V. S. el darnos la posesion de él, señalandonos los limites de terreno, que estamos poseyendo, y poniendonos por linderos de Norte á Sur desde el Torreon, hasta la antigua mision de Abó, y de Oriente á Poniente desde la Mesa llamada de Jumanes, hasta la Sierra, todo esto para pasteos y demas usos comunes, trabesias y servidumbres necesarias á toda poblocion construida sobre todos los solidos fundamentos de propiedad comun particular y habitada por los mismos; pidiendo á mas en circunstancia que para que cualesquiera individuos de los anotados, ú otros que en lo susesivo sin perfuicio de estos se admitieren en la nueva poblacion del Manzano, pueda adquirir legitima propiedad, ha de fabricar casa formal de terrado adobe, en la Plaza en donde se ba á construir la capilla (cuya licencia tenemos) y ha de hacer introduccion de suo bienes de toda clase, contribuyendo en todas las obras de comunidad, procurando el ingreso y adelanto de la poblacion, defendiendo con las armas los hogares de su Pueblo en todo su termino, contra cualquiera enemigo interior ó esterior y ultimamente que el que no habitare en dicha poblacion con la familia que le corresponde, pierda, habitando en otra, el derecho de propiedad que habia adquirido, por todo lo espuesto. A V. S. pedimos todos y cada uno se sirva por medio de una comision de su seno, mandar se nos señale los terminos de la poblacion en los puntos que llebamos referidos, y verificado se nos oblique á poner las masoneras correspondientes, para gobierno de los poblado res y publico de todo el Territorio, dandonos dicho terreno, á nombre del Supremo Gov. de la Nacion Mejicana, á cuya masa pertenecemos, pasando en seguida esta nuestra solicitud á la Exma. Diputacion Territorial, para que de S. E. emane la aprobacion correspondiente.

Tomé, *Sepbre.* 22 *de* 1829.

JOSÉ MAN'L TRUJILLO.†

El Ayuntamiento de la Jurisdiccion de Tomé, á consecuencia de la solicitud que antesede, en sesion de este dia ha acordado se eleve dicha solicitud á la Exma. Diputacion Territorial, esponiendo que la enunciada corporacion no encuentra embarazo alguno para que se les conceda á los impetrantes el terreno que solicitan, pues el unico que se encontró de las tierras de labor que en el terreno solisitado, le corresponden al Señor Teniente coronel retirado C. Bme. Baca, ha quedado vensido con que disfrute como nuevo repoblador de las que adquirio por posesion y por compra que hizo á los que lo poblaban ofresiendo que aunque no pasara á residir aquel punto lo fomentara, como lo ha verificado, y cultivará las tierras que reconzcan por suyas.

Tomé, 7bre. 25 de 1829.

JACINTO SANCHEZ.

Juan Baca, Secreto. into.

Secretaria de la Exma. Diputacion Territorial de Nuevo Méjico:

En sesion de 28 de Noviembre procsimo anterior, ha acordado esta Diputacion se ponga á la presente instancia, el decreto que sigue:— "Mediante el informe que antesede del Ayuntamiento de la Jurisdiccion de Tomé, el Alcalde de dicha Jurisdiccion pondrá en posesion á los impetrantes del terreno que solicitan, señalando á cada uno las tierras de labor que puedan cultivar defando las sobrantes para los demas individuos que en lo susesivo se quieran transportar á dicho terreno limitandose los linderos á una legua por cada rumbo."

Señores Sarracino, Baca y Caleza Baca.

Manzano, 24 de Dbre. de 1829.

En cumplimiento á lo dispuesto por la Exma. Diputacion Territorial, segun el acuerdo que antecede, pasé á este puesto del Manzano hoy dia de la fecha, y hallando reunidos á todos sus moradores, se les leyó el decreto, para su conosimiento, y en seguida, pasé á darles posesion del sitado puesto, en nombre de la nacion á asignandoles por centro de dicho terreno el alto del Pino de la Virgen que está en el centro de la labor, pues hai lo pidieron dichos pobladores, y habiendoles medido su legua por cada viento como la Exma. Diputacion lo dispuso en su anterior decreto, se les señaló por linderos, por el Norte, dos sabinos huerfanos que están en la cañada del alto que llaman del difunto Blas, por el Poniente la cesa que está al lado de dicho Poniente del (lado) de arriba: por el Sur, el alto que está al otro lado del arroyo de la sienega: por el oriente, con la mesa Colorado que llaman el Rancho de Don Pedro de la Torre, y habiendoles dado su posesion, pasé á la cabezera de la labor, y habiendoles ingsinuado les iba á repartir por suertes la tierra de labor arreglado al decreto que antesede, me respondieron todos unanimes, que les hiciera el honor de desarlos á cada uno en su tierra que tenian frabicado, lo que les concedi por pareserme asi conveniente, y que no quedara ninguno disgustado, y para su debida constancia, lo firmé con los de mi asistencia de que doy fé.

JACINTO SANCHEZ.

De Assa. Juan Jé. Sanchez.
De Assa. Nereo Antonio Montoya.

Pobladores del Manzano.

José Manl. Trujillo.
Bernardino Chavez.
Joaquin Sanchez.
Antonio Torres.

Diego Gonzales.
José Anto. Torres.
José Ma. Marquez.
Jn. Marquez.

Mariano Torres.
Gertrudis Benavides.
Santos Marquez.
Tomas Sanchez.
José Sisneros.
Ramon Sisneros.
Diego Sisneros.
Estanislado Otero.
José Ma. Perea.
Juan Perea.
José de Jesus Baldonado.
Anto. Mirabal.
Anastacio Mirabal.
Juan Chavez.
Jn. Gonzales, 2d.
Jn. Esteban Chavez.
Faustin Sanchez.
Francisco Belasquez.
Jn. Belasquez.
Anto. Candelaria.
Manuela Serna.
Anto. José Garcia.
Matias Montoya.
Anto. Torres.
Reyes Torres.
Jn. Archuleta.
José Leon Perea.
Juan de Herrera.
José Maul. Garcia.
Francisco Garcia.
Franco. Herrera.
Nicholas Salazar.
Rafael Montoya.
Matilde Montoya.
Jesus Savedra.
Nepomoseno Luera.
José Rafael Chavez.
Juan Luera.
Luis Romero.
Manuel Salas.
Franco. Serna.
Marcos Sedillo.
Juan Perea.
Manuel Trujillo.
Ygnacio Sedillo.
Ysidro Serna.
Jesus Serna.
Trenidad Salas.
Juan de Jesus Samora.
José Torres.
Anto. José Otero.

Ana Ma. Barela.
Grego. Sedillo.
Juan Sedillo.
José Sedillo.
Rafael Sedillo.
Alfonso Sedillo.
Juan Montaño.
Diego Sanchez.
José Mirabal.
Juan Castillo.
José Dolores Jaramillo.
Miguel Chavez.
Eulogio Saez.
Nereo Montoya.
Miguel Lucero.
Domingo Lucero.
José Maria Gonzales.
José Antonio Montoyo.
Francisco Torres.
Gaudalupe Perea.
Juana Peralta.
Son 67.
Yden mas.
José Sanchez.
Pedro Chavez.
Rafael Montoya.
Eugenio Cordoba.
Julian Sanchez.
Miguel Archuleta.
Domingo Sanchez.
Francisco Padia.
Nuevos Pobladores.
Pablo Gallego.
Alfonso Jaramillo.
José de Jesus Maldonado.
Santiago Lucero.
Toribio Mirabal.
Antonio José Luna.
Sipriano Torres.
Nicholas Torres.
Candido Chavez.
Juan Lucero.
José Ma. Torres.
Juan Cruz Telles.
Miguel Chavez.
José Padia.
Santiago Otero.
Juan Otero.
Ysidro Otero.
José Anto. Romero.
Juan José Romero.

Romulo Chavez.
José Sanchez y Curvo.
Martin Gurulé.
Desiderio Sanchez.
Juan de Jesus Maldonado.
Pablo Padia.
Manuel Sanchez Samora.
Manuel Sanchez y Chavez.
Luis Flores.
Franco. Romero y Luera.
Franco. Romero y Campos.
Doroteo Salas.
Antonio Romero y Baca.
Cruz Romero.
Franco. Garcia.
Luciano Garcia.
José Manuel Bustos.
Juan Montoya.
Manuel Torres.
Juan Sanchez.
Ramon Sanchez.
Julian Mirabal.
Luciano Chavez.
Lorenzo Roibali.
Domingo Archuleta.
Francisco Gonzales.
Juan Marquez.
Fernando Chavez.
Miguel Gerulé.
Nicholas Perea.
Francisco Sedillo.
Bernabé Salas.
Dario Apodaca.

Bibian Torres.
José Sanchez y Torres.
Lorenzo Torres.
José Sanchez Serna.
José Sais.
Manuel Lucero.
José Lucero.
Mateo Martin.
Roque Griego.
Gorge Tarin.
José Montoya.
José Montoya y Carvo.
Juan Agustin Romero.
José Jaramillo.
Antonio Peralta.
Jose Montoya y Garcia.
Juan José Torres.
Antonio Torres.
Juan Jaramillo.
Juan Lujan.
Juan Gonzales.
Juan Trujillo.
Juan José Chavez.
José Chavez Montoya.
José Chavez.
Bicente Baca.
Melquiades Padia.
Jesus Ma. Luera.
Franco. Torres.
Ygnacio Romero.
San G. Armiso.
Juan Aragon.

SURVEYOR GENERAL'S OFFICE, TRANSLATOR'S DEPARTMENT,
Santa Fé, New Mexico, August 23, 1859.

The above is a true copy of the original on file in this office.
DAVID V. WHITING,
Translator.

GRANT—TRANSLATION.

To the Illustrious Corporation of Tomé:

Citizen José Manuel Trujillo, for himself, and in the name of the settlers of Manzano, whose names appear on the margin, with due respect represents to your excellencies: That not having the deed of possession to the said town in which they have settled, and the site of said town being known to be owned by no one, we request your excellency to be pleased to grant us the possession thereof, giving us the land which we are now occupying; giving us as boundaries from north to south, from Torreon to the old mission of Abó, and from east to west, from the table lands called Jamanes to the mountain; all of which is to be for pasture grounds and other common purposes, cross roads and other uses necessary for every town established upon all the solid basis of common and private property, and inhabited by the same; requesting further, as a condition for any of the above-mentioned individuals, or any others to be admitted in future without injury to the former, to the new town of Manzano, to acquire legal property therein, that he shall construct a regular terraced house of adobe in the square where the chapel is to be constructed, (for which permission has been granted us,) and he shall bring with him his property of every description, contribute to all community labor, procure the increase and prosperity of the town, defending with arms the firesides of his town to the fullest extent against any domestic or foreign enemy; and finally, that the person who will not reside in said town with the family belonging to him, and who shall remove to another settlement, shall lose all right he may have acquired to his property.

In view of what has been above stated we all, and each of us, request that your excellencies will be pleased, through a committee of your body, to establish the boundaries of the town at the points above set forth, which being done, that we be compelled to establish the proper monuments for the information of the settlers and the public within the entire territory, granting us the said land in the name of the supreme government of the Mexican nation, to which government we belong, referring thereupon this our petition to the most excellent territorial deputation, in order that the proper approval may issue therefrom.

TOMÉ, *September 22, 1829.*

JOSÉ MANUEL TRUJILLO.

The corporation of the jurisdiction of Tomé, in view of the foregoing petition, in session of to-day, has resolved to refer said petition to the most excellent territorial deputation, with the remark that this corporation knows of no obstacle against granting to the petitioners the land they solicit, the only objection found being in regard to the arable land therein situated belonging to retired Lieutenant Colonel Bartolome Baca, who will be satisfied with the land which, as a new settler, he may acquire, together with that which he has purchased from other settlers, promising that although he will not establish his residence there, he will cultivate and improve the lands which may be recognized as his.

TOMÉ, *September 25, 1829.*

JACINTO SANCHEZ.

JUAN BACA,
   Acting Secretary.

Office of the secretary of the most excellent territorial deputation of New Mexico.

In session of the 28th of November last past, this deputation resolved that the following decree be added to the foregoing proceedings:

" By virtue of the foregoing report of the corporation of Tomé, the justice of that jurisdiction will place the petitioners in possession of the land they ask for, giving to each one the tillable land he may be able to cultivate, leaving the remainder for such other individuals who in the future may establish themselves therein, limiting the boundaries to one league in each direction."

JOSÉ ANTONIO CHAVEZ,
President.

RAMON ABREU,
Secretary.

MANZANO, *December* 24, 1829.

In compliance with the directions of the most excellent territorial deputation, as herein before expressed, I proceeded to this settlement of Manzano on the day of the date, and all the inhabitants thereof being assembled, the decree was read to them for their information, and thereupon I proceeded to give them possession of the aforesaid site in the name of the nation; establishing as the centre of said land the "Alto del pino de la Virgen," (heighth of the pine of the Virgen,) which is situated in the middle of the fields, the settlers having asked for that point, and having measured their league in the direction of the four cardinal points of the compass, as directed by the most excellent deputation in their foregoing decree, their boundaries were given to them as follows: On the north two solitary cedar trees in the cañon del alto, called the cañon of the deceased Ulas; on the west the summit of the hill, which is on the western side of the upper (torn); on the south the rise which is on the opposite side of the gulf of Cienega; on the east the mesa Colorado, called the Rancho of Don Pedro de la Torre; and having placed them in possession, I proceeded to the head of the tillable land, and having intimated to them that I was going to divide out their lands by lot in accordance with the foregoing decree, they unanimously answered, requesting me to do them the honor to let them retain the land they had already improved, which request I deemed proper to comply with, in order that no one should be dissatisfied. In testimony whereof I signed with my attending witnesses, to which I certify.

JACINTO SANCHEZ.

Attending,
   JUAN JOSÉ SANCHEZ.
Attending,
   NERIO ANTONIO MONTOYA.

PRIVATE LAND CLAIMS IN NEW MEXICO. 71

Settlers of Manzano.

José Manuel Trujell
Bernardino Chavez
Joaquin Sanchez
Antonio Torres
Diego Gonzalez
José Antonio Torres
José Maria Marquez
Juan Marquez
Mariano Torres
Gertrudis Benavideo
Santos Marquez
Tomas Sanchez
José Cisneros
Ramon Cisneros
Estanislao Otero
José Maria Perea
Juan Perea
José de Jesus Baldonado
Antonio Mirabal
Anastacio Mirabal
Juan Chavez
Juan Gonzalez, jr.
Juan Esteban Chavez
Faustin Sanchez
Francisco Velasquez
Juan Velasquez
Antonio Candelaria
Manuela Sena
Antonio José Garcia
Matias Montoya
Antonio Torres
Reijes Torres

Juan Archuleta
José Leon Perea
Juan de Herrera
José Manuel Garcia
Francisco Garcia
Francisco Herrera
Nicolas Salazar
Rafael Montoya
Matilde Montoya
Jesus Saavedra
Ana Maria Barela
Francisco Sedillo
Juan Sedillo
José Sedillo
Rafael Sedillo
Alfonso Sedillo
Juana Montaño
Diego Sanchez
José Miribal
Juan Castillo
José Dolores Juramillo
Miguel Chavez
Eulogia Saez
Nerio Montoya
Miguel Lucero
Domingo Lucero
José Maria Gonzalez
José Antonio Montoya
Francisco Torres
Guadalupe Perea
Juana Peralta.

Amounting to 61.

Further.

José Sanchez
Pedro Chaves
Rafael Montoya
Eugenio Cordova

Julian Sanchez
Miguel Archuleta
Domingo Sanchez
Francisco Padilla.

New Settlers.

Pablo Gallegos
Alfonso Jaramillo
José de Jesus Maldonado
Nepomuceno Luero
José Rafael Chaves

Juan de Jesus Zamora
José Torres
Antonio José Otero
Manuel Chaves
José Sanchez y Cueva.

Juan Luera	Martin Gurule
Luis Romero	Tiburcio Sanchez
Manuel Salas	Juan de Jesus Maldonado
Francisco Sena	Pablo Padillo
Marcos Sedillo	Cepriano Torres
Juan Perea	Nicolas Torres
Manuel Trajillo	Bian Torres
Ignacio Sedillo	José Sanchez y Torres
Pedro Sena	Lorenzo Torres
Jesus Sena	Cruz Flores
Trinidad Salas	Manuel Sanchez y Chaves.

SURVEYOR GENERAL'S OFFICE,
Santa Fé, New Mexico, May 18, 1859.

The foregoing is a correct translation of the original on file in this office.

DAVID V. WHITING,
Translator.

SURVEYOR GENERAL'S OFFICE,
Santa Fé, New Mexico, August 10, 1859.

The above is a true copy of the original on file in this office.

WM. PELHAM,
Surveyor General.

TESTIMONY.

SIMON DELGADO, sworn:

Question. Do you know the town called Manzano, and for how long have you known it?

Answer. I do. I have known it to have been settled from 1836 up to this date.

Question. Do you know if the town was in existence in the year 1846?

Answer. It was in existence at that time.

Question. Do you know any of the original settlers of that town?

Answer. I knew Felomena Sanchez, Ramon Cisneros, Juan Montoya, Juan Lucero, Santiago Otero, Juan Otero, Ysidro Otero, Manuel Lucero, José Lucero, Juan Sanchez, Ramon Sanchez, Fernando Chaves, José Chaves, Jesus Lucero, José Maria Marquez, Tomas Sanchez, Diego Cisneros, and others.

Question. Did you know these persons to be living at Manzano in 1846?

Answer. I knew they lived there. I resided then at the Bosque de los Pinos, and traded with many of them.

Question. Have you any interest in this claim?

Answer. I have none.

SIMON DELGADO.

Sworn and subscribed before me this 6th day of August, 1857.

WILLIAM PELHAM,
Surveyor General.

TOWN OF MANZANO.

FRNCISCO BACA, sworn:

Question. Did you know Ramon Abreu?

Answer. I did.

Question What office did he hold in the year 1829 under the Mexican government?

Answer. He was always in office as secretary of the territorial deputation.

Question. Are you acquainted with the signature of Ramon Abreu, and is his signature to the proceedings of the territorial deputation in this case genuine?

Answer. I am well acquainted with his signature, and the one shown to me is genuine.

FRANCISCO BACA Y ORTIZ.

Sworn and subscribed before me this 25th day of July, 1859.
WILLIAM PELHAM,
Surveyor General.

SURVEYOR GENERAL'S OFFICE,
Santa Fé, New Mexico, August 12, 1859.

The above is a true copy of the original on file in this office.
WILLIAM PELHAM,
Surveyor General.

REPORT.

TOWN OF MANZANO *vs.* THE UNITED STATES.

This case was set for trial on the 10th day of May, 1859.

On the 22d September, 1829, José Manuel Trujillo, for himself and in the name of the settlers of Manzano, petitioned the corporation of Tomé for a tract of land situate in the county of Valencia, with the boundaries therein set forth. The deputation, on the 25th of the same month, referred the petition to the territorial deputation, which, on the 28th of the following November, ordered the justice of the peace of the jurisdiction of Tomé to place the parties in possession, limiting the boundaries to one league in each direction, giving unto each one what he could cultivate, and leaving the remainder for any one who in the future should desire to remove there.

The land has been in the constant occupancy of the parties and their assigns from the date of the grant up to the present time. The grant is deemed to be a good and valid one, and therefore approved and ordered to be transmitted to Congress, with the request that there be confirmed to the town of Manzano one league towards the four cardinal points of the compass, as granted by the territorial deputation.

WILLIAM PELHAM,
Surveyor General.

SURVEYOR GENERAL'S OFFICE,
Santa Fé, New Mexico, August 10, 1859.

SURVEYOR GENERAL'S OFFICE,
Santa Fé, New Mexico, August 20, 1859.
The above is a true copy of the original on file in this office.
WILLIAM PELHAM,
Surveyor General.

CLAIM NO. 24.

TOWN OF SAN ISIDRO.

Schedule of documents composing claim No. 24.

No. 1. Notice—Spanish.
    2. Notice—Translation.
    3. Grant—Spanish.
    4. Grant—Translation.
    5. Report.

NOTICE—SPANISH.

ESTADOS UNIDOS DE AMERICA, }
Territorio de Nuevo Mejico. }
SANTA FÉ, *Enero* 28 *de* 1857.

Al agrimensor general del Nuevo Mexico se le avisa por el presente que bajo las prevenciones de la seccion octaba del decreto del Congreso aprobado el dia 22 de Julio de 1854, titulado un decreto para crear los destinos de agrimensor general del Nuevo Mejico, Kansas y Nebraska, para conceder donaciones á los pobladores actuales y para otros fines.

Nosotros, Dolores Perea, Francisco Sandobal, José Andres Sandobal, Antonio Baca, Desiderio Valdez, José Antonio Montoya, representantes legales de Antonio Armenta y Salvador Sandobal, reclamantes originales, reclamamos un pedazo de terreno poblado conocido y mencionado ser el Rancho de San Ysidro en Jemes en el condado de Santa Ana Territorio de Nuevo Mejico, et tal reclamo es hecho por una donacion hecha bajo la autoridad del gobierno Español y concedido por el Señor Don Juan Bautista de Ansa, gobernador del Nuevo Mejico, el dia dies y seis de mayo de 1786, año y posesion judicial del Alcalde Mayor Don Nerio Antonio Montoya en la misma fecha siendo el dicho reclamo incompleto por faltarle la cadena de titulo del agraciado original á los reclamantes actuales. No choca con ninguno otro la cantidad de tierra reclamada consta segun el antedicho titulo de dos mil novecientas varas la localidad en el condado de Santa Ana, sus linderos por el norte con tierras de Jemes por el sur con tierras del pueblo de Zia por el poniente la Sierra del Ojo del Espiritu Santo en los bancos que comunmente llaman, por el oriente con tierras del mencionado Alcalde Mayor Nerio Antonio Montoya que es el camino que baja de Cochiti a Jemes. Los reclamantes actuales son los herederos de los agraciador originales pero su ausencia de evidencias escritas suplicamos que sea confirmada la merced á los herederos legales de los agraciados originales.

FRANCISCO SANDOBAL,
Por los reclamantes.

SURVEYOR GENERAL'S OFFICE, TRANSLATOR'S DEPARTMENT,
Santa Fé, New Mexico, August 23, 1859.

The above is a true copy of the original on file in this office.

DAVID V. WHITING,
Translator.

NOTICE—TRANSLATION.

UNITED STATES OF AMERICA,
Territory of New Mexico.

SANTA FÉ, *January* 28, 1857.

The surveyor general of New Mexico is hereby informed that under the provisions of the eighth section of the act of Congress, approved July 22, 1854, entitled "An act to establish the offices of surveyor general of New Mexico, Kansas and Nebraska, to grant donations to actual settlers therein, and for other purposes," we, Dolores Perea, Francisco Sandoval, José Andres Sandoval, Antonio Baca, Desiderio Valdez, and José Antonio Montoya, legal representatives of Antonio Armenta and Salvador Sandoval, original grantees, claim a tract of settled land known and described as the Rancho de San Ysidro, at Jemez, in the county of Santa Ana, Territory of New Mexico, said claim originates from a grant made under the authority of the Spanish government, by Juan Bautista de Anza, governor of New Mexico, on the sixteenth day of May, 1786, and judicial possession given by Nerio Antonio Montoya, chief justice, on the same date. Said claim is inchoate, the chain of title being incomplete from the original grantee to the present claimants. It does not conflict with any other claim. The amount of land claimed, according to the grant aforementioned, amounts to two thousand nine hundred varas. It is situated in the county of Santa Ana. Its boundaries are: on the north, lands of Jemez; on the south, lands of the pueblo of Zia; on the west, the mountain of the Espiritu Santo Spring, at the place commonly called Los Bancos; on the east, lands of the aforementioned chief justice, Nerio Antonio Montoya, which is the road leading from Cochiti to Jemez. The present claimants are the heirs of the original grantees, but, in the absence of documentary evidence, we pray that the grant be confirmed to the legal representatives of the original grantees.

FRANCISCO SANDOVAL,
For claimant.

Surveyor General's Office, Translator's Department,
Santa Fé, New Mexico, July 25, 1859.
The foregoing is a correct translation of the original on file in this office.
DAVID V. WHITING,
Translator.

Surveyor General's Office,
Santa Fé, New Mexico, July 25, 1859.
The above is a true copy of the original on file in this office.
WM. PELHAM,
Surveyor General.

GRANT—SPANISH.

Vale, por del sello segundo. [SELLO.] Un real.

Sello Tercero, un real, años de mil setecientos ochenta y seis, y ochenta y siete.

 Señor Coronel Don Juan Baretista de Ansa, gobernador politico y militar de esta provincia del Nueva Mejico. Antonio de Armenta, actual alcalde mayor y capitan á guerra de los pueblos de la nacion Queres y Salbador Antonio Sandobal soldadó reformado de este real presidio los dos en comun y cada uno de por si parecemos ante V. S. con la mayor sumision y rendimiento y en la mejor forma que nos convenga y decimos que los dos nos hallamos sin tierras propias de labor que cultivar para la mantencion de nuestras familias ni egidos con pastos para poder criar algunos animales presisos para el mismo fin, con lo cual pedimos y suplicamos á V. S. sea muy servido de hacernos merced en nombre de S. M. Que Dios guarde de un pedazo de tierras de labor y pastos realengos que esta desde donde finaliza la legua perteneciente al pueblo de Xemes por la parte del sur hasta el lindero del pueblo * * [torn] * * por la parte del Norte por el oriente hasta lindar con tierras del alcalde mayor Don Nereo Antonio Montoya por el poniente la Sierra Ojo del Espiritusanto que en hacer como llebamos pedido esperamos recivir de la beninidad de V. S. reciviremos merced y alivio en nuestras necesidades y juramos en la mas debida forma no ser de malicia esta peticion. Antonio de Armenta, y Salbador Antonio Sandobal. En la villa de Santa Fé en quatro dias del mes de mayo de mil setecientos ochanta y seis años ante mi el coronel de caballeria de los reales exercitos de S. M. Don Juan Barrista de Ansa, gobernador politico y militar de esta provincia del Nuevo Mejico se presento la antecedente peticion por los contenidos en ella que hube por tal y admitida, y en atencion a su solicitud de no resultar perjuicio de tercero concedia y concedi en nombre de S. M. que Dios Guarde á los espresados Don Antonio de Armenta, actual alcalde mayor de la jurisdiccion de los Queres y al sargento miliciano de la misma jurisdiccion la merced de tierras que priden con la cabidad de que las cultiven en la conformidad que previenen las reales leyes y de la que no esten comprendia en las que pertenescan á los pueblos de Sia y Xemes ni de otro conlindante y á efecto de darles real y personal posesion con las calidades referidas comisiono y day facultad quanta de derecho se requiere al alcaldo mayor de la jurisdiccion de San Carlos de la Alameda Don Nereo Antonio Montoya para que en virtua de esta comision presediendo sitacion y presencia de los conlindantes y no resultando el y nunciado perjuicio lo verifique midiendo las varas que tenga á todos rumbos las que se espresaran en el correspondiente anto de posesion como los luggares en que deban poner las moyoneras que á falta de las de cal y canto efectuaran con prèdra seca señidas con madera de sabina suficientemente enterradas que asi mismo deberan concluirse en el termino de dos meses despues de la pocecion y de no verificarlo en el dicho termino perderan el derecho á la merced concedida y coluido todo se me hara remicion del original que resulte para trasladarlo en el libro de gobierno de mi cargo asi loprovidensie mande y firme con los tesrigos de mi asistencia á falta de escribano publico ni real que nolo hay de ninguna clase en todo este gobierno de que day fe. (Otro si consedida esta merced tambien con la coalidad de que no sean perjudicados en su primacia y uso de aguas los men cionados pueblos de Sia Xemes. Juan Bauptista de Ansa. Asistencia Francisco Perez Serrano. Asistencia Cristobal Maria Larrañaga. En este puesto de San Ysidro de los Dolores en diez y seis dias del mes de mayo de mil setecientos ochenta y seis años, yo Don Nereo Antonio Montoya alcalde mayor y Capitan á Guerra de la jurisdiccion de San Carlos de la Alameda, en virtud de la comision que me es conferida por el Señor Don Juan Bautista de Ansa, Coronel de caballeria de los reales exercitos de S. M. Gobernador politico y militar de esta provincia del Nuevo Mejico allandome en el espresado paraje con sitacion de los hijos del Pueblo de San Diego de los Xemes y de los hijos del pueblo de Sia que son los conlindantes con dichas tierras, y haviendoles medido su legua que les perte nece con dosientas y sesenta y dos varas mas con las quales quedaron conformes por tener unos indios unas mil piyas ya sembradas y por no quitarselas se las hube de dejar por no agravarlos salvo el dictamen de V. S. como asi pase al pueblo de Sia y les medi su legue perte neciente al dicho pueblo con mas mil seiscientas y treinta y dos varas que huvieran los dichos indios de compra que ysieron á Juan Galban por manifestado la escritura de dicha compra y de estas dichas tienas les señale y añadi mil varas mas por havermelas pedido dichos indios, y haviendome manifestado dichos indios una Benta dada por el difunto Miguel Montoya la cual sita sus linderos en una cañada que comunmente llaman el Rito Salado que esta cañada son egidos de agostaderos de ganados cuios linderos de dicha tierra son los mismos que cita la escritura por la parte del Norte una loma Colorada, por el Sur una mesa Blanca y por el virente el mismo rio de Xemes y haviendome entera do de dichos dos instrumentos y no haber allado en ellos mas de solo lo mencionado arriba les di á entender á los dichos dos pueblos de lo que eva suyo tanto á los de Sia por compra como á los de Xemes por merced que S. M. les hizo y pareciendome no tener derecho alguno ambos dos pueblos al pedazo que vealengo esta y ser la mente de Vaestro Soberano que sus tierras se pueblen con sus vasallos en aquello sobrante que hubiere y no hallando yo impedimento ninguno y gosando de la comision que su V. S. me confiere pase á la tierra sobrante de ambos dos pueblos á la que huve de medir y medida que fue salieron dos mil novecientas varas y no resultando quien mejor derecho tubiera y estando presentes hambos dos pueblos y el alcalde mayor Don Antonio de Armenta y el Sargento miliciano Salbador Antonio Sandobal y entendidos de todo los coji de la mano los pasie por dichas tierras arrancaron sacate tiraron piedras á los quatro Bientos y dijimos todos á una tres veses viva el Rey Nuestro Señor (que Dios Guarde) en señal de berdadera posison la que les dixe y aprendieron quieta y pacifica sin contradicion alguna y sus linderos son los siguientes por la parte del Norte con las tierras de Xemes por la parte del Sur con tierras del Pueblo de Sia por la parte del poniente la Sierra del ojo del Espiritu santo, en los bancos que comunmente llaman por el oriente con tierras del mencionado alcalde mayor Don Nereo Antonio Montoya que es el camino que baja de Cochiti á Xemes y señalandoles los linderos y no resultando perjericio alguno quedando conformes con ellos les mande pusieran mojoneras estables y para que asi conste lo firme yo dicho comisionado y alcalde mayor Don Nereo Antonio Montoya á una con dos testigos de mi asistencia con quienes actuo á falta de escribano publico ni real que no lo hay en este reino de que doy fe. Nereo Antonio Montoya. Testigo, Thorivio Gonzales; testigo, Salvador Lopez.

Concuerda este testimonio con su original á que me remito donde yo el espresado alcalde mayor y Capitan á Guerra Don Nereo Antonio Montoya, saque esta copia á pedimento verbal de la parte, el que va cierto y verdadero y al verlo sacar y corregir se hallaron presentes los testigos de mi asistencia, va entre fojas utiles y es fecho en este Pueblo de Zia en diez y seis dias del mes de maio de mil setecientos ochenta y seis años, firmado de mi mano á falta de escribano publico ni real que no lo hay en este reino, y en el presente papel sellado en este dicho reino del Nuevo Mejico de que doy fe.

En testimonio de verdad hago mi firma acostumbrada.

NEREO ANTONIO MONTOYA.

Testigo, THORIVIO GONZALES.
Testigo, SALVADOR LOPEZ.

SURVEYOR GENERAL'S OFFICE, TRANSLATOR'S DEPARTMENT,
Santa Fé, New Mexico, August 23, 1859.

The above is a true copy of the original on file in this office.

DAVID V. WHITING.
Translator.

GRANT TRANSLATION.

Equivalent to seal second. [SEAL.] One rial.
Seal third. One rial. Years one thousand seven hundred and eighty-six and eighty-seven.

Antonio Armenta, the present senior justice and war captain of the towns of the Queres nation, and Salvador Antonio Sandoval, a re-enlisted soldier of this royal garrison, the two together, and each one for himself, appear before your excellency with the greatest submission and humility, and in the most convenient manner to us, and state that both of us are without arable lands of our own to cultivate for the support of our families; nor pasture lands upon which to raise a few animals necessary for the same object. We therefore pray and request your excellency to be much pleased to grant unto us in the name of his Majesty, whom may God preserve, a vacant piece of land for cultivation and pasturage, situate at the termination of the league belonging to the town Jemez, on the southern side, to the boundary of the Pueblo of (torn) on the northern side; on the east to the boundary of the lands of the senior justice, Nerio Antonio Montoya; on the west, the mountain of the Espiritu Santo Spring; that in doing as we request we will be indebted to your kindness, and will receive grace and aid in our necessities. And we swear in due form that this petition is not made through malice, &c.

     ANTONIO DE ARMENTA.
     SALVADOR ANTONIO SANDOVAL.
Col. DON JUAN BAUPTISTA DE ANSA,
 Political and Military Governor of this province of New Mexico.

Decree.

In the city of Santa Fé, on the fourth day of the month of May, in the year one thousand seven hundred and eighty-six, before me, Juan Bauptista de Ansa, colonel of cavalry of the royal armies of his Majesty, political and military governor of the province of New Mexico, came the foregoing petition, the contents whereof having been ascertained and admitted, and in attention to their request, and no injury resulting to any third party, I did and do grant, in the name of his Majesty, whom may God preserve, to the aforesaid Don Antonio de Armenta, the present senior justice of the jurisdiction of the Queres, and to the militia sergeant of the same jurisdiction, the grant of land they ask for, on condition that they cultivate the same in conformity with the provisions of the royal decrees, and which may not be included in the towns of Cia and Jemez, or any other person thereto adjoining, and for the purpose of giving them the royal and personal possession in the terms before mentioned.

I commission and grant such authority as is required by law to Don Nerio Antonio Montoya, senior justice of the jurisdiction of San Carlos de la Alameda, who by virtue of this commission and previous citation and attendance of the adjoining residents, and no injury resulting to any third party, that he will place them in possession, measuring the number of varas it may contain in each direction, which will be noted in the proper deed of possession as the places designated for the establishment of the proper monuments, which, in the absence of cement and mortar, are to be constructed of stone, bound together with cedar timber sufficiently well set in the ground, and which shall be erected within the period of two months after possession, and if not complied with in that time they shall forfeit their right to the grant made, and upon the completion of all the originals will be returned to me to be transferred to the government book under my charge.

I have so provided, ordered, and signed, with my attending witnesses, in the absence of a royal or public notary, there being none of any description in this government, to which I certify.

Addition.—This grant is made with the further condition that the aforementioned pueblos of Cia and Jemez shall not be disturbed in their pre-emption and the use of the water.

JUAN BAPTISTA DE ANSA.

Witnesses:
   FRANCISCO PEREZ SERRANA.
   CRISTOBAL MARIA DE LUNAÑAGA.

Possession.

At this point of San Isidro de Los Dolores, on the 16th day of the month of May, in the year one thousand seven hundred and eighty-six, I, Don Antonio Nerio Montoya, senior justice and war captain of the jurisdiction of San Carlos de la Alameda, by virtue of the commission conferred upon me by Don Juan Bauptista de Ansa, colonel of cavalry of the royal armies of his Majesty, political and military governor of this province of New Mexico, being at the aforementioned place, having summoned the natives of the Pueblo of San Diego, Jemez, and Cia, who are adjacent residents, and having measured the league belonging to them, with two hundred and sixty-two varas more, with which they expressed themselves satisfied. Some of the Indians having planted some small patches, and not to offend them I allowed them to retain possession of them, with your excellency's permission. I also proceeded to the pueblo of Cia and measured the league belonging to that pueblo, with the further amount of one thousand six hundred and thirty-two varas which the Indians purchased from Juan Galvan, as shown by the title-deeds of said purchase, and the aforementioned lands I assigned and added thereto one thousand varas more, the Indians having asked me for it, and the said Indians having shown to me a sale made by the late Miguel Montoya, which boundaries are in a cañon commonly called El Rito Salado; that this cañon is the pasture ground and summer range of their cattle; the boundaries of which land are the same called for in the title-deed; on the north a red hill, on the south a white tableland, and on the east the Jemez river itself; and having informed myself of the contents of the two deeds, and having found in them only what has been above stated, I gave the two pueblos to understand what belonged to each of them—that of Cia what they had acquired by purchase, and that of Jemez what had been granted to them by his Majesty; and believing that neither of the pueblos were entitled to the piece of ground which is unoccupied, and it being the intention of our sovereign that his lands shall be settled upon by his subjects wherever there may be any surplus, and finding no impediment, and by virtue of the commission which I hold from his excellency I proceeded to the land lying between the two pueblos, which, upon being measured, was found to contain two thousand nine hundred varas, and no person appearing who claimed a better right, both pueblos being present, as well as the senior justice, Antonio de Armenta, and the militia sergeant, Salvador Antonio Sandoval, and being informed of all the circumstances, I took them by the hand, walked with them over the land, they pulled up grass, threw stones towards the four winds of heaven, and we all exclaimed three times, "Long life to the king, our sovereign," (whom may God preserve,) in proof of legal possession which I gave them, and they received quietly and peacefully, without any opposition; the boundaries whereof are as follows: On the north, the lands of Jemez; on the south, the lands of the pueblo of Zia; on the west, the mountain of the Espiritu Santa Spring, at the place commonly called Los Bancos; on the east, the lands of the aforementioned senior justice, Antonio Nerio Montoya, which is the road leading from Cochiti to Jemez. And having assigned their boundaries, and no injury resulting thereby, and being satisfied with them, I directed them to erect permanent boundaries; and in order that it may so appear, I, Nerio Antonio Montoya, as commissioner and senior justice, at the same time, signed with two attending witnesses with whom I act in the absence of a royal or public notary, there being none in this kingdom; to which I certify.

NERIO ANTONIO MONTOYA.

Witness:
    FORIBIO GONZALEZ,
    SALVADOR LOPEZ.

This copy agrees with the original, to which reference is made, from whence I, Nerio Antonio Montoya, senior justice and war captain, took this copy at the verbal request of the party, which is true and correct, my two attending witnesses being present when it was made. It is constructed on three written pages, and is taken at this pueblo of Zia, on the 16th day of the month of May, in the year one thousand seven hundred and eighty-six; signed with my hand, in the absence of a public or royal notary, there being none in this kingdom. It is (torn) stamped paper in this said kingdom of New Mexico, to which I certify.

To this copy I attach my customary signature.

NERIO ANTONIO MONTOYA.

Witness:
    FORIBIO GONZALEZ,
    SALVADOR LOPEZ.

SURVEYOR GENERAL'S OFFICE, TRANSLATOR'S DEPARTMENT,
Santa Fé, New Mexico, June 7, 1859.
The above is a translation of the original on file in this office.
DAVID V. WHITING,
Translator.

SURVEYOR GENERAL'S OFFICE, SANTA FÉ,
New Mexico, July 25, 1859.
The above is a true copy of the original on file in this office.
WM. PELHAM,
Surveyor General.

REPORT.

TOWN OF SAN YSIDRO *vs.* THE UNITED STATES.

This case was set for trial on the 16th May, 1859.

Francisco Sandoval, one of the heirs, and the petitioner, sets forth in his said petition that himself and the other persons therein mentioned are the heirs and legal representatives of Antonio Armenta and Salvador Sandoval, and claim the land by virtue of a grant made to the said Armenta and Sandoval on the 4th May, 1786, by Juan Bauptista de Anza, political and military governor of the province of New Mexico.

The papers filed and acted upon by this office are certified copies of the original, (testimonio,) and made by the justice of the peace who placed the parties in possession.

The document filed being more than fifty years old, and beyond the period of a lifetime, presumes that the signature cannot be proven, and that they are assumed as genuine unless they are proven to be fraudulent and counterfeit, and as no such attempt has been made the grant is deemed to be good and valid; and as the chain of title from the original grantees to the present claimants is complete, the grant is approved to the legal representatives of the original grantee, and is ordered to be transmitted to Congress for its action in the premises.

WM. PELHAM,
Surveyor General.

SURVEYOR GENERAL'S OFFICE,
Santa Fé, New Mexico, June 8, 1859.

SURVEYOR GENERAL'S OFFICE,
Santa Fé, New Mexico, August 25, 1859.
The above is a true copy of the original on file in this office.
W. PELHAM,
Surveyor General.

CLAIM NO. 25.

TOWN OF CAÑON DE SAN DIEGO.

Documents composing claim No. 25.

1. Notice—Spanish.
2. Notice—translation.
3. Grant—Spanish.
4. Grant—translation.
5. Testimony.
6. Report.

NOTICE—SPANISH.

Sor. Agrimensor General de este Territorio de Nuevo Mejico:

El abajo firmado por si y á nombre de los poseedores actuales desde el año de 1846 de la merced real del cañon concedida por el Sor. Governador Don Fernando Chacon en 6 Marzo de 1798, años y entregada á los peticionarios que constan sus nombres en dicha merced por el Alcalde Mayor Don Antonio Armenta, con fecha, No. 14 de Marzo de dicho dia mes y año cuyos linderos son por el norte el Vallecito de la Cueba, por el sur á donde finaliza la legua de dichos Indios, por el oriente hasta conlindar con los vecinos del Vallecito, y por el poniente mirando al arroyo del medio y mirando al Rito de la Jara cuya merced y reclamo esperamos sea bien admitida y aprobada por las evidencias que presentamos, y juramos no ser de malicia.

CAÑON DE SAN DIEGO, *Junio* 4, de 1859.

JESUS BACA.
FRANCISCO GARCIA.
PABLO GALLEGO.

SURVEYOR GENERAL'S OFFICE, TRANSLATOR'S DEPARTMENT,
Santa Fé, New Mexico, September 10, 1859.

The above is a true copy of the original on file in this office.

DAVID V. WHITING, *Translator.*

NOTICE—TRANSLATION.

Honorable Surveyor General of the Territory of New Mexico:

The undersigned, for themselves and in the name of the actual settlers since the year 1846 of the royal grant of the cañon, granted by Governor Don Fernando Chacon on the 6th of March, 1798, and delivered to the owners, whose names appear in said grant, by Don Antonio Armenta, senior justice, on the 14th of March, of said day, month, and year, the boundaries of which are: On the north, the Vallecito de la Cueva; on the south, the termination of the league of the Indians; on the east, the lands of the settlers of Vallecito; and on the west, in the direction of the middle arroyo and the Rito de la Jara, which

grant and claim we trust will be admitted and approved by the evidence we present; and we swear that we do not act through malice.
CAÑON DE SAN DIEGO, *June 4, 1859.*

> FRANCISCO GARCIA.
> JESUS BACA.
> PABLO GALLEGO.

SURVEYOR GENERAL'S OFFICE, TRANSLATOR'S DEPARTMENT,
Santa Fé, New Mexico, June 13, 1859.

The foregoing is a correct translation of the original on file in this office.

> DAVID V. WHITING, *Translator.*

SURVEYOR GENERAL'S OFFICE,
Santa Fé, New Mexico, August 5, 1859.

The above is a true copy of the original on file in this office.

> WM. PELHAM,
> *Surveyor General.*

GRANT—SPANISH.

Testimonio. [SEAL.] Corregido.

Sello Tercero, dos reales, años de mil setecientos noventa y ocho, y noventa y neuve.

Sor. Teniente Coronel y Gobernador de esta Provincia:

Francisco y Antonio Garcia de Noriega hermanos é ynterpretes de la Nacion Navajo en conjunto de Miguel Garcia, Joaquin Montoya, Salvador Garcia, Josef Manuel Garcia, Juan Josef Gutierres, Juan de Agilar, Blas Nepomoceno Garcia, Bartolome Montoya, Jose Montoya, Tomas Montoya, Juan Domingo Martin, Joseph Gonzales, Salvador Lopes, Antonio Abad Garcia, Miguel Gallego, Marcos Apodaca, José Miguel Duran, y Josef Maria Jaramillo, parecemos ante V.S. en la mas bastante forma que en derecho se requiere y sea necesario y decimos que se hallan en el Cañon de San Diego desde los linderos de las tierras que pertenecen á los naturales de el Pueblo de Xemes, cantidad de tierras realengas é inavitadas y en consideracion de que de su habitacion resulta un grande beneficio asi á esta Provincia, como en utilidad de nuestras familias, presentes y desendientes, de ellas poblando y amparando con nuestras asistencias y vienes estas soledades, suplicamos á V.S. se digne concedernos esta assistencia, y establecimiento que impetramos á los espresados sugetos sirviendose V.S. de mandar en nombre de Su Magestad que Dios Guarde se nos ministre desde los linderos que á los naturales toca por merced fuera de los terminos de su legua, siendo nuestro pedimento por la linea del Oriente á el Poniente hasta el arroyo de enmedio que llaman los Torriones, y de la linea que corre de el Sur á el Norte hasta el Vallecito de la Cueba, que se halla adelante del Salto de el agua, y por la linea trasversal desde el dicho arroyo de enmedio hasta el Rito de la Jara, asimismo protestamos no ser perjudicales con nuestras personas y vienes de Campo á unos cuantos arboles que tienen los mencionados naturales por suyos aunque estan plantados fuera de las tierras que les pertenecen, por tanto. A V.S. suplicamos rendidameste se digne mandar hacer como pedimos concediendonos este realengo que en ello reciviremos merced y juramos en devida forma no ser de malicia este nuestro pedimento, y lo firmo uno que los demas no saben. José Miguel Garcia. Decreto. Santa Fé seis de Marzo de mil setecientos noventa y ocho años. En atencion á la solicitud que antecede de Josef Miguel Garcia, y de los demas vecinos que á su nombre se espresan sobre poblar el cañon conveido por San Diego de Jemes en donde interenariamente vivian destacados los interpretes de la nacion Navajo, rengo en concederles en nombre del Rey Nuestro Senor, el espresado terreno, con la precisa circumstancia de que ha de ser poblado lo menos por veinte vecinos, que las tierras se han de distribuir por ignales partes sin quedarles á estos accion ni facultad, como ignalmente á ninguno de sus desendientes á vender ni enagenar las tierras de que se les hace merced por ser la voluntad de S. M. segun sus ultimas disposiciones pasen de padres á hijos ó herederos por linea recta, y si por conveniencia propria quisiese algun colon separarse bajo cualesquiera pretesto que sea, debera quedar su posesion á suerte á beneficio del que le reemplase en lo que siempre se debera atender á los vecinos del propio sitio que se establescan ó casen, sin que por esto se le exiba el menor estipendio por el que se ausenta voluntariamente, ó es arrojado ó desterrado á causa de su mala conducta por la justicia. Que ademas del reparto referido se ha de dejar el correspondiente terreno, asi para pastos y abrevaderos, como para que pueda estenderse dicha poblacion si se verifica (como es regular) (torn) mando al alcalde mayor de aquella jurisdiccion Don Antonio Armenta, ponga á los pretendientes en la referida posesion bajo las demas reglas que previene e derecho. Chason. Posesion. En este Cañon de San Diego de los Jemes en catorce dias del mes de marzo de mil setecientos noventa y ocho años, yo Don Antonio de Armenta alcalde mayor del Pueblo de Jemes en virtud de la facultad que me es conferida por my superior Gefe el Señor Don Fernando Chacon Caballero del orden de Santiago, Teniente Coronel de los reales ejercitos, Gobernador Politico y militar de esta Provincia del Nuevo Mejico hallandome en el espresado paraje con citacion de los hijos del dicho pueblo de Jemes, á quienes haviendoles medido su legua les perpenece, halle sobrante dos mil y cien varas, que tenian mas antes de llegar al mencionado coñon de San Diego, que todas estas las llamaban sujas sin tener ningun derecho á ellas, por ninguna via y pareciendome notener derecho alguno al pedaso de tierra que llevo dicho, y ser la mente de Nuestro Soberano que sus tierras se pueblen con sus Basallos, en aguello sobrante que hubiere y no hallando yo impedimento ninguno, y usando de la facultad que me es conferida pase á las tierras sobrantes, y no resultando quien mejor derecho tubiera, y estando presentes Francisco Garcia, Antonia Garcia, Ynterpretes de la Nacion Navajo, Miguel Garcia, Joaquin Montoya,

Salvador Garcia, Josef Manuel Garcia, Juan Josef Gutierres, Juan de Agilar, Juan Blas Nepomoreno Garcia, Bartolo Montoya, Bartolome Garcia, Tomas Montoya, José Montoya, Juan Domingo Sangil, Salvador Lopes, Josef Gonzales, Antonio Abad Garcia, Miguel Gallego, Marcos Apodaca, Josef Miguel Duran, Josef Jaramillo, y otro mas Blas Baca, Todos interesados y entendidos de todo los cogi de la mano, los pacie por dichas tierras arrancaron sacàte, tiraron piedras á los cuatro vientos y dijimos todos á una tres veces viva el Rey Nuestro Señor (Q.D.G.) en señal de verdaderia posesion, la que aprendieron quieta y pacificamente sin contradicion alguna, porque despues de haber hecho todas estas ceremonias les entregue á cada uno de dichos pobladores á trecientas varas con las que quedaron mui conformes con dicha cantidad quedando lo sobrante á beneficio de todos y sin que quedara ningun otro pedaso de tierra en que puedan entrar otros y para evitar el que por este motivo quieran venir otros á entrometerse, y á dar perjuicio asi vecinos, como indios, y asi mismo les di á entender cuales eran sus linderos, que son, por el norte el Vallecito de la Cueba, por el Sur á donde finaliza la legua de dichos indios, por el Oriente hasta conlindar con el lindero de los vecinos del Vallecito y por el Poniente la Bentana mirando al arroyo de enmedo mirando al Rito de la Jara, y no resultando perjuicio alguno quedaron todos conformes, y para que asi conste lo firme yo dicho alcalde mayor á una con, dos testigos de mi assistencia con quienes actuo á falta de escribano publico ni real que no los hay en toda esta governacion de que doy fee. Antonio de Armenta; testigo, Salvador Lopez; testigo, Josef Miguel Garcia; En el margen Blas Baca vale.

Concuerda este testimonio con su original á que me remito, donde yo el espresado Alcalde Mayor D. Antonio de Armenta saque esta copia á pedimento berval de la parte, el que va cierto y verdadero, y al verlo sacar y corregir se hallaron presentes los testigos de mi assistencia y queda su original en el archivo del cargo del Senor Governador Don Fernando Chacon, y es ficho en este Pueblo de Jemes en diez y seis dias del mes de marzo de mil setecientos noventa y ocho años firmado de mi mano á falta de escribano publico ni real que nolo hay en toda esta Governacion de que doy fee.

En testimonio de verdad hago mi firma acostumbra da.

ANTONIO DE ARMENTA.

Testigo: SALVADOR LOPEZ.
Testigo: JOSÉ MIGUEL GARCIA.

FERNANDO CHACON.

SURVEYOR GENERAL'S OFFICE, TRANSLATOR'S DEPARTMENT,
Santa Fe, New Mexico, September 10, 1859.

The above is a true copy of the original on file in this office.

DAVID V. WHITING,
Translator.

GRANT—TRANSLATION.

Seal Third. [SEAL.] Two Rials.

For the years one thousand seven hundred and ninety-eight and ninety-nine.

To the Lieutenant Colonel and Governor of this Province:

Francisco and Antonio Garcia, brothers, and interpreters of the Navajo nation, in unison with Miguel Garcia, Joaquin Montoya, Salvador Garcia, José Manuel Garcia, Juan José Gutiewez, Juan de Aguilar, Blas Neponuceno Garcia, Bartolomew Montoya, José Montoya, Tomas Montoya, Juan Domingo Martin, José Gonzales, Salvador Lopez, Antonio Abad Garcia, Miguel Gallego, Marcos Apodaca, José Miguel Duran, and José Maria Jaramillo, appear before your excellency in the most approved manner the law requires and may be necessary, and state that a quantity of vacant and uncultivated land lies in the cañon of San Diego, adjoining the boundaries of the lands belonging to the Indians of the town of Jemez; and whereas the settlement thereof would be beneficial to the province, and advantageous to our present families and descendants to be settling upon these lands with our property and cultivating the same, we pray your excellency to be pleased to grant this aid and settlement that we petition for, to the persons herein mentioned; being pleased at the same time to order, in the name of his Majesty, (whom may God preserve,) that we may receive from the boundaries beyond the land granted to the Indians of the pueblo, our petition calling for from east to west to the middle arroyo called Los Torreones, and the line running from north to south, to the Vallecelo de la Ceuva, which is in front of the waterfall, and in a transverse line from said middle arroyo to the Rito de la Jara. We also protest that we will not injure, with our persons or stock, a few trees which the Indians claim as their own, although they are planted beyond the limits of the lands which belong to them. Therefore we humbly pray your excellency to be pleased to order our request to be complied with, granting us the vacant land asked for; by doing which we will receive grace, and we swear, in due form, that our petition is not made through malice; and one signed, the others not knowing how.

JOSÉ MIGUEL GARCIA.

Decree.

SANTA FÉ *March* 6, 1799.

In view of the foregoing petition made by José Miguel Garcia and other citizens therein mentioned, in regard to settling in the cañon known as San Diego de Jemez, where the interpreters of the Navajo nation were temporarily stationed, I grant to them the aforesaid land in the name of the King, our sovereign, with the express condition that it is to be settled by at least twenty citizens; that the lands are to be distributed in equal parts, and that they are not allowed or authorized, for themselves or their heirs, to sell or dispose of the lands granted to them. It being his Majesty's will, according to his last orders, that the lands should descend from father to son, or his heirs, in a direct line; and if any colonist, to suit his own convenience, should desire to remove, under any pretext whatsoever, his possession or share shall remain for the benefit of the one taking his place, in which case the residents of the same place, or persons marrying there, shall be preferred, and for which no remuneration whatever shall be exacted by the person voluntarily absenting himself, or expelled or banished by the authorities on account of his bad conduct; that besides the subdivision above mentioned, a sufficient amount of land is to be left for pastures and watering places, as well as to allow for the increase of the settlement, if such may be the case, (which is likely to occur,)—(torn)—order the chief justice of that jurisdiction, Don Antonio Armenta, to place the parties in possession under the rules prescribed by law.

CHACON.

Possession.

In the cañon of San Diego de los Jemez, on the fourteenth day of the month of March, in the year one thousand seven hundred and ninety-eight, I, Don Antonio de Armenta, chief justice of the pueblo of Jamez, by virtue of the authority conferred upon me by my superior chief, Don Fernando Chacon, gentleman of the order of Santiago, lieutenant colonel of the royal armies, political and military governor of this province of New Mexico, being at the aforementioned place, and having summoned the natives of said pueblo of Jemez, to whom having measured the league belonging to them, I found a surplus of two thousand one hundred varas, which they had before arriving at the cañon de San Diego, all of which they claimed as their own, without having any right to them in any manner; and believing that it is the wish of our sovereign that his lands be settled upon by his subjects wherever a surplus may be found, and finding no impediment whatever, and using the authority in me vested, I proceeded to the surplus lands, and finding no one with a better title, and Francisco Garcia, Antonio Garcia Navajo, interpreters, Miguel Garcia, Joaquin Montoya, Salvador Garcia, José Manuel Garcia, Juan José Gutierrez, Juan de Aguilar, Juan Blas Pomuceno Garcia, Bartolo Montes, Thomas Montoya, José Montoya, Juan Domingo Sangil, Salvador Lopez, José Gonzalez, Antonio Abad Garcia, Migull Gallego, Marcos Apodaca, José Migull Duran, and José Jaramillo, being present, all interested and well informed in regard to the matter, I took them by the hand, walked with them over said lands, they pulled up grass, threw stones towards the four winds, and we all cried at once, three times, " live the King our sovereign!" (whom may God preserve.) in proof of legal possession, which they received quietly and peaceably without any opposition whatsoever, because, after concluding with all these ceremonies, I delivered to each one of said settlers three hundred varas, with which they were well satisfied, leaving the remainder for the benefit of all, and without any other land being left for any other person to enter ; and in order to prevent any other from coming in to meddle and create difficulties between the citizens, as well as the Indians, I gave them to understand which were their boundaries, which are: on the north, the Vallecito de la Cueva; on the south, the termination of the Indian league; on the east, the boundary of Vallecito ; and on the west, the opening towards the middle arroyo and the Rito de la Jara; and no injury resulting to any one they were all satisfied ; and in order that it may so appear, I, the said chief justice signed, with my two attending witnesses, in the absence of a public or royal notary, there being none within the limits of all this government, to which I certify.

ANTONIO DE ARMENTA.

Witnesses :
  Salvador Lopez.
  José Miguel Garcia.

This copy agrees with its original, to which reference is made, and from whence I, the said Don Antonio de Armenta, chief justice, took this copy at the verbal request of the parties. It is correct and genuine, and my attending witnesses were present when it was made and compared, and the original remains in the archives in charge of the governor, Don Fernando Chacon; and it is made at this pueblo of Jemez, on the sixteenth day of the month of March, in the year one thousand seven hundred and ninety-eight, signed with my hand, in the absence of a public or royal notary, there being none in this government, to which I certify.

In testimony of the truth, I hereto attach my customary signature.

ANTONIO ARMENTA.

Witnesses :
  Salvador Lopez.
  José Miguel Garcia.

Surveyor General's Office, Translator's Department,
    Santa Fé, New Mexico, June 3, 1859.

The foregoing is a correct translation of the original on file in this office.

TRANSLATOR.

Surveyor General's Office,
    Santa Fé, New Mexico, August 5, 1859.

The above is a true copy of the original on file in this office.

WILLIAM PELHAM,
Surveyor General.

TESTIMONY.

Town of Cañoncito.

Francisco Sandoval sworn :

Question. Have you any interest in this grant ?
Answer. None.
Question. How old are you, and how long have you resided in the Territory ?

Answer. Sixty-two years; I have lived in this Territory all my life.

Question. What have been your opportunities of knowing the town of Cañoncito?

Answer. I was born in the neighborhood, and have always resided there.

Question. How many inhabitants live in the town?

Answer. About three hundred.

Question. How long has the town been in existence, and was it occupied when the United States took possession of the Territory?

Answer. It was founded about sixty years ago; it was in existence when the United States took possession.

FRANCISCO SANDOVAL.

Sworn and subscribed before me this 6th day of June, 1859.
DAVID V. WHITING,
Notary Public.

Jesus Gonzalez, sworn:

Question. Have you any interest in this case?
Answer. I have none.
Question. How old are you?
Answer. Forty-two years old.
Question. What have been your opportunities for knowing the town of Cañoncito?
Answer. I live in the neighborhood, and have always lived there?
Question. Was the town in existence in 1846, when the United States took possession of the country?
Answer. It was.

his
JESUS + GONZALEZ.
mark.

Sworn and subscribed before me this 6th day of June, 1859.
DAVID V. WHITING,
Notary Public.

Surveyor General's Office,
Santa Fé, New Mexico, August 5, 1859.

The above is a true copy of the original on file in this office.
WILLIAM PELHAM,
Surveyor General.

REPORT.

Town of Cañon de San Diego vs. The United States.

This ase was set for trial on the 6th day of June, 1859.

The parties claim the land embraced within the limits of the town, by virtue of a royal grant made by Fernando Chacon, governor of the province of New Mexico, on the 6th March, 1798, and possession given him by the justice of the peace on the fourteenth of the same month and year.

The evidence shows that the town has been in continuous occupation of the claimants, and was in existence when the United States assumed sovereignty over the country.

The papers acted upon by this office are the originals filed by the claimants.

The grant is approved and ordered to be transmitted to Congress, with the request that it be confirmed to the original grantees and those claiming under or through them.

WM. PELHAM,
Surveyor General.

SURVEYOR GENERAL'S OFFICE,
Santa Fé, New Mexico, June 10, 1859.

SURVEYOR GENERAL'S OFFICE,
Santa Fé, New Mexico, August 30, 1859.

The above is a true copy of the original on file in this office.

WM. PELHAM.
Surveyor General.

CLAIM NO. 26.

JUAN B. VIGIL ET AL.

Documents composing claim No. 26.

1. Notice.
2. Grant, &c.—Spanish.
3. Grant—translation.
4. Order of possession—translation.
5. Resignation of Chacon—translation.
6. Conveyance—Spanish.
7. Conveyance—translation.
8. Proclamation of General Kearney.
9. Testimony.
10. Report.
11. Notice of appeal.

UNITED STATES OF AMERICA, *Territory of New Mexico:*

To the Hon. William Pelham, surveyor general of the Territory of New Mexico:

Your petitioners, Juan Bautista Vigil y Alorid, Antonio José Rivera, and Michael Houck—the two first mentioned, residents of the Territory of New Mexico, and the last mentioned, a resident of the State of Missouri—respectfully represent: That they are the claimants and legal owners in fee of a certain tract of land known as the grant or merced of "Jornada del Muerto," situated in the counties of Socorra and Doña Ana, and bounded as follows: on the north by the little table-land of the Contadero; on the east by the Sandia range of mountains, with its spurs; on the south by the old site of Doña Ana, at Roblerito; and on the west by the Rio del Norte.

Said petitioners claim a perfect title to said land by virtue of a certain grant made by the departmental assembly on the 10th day of January, 1846, and confirmed on the 4th day of February of the same year by Governor Manuel Armijo, who, according to law, as governor of New Mexico, directed and authorized Albino Chacon, justice of original jurisdiction of the city of Santa Fé and central district, to place the petitioners in possession; which act was duly performed on the 15th day of March, 1846, as will appear from the accompanying original documents, from folio 1 to 7.

Your petitioners would further represent that Michael S. Houck, one of the original petitioners, (signed "José Miguel Houck,") though excluded by the act of the departmental assembly of January 6, 1846, (see folio 4 of the accompanying documents,) from interest in the grant, yet said interest was to be extended to him upon his presenting his papers of naturalization, (see decree of governor of the department, folio 5 of accompanying documents;) and for evidence that he did present said papers, and received in due form from Santiago Abrin, departmental governor, a certificate of citizenship, (see folios 6 to 8, accompanying documents,) all of which places Michael S. Houck on the same footing in regard to this claim as the other two original grantees.

Petitioners claim that said grant was made according to law, according to the Spanish laws and regulations which were declared and recognized by the government of Mexico to be in force and effect at that time.—(See collection of decrees and orders of the Cortes of Spain, published in Mexico by Mariano Galvan in 1829, page 56, and from page 91 to 101; and also decrees of Mexico, of June 4 and September 18, 1823, pages 123 and 180, 2d vol. Colecion de Decretos; see also Howard's Reports, page 24, vol. 1; 6 Peters, 691; Holcomb's Digest, 358 to 356.)

The said claimants are unable to show the quantity of land contained in said tract, as it has never been surveyed, and can only show its extent by the bounds and well known points and limits by which it is above described.

The petitioners herewith file, as proof, original documents marked in folios from 1 to 9, by which they hope to prove the justice of their claim both in law and equity, and that the same may be confirmed to them; giving notice that, on the north side of said land, about twenty-seven or thirty miles are in dispute with other deeds appearing personally to belong to the heirs of the late Pedro Armendaris, and to avoid disputes the original and present claimants have agreed that their northern boundary shall be the southern boundary called for by the deeds of the said Armendaris.

All of which is most respectfully submitted.

J. HOUGHTON,
Attorney for claimants.

SURVEYOR GENERAL'S OFFICE,
Santa Fé, New Mexico, August 31, 1859.
The foregoing is a true copy of the original on file in this office.
WM. PELHAM,
Surveyor General.

GRANT—ORIGINAL.

Asamblea departamental de Nuevo Méjico.

La asamblea departamental, ha resuelto, se debuelva á V. E. la presentacion de los ciuda danos Antonio Jose Rivera, Juan Bautista Vigil y Alarid, y el estrangero Miguel Hauk, la cual ha decretada conforme con la resolucion de dicha asamblea.

Reitero á V. E. las protestas de mi consideracion y aprecio.

Dios y Livertad Santa Fé, Enero 12, 1846.
J. MANUEL GALLEGOS.
NICHOLAS QUINTANA Y ROSAS,
Secretario.

Exmo. Sor. GOVERNOR *del departamento.*

Sello Tercero. [SEAL.] Un Peso.

Anos de mil ochocientos y mil ochocientos cuarenta y cuatro cuarenta y cinco.

Los individuos que suscriben esta solicitud animados del mas puro patriotismo y de ser utiles á la sociedad en que viven; haciendo uso del derecho de peticion y del que les favorece por las leyes rigentes de colonizacion en esta republica Mejicana á que tienen el honor de pertenecer, como cuidadanos y uno como naturalizado en la misma; con el respecto devido hacemos presente á la Exma. Asamblea departamental, por conducto de V. E. la presente solicitud, contraida á pedir se nos mercene por dicho honorable cuerpo en la forma ordinaria segun la facultad 5ª parte segunda que le señala el articulo 134 de las Bases organicas elterreno conocido por la Jornada del Muerto poniendo por linderos, la Mecita del Contadero por el Noroeste; por el Oeste el Rio del Norte; por el sur el parage antiguo de Doña Ana; y por el Este la Cordillera de la Sierra de Sandia y sus chorreras por dicho rumbo; conseguida la solicitud y puestos en posesion de dicho torreno se comprometen solemne mente los que firman primero; á construir dos norias en los parajes mas sentricos de la Jornada, con sus correspondientes targeas para alivio y aucilio de los caminantes que hasta la fecha han sufrido perdidas incalculables de bestias caballares y mulares y ganado major y menor, de lana y pelo; y loque es mas muchas victimas humanas que ha deborado la absoluta falta de equa que tenaran segura los caminantes, á *muy poca costa,* estando en corriente dichas norias: Segundo, con igual solemnidad ofrecen plantar dos talleres de fabricas utiles al departamento, y en las cuales se reciviran los delincuentes destinados, por los jueces y autoridades del departamento, á compurgar algun delito, conforme á lo que sobre la meteria disponen ó disprisieren las leyes de la materia y los decretos de dicha honorable asamblea. Tercero, que ambas cuatro cosas que deben pertenecer á la Maguinaria Moderna, se obligan los licitantes á tenerlas concluidas en el termino mas pronto posible, y que no pase de cinco años; obligandose tambien á tener un par de canones de artilleria y las armas suficientes al numero de hombres operarios que ecsistan para repeler á los indios barbaros en caso de que, como á la presente se hallen sublevados; por todo lo espuesto y por el bien y beneficio publico que debe resultar de las obras propuestas en esta solicitud.

A. V. E. podimos y suplicamos se sirva dar el curso correspondiente á esta solicitud, dispensandole la recomendacion, que de si arroya la peticion, para alcanzar y conseguir la adguicicion del terreno á que se refiere la misma. Juramos, &c. Santa Fé, Deciembre 28 de 1845.

Otro si decimos: que la mercenacion de terreno en la siempre memorable forma del muerto, á que se refieren los que firman esta solicitud, piden que se les conseda sin perjuicio de tercero de mejor derecho, *fha ut supra.*

Por mi Patron. ANTONIO JOSÉ RIBERA.
JUAN BAUTISTA VIGIL Y ALARID.
JOSÉ MIGUEL HAUCK.
J. ALBINO CHACON.

SANTA FÉ, *Enero* 10, 1846.

Se les concede por esta asamblea, á los Cuidadanos José Antonio Rivera y Juan Bautista Vigil y Alarid, el terreno pedido en el punto conocido por la Jornada del Muerto, para abrin norias y hacer una siembra hasta donde alcanzen sus facultades, quedando sin un derecho esclusivo á los pastos, y sin que en esta coneccion tenga parte alguna el estrangero Miguel Hauk, porque segun el articulo 9° de la ley de 11 de Marzo de 1842 le prohibe adquirir terrenos en los Departamentos fronterizos, sin previo consentimiento del Supremo Gobierno de la Nacion.

JOSÉ CHAVEZ.
NICOLAS QUINTANA Y ROSAS,
Secretario.

SANTA FÉ, *Enero* 10 *de* 1846.

Pase esta Ynstancia á la Exma. Asamblea para que si considera util al bien procumunal las proposiciones que como condiciones del pedido y la consecion, hacen los postulantes; conceda el terreno que se solicita disponiendo que conforme á las leyes se pongan los mismos en la posesion correspondiente; omitiendo el Gobierno recomendar á S. E. la honorable Asamblea Departamental este pedido que por su misma naturaliza y circunstancias, *hasta ahora no proyectadas* la trahe en si mismo la referida solicitud.

ARMIJO.
MIGUEL E. PINO, Oficial 1°.

Sello Tercero. [SEAL.] Cuatro Reales.

Anos de mil ochocientos y mil ochientos cuarenta y seis cuarenta y siese.

En la cuidad de Santa Fé capital del Departamento de Nueva Mejico, á los seis dias del mes de Febrero de mil ochocientos cuarenta y seis, yo el Cuidadano José Albino Chacon Alcalde 1º del Ayuntamiento de esta cuidad y Juez de 1ª Ynstancia del distrito del centro, dije: que mediante la Superior orden que con fecha cuatro del corriente mes me ha sido dirijida por la Secretaria de Gobierno, y haviendore presentado en este jusgado los cuidadanos Juan Bautista Vigil y Alaria y Antonio José Ribera con el decrcto de concesion de terreno en la Jornada del Muerto, que la Exma. Asamblea Departamental les dio en diez de Enero proximo pasado á dichos individuous, y el E. S. Gobernador confirmo en su superior disposicion oficial de cuatro del corriente mes; en cuya virtud prosedase por mi el presente Juez á darseles la posesion corporal Velquasi, de dicho terreno á los dos espresados agraciados, bajo la condicion de que si Don Miguel Hauck, presentare la constancia de que habla la superior comunicacion arriba sitada, se le declarará por participe á dicho terreno en iqualdad de derechos á sus socios segun su escrito de peticion. Y por este auto asi lo probeo mando y firmo con testigos de asistencia doy fee.

J. ALBINO CHACON.

De asist'a: JESUS MARIA TAFOYA.
De asist'a: TELESFORO SALAZAR.

SANTA FE, *Febrero* 7 *de* 1846.

Agreguese á estos ubos copia testimoniada de la superior orden del E. S. Gobor. de cuatro del coriente segun se dispone por la misma. Decretelo asi yo el Cuidadano José Albino Chacon, alcalde 1º y Juez en 1ª. Ynstancia del distrito actuando con testigos de asistencia doy fee.

J. ALBINO CHACON.

De asist'a: JESUS MARIA TAFOYA.
De asist'a: TELESFORO SALAZAR.

SECRETARIA DE GOBIERNO DEL DEPARTAMENTO: El Exmo. Sor. Gobor. me manda prevenir á V. que tan luego como le sea presentada el documento que acredite la mercenacion de terreno dado por la Exma. Asamblea Departamental, en 10 de Enero proximo pasado, á Don Juan Bautista Vigil y Alarid, y á Don Antonio José Ribera, en el terreno conocido por la jornada del muerto, y de cuya donacion se escluye al naturalizado Miguel Salomon Hauck, teniendolo por estrangero, y cuyo individuo si presentare la correspondiente carta de naturaleza, en este caso será tenido por agraciado como á los otros interesados arriba mencionados, á quienes prosedera V. á poner en posesion de dicho terreno, demandandoles los linderos que señalaron en su peticion, por no haber alteradolos la Exma. Asamblea, que solo restringio el derecho esclusivo de los pastos que seran comunes á los transitantes que ban y vienen por el camino, y nunca á los asendados ó pastores de este y de otros departamentos; previniendole ademas, de orden de S. E. que al documento de mercenacion agregase V. una copia legalizada de esta comunicacion para que sirva de resguardo á los interesados, y puedan estos con mayor seguridad emprender las obras de habrir norias que seran muy utiles al publico librandose de muchas perdidas y asegurando su vida, y la de sus animales á muy poca costa. Todo lo que de orden de S. E. digo á V. para su cumplimiento y ejecucion, avisando del recivo de lo presente. Dios y libertad Santa Fé, Febrero cuatro de mil ochocientos cuarenta y seis. Nicolas Quintana, Prosecretario. Sor. Alcalde y Juez de 1ª Ynstancia de esta Capital. Santa Fé.

Es copia fiel y legalmente sacada de su original que obra en la papelera de mi cargo para archivarse confrontada y emendada por mi y los de mi asistencia con quienes actuo por receptoria doy fe.

J. ALBINO CHACON.

De asist'a: Jesus Maria Tafoya.
De asist'a: Telesforo Salazar.

En cumplimiento del anterior auto y de la superior orden que antesede de cuatro del proximo pasado Febrero, que se sita y consta en testimonio legalizado arriba, he pasado de ida y vuelta, por el terreno *merced*, dado a los espresados en el mismo decreto de la Exma. Asamblea; por los conocimientos practicos que tengo del espresado terreno de la Jornado del Muerto, y segun las leyes, seremonias y costumbres bien recividas en este departamento, he prosedido á darles la posesion que de echo y de derecho les corresponde por no haberse presentado hasta la fha. ningun tercero de mejor derecho ni haber oposicion de parte al terreno baldio que se las ha concedido en propriedad á los agraciados Juan Bautista Vigil y Alarid, y Antonio José Ribera los cuales quedan en posesion quieta y pacifica de dicho terreno del que en señal de verdadera posesion han arrancado yerbas, sacates, tirado piedras dando voces de regocijo en Loor del Supremo Gobierno Mejicano, de cuya venignidad les viene dicho propriedad de la cual reconoceran y defenderan por linderos fijos los puntos siguientes; por el norte la mecita del contadero: por el sur el paraje anbiguo de Doña Ana en Roblerito: por el oriente la cordillera de la Sierra de Sandia y sus chorreras en aguel rumbo: y por el Poniente el Rio del Norte: en cuyos rumdos pondran los interesados las correspondientes mohoneras para evitar confusiones, con advertensia de que si el socio de la compañia José Miguel Salomon Hauck, presentare la correspondiente carta de naturaleza, sera tenido por propetario en igualdad de derechos con los Sres. Vigil y Ribera, pudiendo á mas admitir óno segun les convenga por socios y compañeros en el sitado terreno á la persona ó personas que fuere su voluntad y les merescan confianza. Y para la debida constancia y que este documento les sirva de titulo de posesion á los agraciados doy el presente que autorizo y fermo á los quince dias del mes de Marzo de mil ochocientos cuarenta y seis con los interesados y los testigos de mi asistencia con quienes actuo á falta de escribano doy fee.

J. ALBINO CHACON.
JUAN BAUTISTA VIGIL Y ALARID.
ANTONIO JOSÉ RIVERA.

De asist'a: Telesforo Salazar.
De asist'a: Jesus Maria Tafoya.
Derechos de posesion, 150 pesos.

En la ciudad de Santa Fé, capital del Departmento del Nuevo Mejico, en diez y seis de Septiembre de este año de mil ochocientos cuarenta y seis. Yo el ciudadano José Albino Chacon, Alcalde 1º y Juez en 1ª Ynstancia de esta capital y su distrito dije: que en virtud de haber presentado el Sr. Don José Miguel Salomon Hauck, al jusgado de mi cargo, su carta de naturaliza; agregueso esta original á estos documentos de donacion y tengase por lo mismo al enunciado Hauck por participe y propetario y con los mismos derechos del terreno de la Jornada del Muerto, arriba espresado, que los Sres. socios Don Juan Bautista Vigil y Alarid y Don Antonio José Ribera, segun la determinacion de la Exma. Asamblea de diez de Enero de este año y oficial comunicacion del E. S. Gobernador de cuatro de Febrero del mismo. Yo el juez setado asi lo probeo actuando con testigos de asistencia á la notoria falta de escribano publico doy fee.

J. ALBINO CHACON.

De asist'a: Jesus Maria Tafoya,
De asist'a: Telesforo Salazar.

Razon: Por haber reclamado Don Manuel Armendaris vecino del departmento de Chihuahua, parte del terreno constante en esta merced por el lindero del norte en la mecita del Contadero; se ordena, de orden del E. S. Gobor. actual, á los dueños y propietarios de la Jornada del Muerto, que no prosedan á las sacas de las norias hasta que sea concluido el pleito entre dicho Armendaris y los herederos del finado Don Francisco Xavier Chavez, y por lo mismo el termino delos cinco años para la conclusion de las norias se empesará á contar desde el propio dia en que se feje el dicho lindero del norte; ya sea por parte del dicho Armendaris ó sus coolitigantes los herederos del dicho finado Chavez. Y para que conste puse esta razon que rubrique.

Santiago Abreú Gefe Politico del Territorio de Nuevo Mejico.

Haviendo José Miguel Houck natural del Estado de Virginia, en los Unidos del Norte America, complido con las condiciones y requisitos que previene la ley de 14 de Abril de 1828, del Congreso General que arregla el modo con que debe consederse la carta de naturaleza, á los estrangeros, y acompañando los documentos que lo acreditan, declaro

al referido por las presentes, naturalizado en los Estados Unidos Mejicanos, en virtud de la autoridad que por aquella ley se me confiere.
SANTIAGO ABREÚ,
TEODOSIO QUINTANA, Srio.
SANTA FÉ, Agosto 18 de 1832.

Secretario de Gobierno del Departmento:

El Exmo. Sor. Gobor. me manda pre venir á V. que tan luego como le sea presentado el documento que acredite la mercenacion de terreno dado por la Exma. Asamblea Departamental en 10 de Enero proximo pasado, á Don Juan Bautista Vigil y Alarid y a Don Antonio José Rivera, en el terreno conocido por la Jornada del Muerto, y de cuya donacion se escluyó al naturalizado Miguel Saloman Houck, teniendolo por estrangero, y cuyo individuo, si presentare la correspondiente carta de naturaleza en este caso, sera venido por agraciado como á los otros dos interesados arriba mencionados, á quienes prosedera V. á poner en posesion de dicho terreno, demandandoles los linderos que señalaron en su peticion, por no haber alteradolos la Exma. Asamblea que solo restringio el derecho esclusivo de los pastos que serian comunes, á los transitantes que ban y bienen por el camino, y nunca á los asendados ó pasto res de este, y de otros departamentos, previniendole ademas de ordem de S. E. que al documento de mercenacion agregase V. una copia legalizada de esta comunicacion para que sirva de resguardo á los interesados, y puedan estos con mayor seguridad emprender las abras de abrir norias que seran muy utiles al publico librandose de muchas perdidas, y asigurando su vida, y la de sus animales á muy poca costa.

Todo loque de orden de S. E. digo á V. para su complimiento y ejecucion, avisandose del reciva de la presente.

Dios y libertad, Santa Fé, Febrero 4 de 1846.
NICHOLAS QUINTANA,
Pro. Secretario.

Sor. ALCALDE Y JUEZ,
De 1ª ynstancia de esta Capital.
SANTA FÉ, 13 de Mayo de 1846.

Gobierno Superior del Departamento:

Teniendo por justas, bastantes y legales las causas que V. espone en nota de 19 del corriente; para renunciar el destino de 1er individuo del Ayuntamiento de esta ciudad; el Gobierno haciendo uso de la facultad que le concede el articulo 3° fraccion 12 de la ley Reglamentaria de 20 de Marzo de 1837, he venido en admitirle á V. su renuncia la cual transcribira al Sor. Prefecto para que al regidor que le toque tornar en la vara se encargue desde luego del Jusgado 2° y este del 1° que V. obtenia por eleccion.

Dios y libertad. Santa Fé, Septiembre 21 de 1846.
JUAN BAUTISTA VIGIL Y ALARID.
JESUS MARIA TAFOYA, *Ofl.* 1°

Señor ALCALDE 1° de Santa Fé.
En 21 Septiembre se transcribio al Pref'to.

SURVEYOR GENERAL'S OFFICE, TRANSLATOR'S DEPARTMENT,
Santa Fé, New Mexico, August 24, 1859.

The above is a true copy of the original on file in this office.
DAVID V. WHITING,
Translator.

GRANT—TRANSLATION.

Third seal. [SEAL.] One dollar.

For the year one thousand eight hundred and forty-four and one thousand eight hundred and forty-five.

MOST ECXELLENT SIR: The individuals who subscribe this petition, animated by the purest patriotism and a desire to be useful to the society in which they live, making use of the right of petition, and of those with which they are favored by the existing colonization laws of this Mexican republic, to which they have the honor to belong as citizens, and one of them naturalized in the same, with all due respect present this petition to the most excellent departmental asssembly, through your excellency, the object of which is to ask for a grant from said honorable body in the ordinary manner, according to the fifth faculty, part second, mentioned in article 134 of the organic basis, the land known as the Jornado del Muerto, with the following boundaries: on the northwest, the little table land of the Contadero; on the west, the Del Norte river; on the south, the old site of Doña Ana; and on the east, the range of the Sandia mountains, with its tributaries in that direction. After our petition has been granted, and we are placed in possession of the land, the undersigned solemnly bind themselves, first, to construct two wells at the most central points of the Jornado, with their respective tanks, for the relief of and aid of travellers, who, up to this time, have suffered incalculable losses of horses, mules, cattle, sheep, and goats; and what is worse still, many human victims, who have perished for the absolute want of water, which travellers will be certain of obtaining at a very little expense when said wells are placed in working order. Second, with equal solemnity they offer to establish two factories, which will be of utility to the department, and in which such delinquents as may be sentenced by the justices and authorities of the department to suffer for crime will be received, as the laws and decrees of the honorable assembly now or hereafter may direct in regard to the matter. Third, the petitioners bind themselves to have the four requisites which should belong to modern machinery completed within the shortest possible period, not exceeding five years; obligating themselves, also, to have two field-pieces and a sufficient number of arms, equal to the number of workmen, to repel the hostile Indians in case they may revolt, as is now the case. In view of all that has been stated, and for the welfare and benefit of the public which will result from the works proposed in this petition, we pray and request your excellency to be pleased to transmit this petition through its proper channel, adding thereto a recommendation of the merits of the petition, in order to obtain the requisition of the land therein referred to. We swear, &c.

SANTA FÉ, *December* 28, 1845.

The undersigned further request that the grant to the land in the ever memorable Jornado del Muerto be made without injury to any third party who may show a better title. Date ut supra.

For my patron.
     ANTONIO JOSÉ RIVERA.
     JUAN BAUTISTA Y ALARID.
     JOSEPH M. HOUCK.
     JOSÉ ALBINO CHACON.

SANTA FÉ, *January* 10, 1846.

This petition is referred to the most excellent assembly in order that if they consider the offers which, in the form of conditions, the petitioners make beneficial to the Commonwealth, that the land asked for be granted to them, directing that they be placed in legal possession, as the law directs. This government omits to recommend the petitions to its excellency the honorable departmental assembly, as the nature and circumstances connected therewith, *and never heretofore planned,* is explained in said petition.

               ARMIJO.
MIGUEL E. PINO, *First Clerk.*

This assembly grants to citizens Antonio José Rivera and Juan Bautista Vigil y Alarid the land asked for at the place known as the Jornado del Muerto for the purpose of constructing wells and cultivating the land, as far as their means will permit, without being entitled to an exclusive right to the pasture, and debarring from any of the privileges of this grant the foreigner, Michael Houck, as he is prohibited by article ninth of the law of March 11, 1842, from acquiring lands in the frontier department, without the previous consent of the supreme government of the nation.

              JOSÉ CHAVES.
NICHOLAS QUINTANA Y ROSAS,
    Secretary.

Seal third. [SEAL.] Four rials.

Years of 1846 *and* 1847.

In the city of Santa Fé, capitol of the department of New Mexico, on the 6th day of the month of February, one thousand eight hundred and forty-six, I, citizen José Albino Chacon, first justice of the corporation of this city, and judge of original jurisdiction of the central district, stated that, by virtue of the superior order of the 4th instant, addressed to me by the secretary of the government, and citizens Juan Bautista Vigil y Alarid and Antonio José Rivera, having presented themselves at my office with the decree of the most excellent departmental assembly, of the 10th of January last, granting to them the Jornado del Muerto, and confirmed by his excellency the governor in his superior official order of the 4th instant, by virtue whereof I, the aforesaid justice, will proceed to give them the legal personal possession of said land to the aforesaid grantees, on condition that if D. Miguel Houck shall present the record referred to in the superior communication, above referred to, he shall be declared as a participant in said land, with the same rights as his associates, as appears by their written petition, and by this decree be so provided, ordered, and signed, with attending witnesses.

I certify.

J. ALBINO CHACON.

Attending: JESUS MARIA TAFOYA.
TELESFERO SALAZAR.

SANTA FÉ, *February* 7, 1846.

Let a certified copy of the superior order of his excellency the governor of the 4th instant be attached to these decrees, as directed therein. I, citizen José Albino Chacon, first justice and judge of original jurisdiction of the district, so decreed, acting with attending.

JOSÉ ALBINO CHACON.

Attending: JESUS MARIA TAFOYA.
TELESFERO SALAZAR.

OFFICE OF THE SECRETARY OF THE GOVERNMENT.

His excellency the governor directs me to require you that so soon as the document is presented to you, accrediting the grant made by the most excellent departmental assembly, on the 10th of January last past, to Don Juan Bautista Vigil y Alarid and Don Antonio José Rivera, to the land known as the Jornado del Muerto, from which the naturalized Michael Solomon Houck is excluded, he being a foreigner, who, upon presentation of the proper naturalization papers, shall in that case be considered as one of the grantees, the same as those above mentioned, whom you will proceed to place in possession of said land, giving them the boundaries called for in their petition, not having been changed by the most excellent assembly, which only restricted the exclusive right of pasturage, which shall be free to travellers who may go and come over the road, and only to the owners of stock and shepherds of this and other departments; requiring you also, by order of his excellency, to attach to the granting deed a legal copy of this communication, for the protection of the parties interested, and give them more security to undertake the work of opening wells, which will be of great utility to the public by preventing many losses, and securing not only their lives, but those of their animals, at very little cost. Of all which you are informed, by order of his excellency, for its due compliance and execution, acknowledging the receipt hereof. God and liberty, Santa Fé, February 4, 1846.

NICHOLAS QUINTANA,
Acting Secretary.

The JUSTICE and JUDGE *of original jurisdiction of the capital, Santa Fé.*

The above is a true and legal copy of the original, among the papers placed under my charge for record, corrected and compared by me and those in my attendance, with whom I act by appointment.
I certify.

JOSÉ ALBINO CHACON.

Attending: JESUS MARIA TAFOYA.
TELESFERO SALAZAR.

In obedience to the foregoing decree and the above superior order of the 4th of February last past, a legal copy whereof appears above, I have gone backwards and forwards over the land granted to the parties referred to in the same decree of the most excellent assembly. From the practical knowledge I have of the aforesaid land of the Jornado del Muerto, and according to the well-received laws, ceremonies, and customs in this department, I proceeded to give them the possession which in fact and by right they are entitled to, no third parties having a better title having presented themselves up to this time, and no opposition being made to the public land which has been granted in fee to the grantees, Juan Bautista Vigil y Alarid and Antonio José Rivera, who remain in the quiet and peaceful possession of said land, from which, in proof of lawful possession, they have pulled up weeds and grass, throwing stones and crying aloud with joy, in honor of the supreme Mexican government, from whose generosity they received said possession, of which they acknowledge and will defend, as permanent boundaries, the following points: on the north, the little table land of the Contadero; on the south, the old site of Doña Ana, at Roblerito; on the east, the range of the Sandia mountain and its tributaries on that side; and on the west, the river Del Norte; in which directions the parties will erect the proper monuments to avoid confusion, with the understanding that if José Miguel Solomon Houck, one of the partners in the company, shall present the proper naturalization papers, he shall be considered as one of the proprietors, holding equal rights with Messrs. Vigil and Rivera; being privileged, further, to admit as associates and partners in said land such persons as they may desire, and in whom they may have confidence. And in testimony thereof, and that this document may be to the grantees a deed of possession, I have executed this, which I authorize and sign on the fifteenth day of the month of March, one thousand eight hundred and forty-six, with the parties interested, and my attending witnesses, with whom I act in the absence of a notary. I certify.

Fees for placing in possession, 150 dollars.

JOSÉ ALBINO CHACON.
JUAN BAUTISTA VIGIL Y ALARID.
ANTONIO JOSÉ RIVERA.

Attending:
TELESFERO SALAZAR.
JESUS MARIA TAFOYA.

In the city of Santa Fé, capital of the department of New Mexico, on the sixteenth day of September of this year, one thousand eight hundred and forty-six, I, citizen José Albino Chacon, first justice and judge of original jurisdiction of this capital and its district, stated that Don José Miguel Solomon Houck, having presented his naturalization papers before the court under my charge, let the original thereof be attached to these granting documents, and therefore the said Houck is to be considered a participant in, and one of the proprietors of, the above-mentioned land of the Jornado del Muerto, with the same rights as the other partners, Messrs. Juan Bautista Vigil y Alarid and Antonio José Rivera, according to the directions of the most excellent assembly, dated the tenth day of January of this year, and the official communication of his excellency the governor, of the fourth of February of the same year. I, the aforesaid justice, so provided, acting with attending witnesses in the known absence of a notary public. I certify.

JOSÉ ALBINO CHACON.

Attending:
JESUS MARIA TAFOYA.
TELESFERO SALAZAR.

NOTE.—Don Manuel Armendaris, resident of the department of Chihuahua, having claimed part of the land contained in this grant on the northern boundary at the little table land of the Contadero, it is ordered, by directions of his excellency the present governor, that the owners and proprietors of the Jornado del Muerto shall not proceed to construct the wells until the suit between the said Armendaris and the heirs of the late Don Francisco Xavier Chaves shall be decided. And therefore the term of five years, limited for the construction of the wells, shall be counted from the day on which the said northern boundary shall be established, be it by the said Armendaris or the heirs of the late Chaves, the other parties to the suit. And in order that it may so appear, I have made this note, which I have subscribed.

[Rubric.]

Santiago Abreú, political chief of the Territory of New Mexico.

José Miguel Houck, native of the State of Virginia, in the United States of North America, having complied with the conditions and requirements provided by the laws of the general Congress of April 14, 1828, which regulated the manner in which naturalization papers are to be granted to foreigners, and accompanying the documents by

which he is identified, I hereby declare the above to be naturalized in the United Mexican States, by virtue of the authority in me invested by said law. Santa Fé, August 18, 1832.
Gratis. SANTIAGO ABREÚ.
TEODOSIO QUINTANA, *Secretary*.

DEPARTMENTAL ASSEMBLY OF NEW MEXICO.
Santa Fé, January 12, 1846.

The departmental assembly has resolved to return to your excellency the petition of citizens Antonio José Rivera, Juan Bautista Vigil, and the foreigner, Miguel Houck, which has been decreed in accordance with the resolution of said assembly.

I reiterate to your excellency the protestations of my consideration and esteem. God and liberty.
JOSÉ MANUEL GALLEGOS,
President.
NICOLAS QUINTANA Y ROSAS,
Secretary.
His excellency the GOVERNOR OF THE DEPARTMENT.

SURVEYOR GENERAL'S OFFICE, TRANSLATOR'S DEPARTMENT,
Santa Fé, New Mexico, July 31, 1859.

The foregoing is a correct translation from the original Spanish now on file in this office.
DAVID V. WHITING,
Translator.

SURVEYOR GENERAL'S OFFICE,
Santa Fé, New Mexico, August 31, 1859.

The foregoing is a correct transcript from the original now on file in this office.
WILLIAM PELHAM,
Surveyor General.

ORDER FOR POSSESSION—TRANSLATION.

OFFICE OF THE SECRETARY OF THE
GOVERNMENT OF THE DEPARTMENT.

*To the Justice of the Peace and Judge of First Instance of this capital,
Santa Fé:*

His excellency the governor directs me to inform you that so soon as the document is presented to you, accrediting the grant of land made by the most excellent departmental assembly, on the 10th of January last past, to Don Juan Bautista Vigil y Alarid and Don Antonio José Rivera, at the point known as the Jornado del Muerto, and from which grant the naturalized citizen, Miguel Salomon Houck, was excluded, being considered as a foreigner, which individual, if he presents the proper naturalization papers in that case, he shall be considered as one of the grantees equally with the other two persons above mentioned, whom you will proceed to place in possession of said land, marking out to them the boundaries which they set forth in their petition, as they have not been charged by the most excellent assembly, who only restricted the exclusive right to pastures, which are declared to be common to travellers going and coming over the road, and not to owners of stock in this and other departments; requiring them, also, by direction of his excellency, to attach to the granting deed a certified copy of this communication for the protection of the parties interested, and that they may, with greater security, undertake the work of opening wells, which will be of great utility to the public, thereby preventing many losses, and saving their lives at very little expense.

Of all which you are informed, by order of his excellency, for its due compliance and execution, acknowledging the receipt hereof.

God and liberty.

NICOLAS QUINTANA,
Pro. Secretary.

SANTA FÉ, *February* 4, 1846.

SURVEYOR GENERAL'S OFFICE, TRANSLATOR'S DEPARTMENT,
Santa Fé, New Mexico, August 29, 1859.

The foregoing is a correct translation of the original on file in this office.

DAVID V. WHITING,
Translator.

SURVEYOR GENERAL'S OFFICE,
Santa Fé, New Mexico, August 31, 1859.

The foregoing is a correct transcript from the original now on file in this office.

WILLIAM PELHAM,
Surveyor General.

RESIGNATION OF CHACON—TRANSLATION.

SUPERIOR GOVERNMENT OF THE DEPARTMENT,
Santa Fé, September 3, 1846.

Considering the reasons given in your note of the 11th instant as just, sufficient, and legal for resigning the office of first individual of the corporation of this city, the government making use of the faculties conferred upon it by article 3d, fraction 12, of the regulatory law of March 20, 1837, I have accepted your resignation, which you will transmit to the honorable prefect, in order that the alderman whose term it is to receive the staff may assume the duties of 2d justice, who will assume those of the first justice, which you obtained by election.

God and liberty.

JUAN BAUTISTA VIGIL Y ALARID.

Jesus Maria Tafoya,
First Clerk.

The First Justice *of Santa Fé.*

On the 21st September it was transmitted to the prefect.

Surveyor General's Office, Translator's Department,
Santa Fé, New Mexico, July 10, 1859.

The above is a correct translation of the original on file in this office.

DAVID V. WHITING,
Translator.

Surveyor General's Office,
Santa Fé, New Mexico, August 31, 1859.

The foregoing is a correct copy of the original on file in this office.

WILLIAM PELHAM,
Surveyor General.

CONVEYANCE—SPANISH.

El dia veinte y tres de Mayo de mil ochocientos cincuenta y nueve, en Santa Fé, Territorio de Nuevo Mejico, Juan Bautista Vigil y Alarid, de la primera parte, y Albino Chacon, de la segunda parte, hicieron y confirmaron el contrato que sigue: A Saver: Juan Bautista Vigil y Alarid, el primera siendo uno y el principal de los agraciados, que con justos, legales y faccientes titulos que presenta se prueva que á el citado Vigil y Alarid, á José Miguel S. Houck y á Antonio José Rivera, que por su patron firmo la peticion, les fue donado y concedido por las autoridades Mejicanas el terreno en este Territorio conocido y llamado la Jornado del Muerto, y reconociendo el dicho Juan Bautista Vigil y Alarid los grandes y utiles servicios que en este asunto ha hecho y esta haciendo Albino Chacon, quien como juez de primera ynstancia, en aquel tiempo actuo en dichos titulos desde el principio hasta darles copia y ponerlos en posesion del terreno referido, en correspondencia á tales servicios y en meritos á ser el dicho Albino Chacon uno de los peticionarios del dicho terreno, y conforme, tambien, á la amplitud conferida á los agraciados en los actos de concesion arriba dichos de admitir ó no en el dicho terreno, uno ó mas socios compañeros á su advitrio, por todo lo cual el dicho Juan Bautista Vigil y Alarid, bajo su responsabilidad se compromete y le ofrecio al dicho Albino Chacon, por si y á nombre de sus compañeros de terreno, los Señores José Miguel S. Houck, y Antonio José Rivera, hacer lo participante del (del) terreno de la Jornado del Muerto en iguales derechos á ellos conferidos, es decir: en una cuarta parte del terreno ó su importe, á lo que el dicho Albino Chacon acepto y se compromete á alludar y emprender costos, si necesario fuere, hasta lograr la concesion final por el gobierno á quien pertenece a hora este Territorio de Nueva Mejico. En fe de lo cual estendieron el presente documento, el que ambos contratantes convienen en presentarse ante alguna de las autoridades de esta ciudad para que lo autorize y certifique en forma firmandolo para constancia las partes con testigos, &ª.

JUAN BAUTISTA VIGIL Y ALARID
y Compañia.
ALBINO CHACON.

Ejecutado firmado y sellado en presencia de—
 Tomas Baca y Ortiz y
 José David Baca.

Territorio de Nuevo Méjico, *Condado de Santa Fé:*

Ante mi, Nicolas Quintana, un juez de paz del condado de Santa Fé, comparecieron presentes Albino Chacon y Juan B. Vigil y Alarid, personalmente conocidos por mi de ser las mismas personas cuyos nombres aparecen en el antecedente documento ó contrato; y ellos declaran de haberlo ejecutado firmado y sellado voluntariamente por y para los fines en el espresados.

En testimonio de lo cual pongo mi nombre oficial, en Santa Fé, hoy el dia 24 de Mayo, A. D. 1859.

NICOLAS QUINTANA,
Juez de Paz.

Surveyor General's Office, Translator's Department,
Santa Fé, New Mexico, August 24, 1859.

The above is a true copy of the original on file in this office.

D. V. WHITING,
Translator.

CONVEYANCE—TRANSLATION.

On the twenty-third day of May, one thousand eight hundred and fifty-nine, at Santa Fé, Territory of New Mexico, Juan Bautista Vigil y Alarid, of the first part, and Albino Chacon, of the second part, made and confirmed the following agreement, to wit: Juan Bautista Vigil y Alarid, the first, being one and the principal of the grantees, who, by just, legal, and sufficient title, which they show, proves that to the aforesaid Vigil y Alarid, José Miguel S. Houck, and Antonio José Rivera, who for his patron signed the petition, was granted and donated by the Mexican authorities the land in this Territory known and called the Jornado del Muerto; and the said Juan Bautista Vigil knowing the great and useful services which have been, and are now being, rendered by Albino Chacon, who, as judge of the first instance, at that time carried out the execution of said title from the beginning to the delivery of the copy and placing the parties in possession of the land aforesaid, as compensation for said services, and in consideration of the said Albino Chacon being one of the petitioners for said land, and in conformity also with the privileges conferred upon the grantees in the aforesaid acts of concession of admitting one or more associates at their will, therefore the said Juan Bautista Vigil y Alarid upon his responsibility binds himself, and did offer to the said Albino Chacon, for himself and in the name of his associates, Messrs. José Miguel S. Houck and Antonio José Rivera, in said land, to give him an equal interest as conferred upon them in said land of the Jornado del Muerto, that is to say: one-fourth interest in the land, or its equivalent, which the said Albino Chacon accepted and binds himself to aid in paying costs, if it becomes necessary to do so, until the final concession is made by the government to which this Territory of New Mexico now belongs.

In testimony whereof, the present document was executed, which both parties agree to submit to one of the authorities of this city to be authorized and certified in form—the parties signing before witnesses—as a matter of record, &c.

JUAN BAUTISTA VIGIL Y ALARID
and associates.
ALBINO CHACON.

Executed, signed, and sealed in presence of—
TOMAS BACA Y ORTIZ.
JOSÉ DAVID BACA.

TERRITORY OF NEW MEXICO, *County of Santa Fé:*

Before me, Nicolas Quintana, a justice of the peace for the county of Santa Fé, appeared Albino Chacon and Juan Bautista Vigil y Alarid, known to me to be the persons whose names appear to the foregoing document or contract, and they acknowledged that they executed, signed and sealed the same voluntarily and for the purposes therein mentioned. In testimony whereof, I hereto attach my official signature, at Santa Fé, this 24th day of May, A. D. 1859.

NICOLAS QUINTANA,
Justice of the Peace.

SURVEYOR GENERAL'S OFFICE, TRANSLATOR'S DEPARTMENT,
Santa Fé, New Mexico, August 9, 1859.

The above is a correct translation of the original on file in this office.

DAVID V. WHITING,
Translator.

SURVEYOR GENERAL'S OFFICE,
Santa Fé, New Mexico, August 31, 1859.

The foregoing is a correct copy of the original on file in this office.

WM. PELHAM,
Surveyor General.

PROCLAMATION OF GENERAL KEARNY.

To the inhabitants of New Mexico, by Brigadier General S. W. Kearney, commanding the troops of the United States in the same:

As by the act of the republic of Mexico a state of war exists between that government and the United States, and as the undersigned, at the head of his troops, on the 18th instant took possession of Santa Fé, the capital of the department of New Mexico, he now announces his intention to hold the department, with its original boundaries, (on both sides of the Del Norte,) as a part of the United States, and under the name of the "Territory of New Mexico."

The undersigned has come to New Mexico with a strong military force, and an equally strong one is following close in his rear. He has more troops than necessary to put down any opposition that can possibly be brought against him, and therefore it would be but folly or madness for any dissatisfied or discontented persons to think of resisting him.

The undersigned has instructions from his government to respect the religious institutions of New Mexico, to protect the property of the church, to cause the worship of those belonging to it to be undisturbed, and their religious rights in the amplest manner to be preserved to them; also to protect the persons and property of all quiet and peaceable inhabitants within its boundaries against their enemies, the Utahs, the Navajoes, and others; and when he assures all that it will be his pleasure as well as his duty to comply with those instructions, he calls upon them to exert themselves in preserving order, in promoting concord, and in maintaining the authority and the efficiency of the laws. And he requires of those who have left their homes and taken up arms against the troops of the United States to return forthwith to them, or else they will be considered as enemies and traitors, subjecting their persons to punishment and their property to seizure and confiscation for the benefit of the public treasury.

It is the wish and intention of the United States to provide for New Mexico a free government, with the least possible delay, similar to those in the United States, and the people of New Mexico will then be called upon to exercise the right of freemen in electing their own representatives to the territorial legislature. But until this can be done the laws hitherto in existence will be continued until changed or modified by competent authority, and those persons holding offices will continue in the same for the present, *provided* they will consider themselves good citizens and willing to take the oath of allegiance to the United States.

The undersigned hereby absolves all persons residing within the boundaries of New Mexico from any further allegiance to the republic of Mexico, and hereby claims them as citizens of the United States. Those who remain quiet and peaceable will be considered good citizens and receive protection; those who are found in arms or instigating others against the United States will be considered as traitors and treated accordingly.

Don Manuel Armijo, the late governor of the department, has fled from it. The undersigned has taken possession of it without firing a gun or spilling a single drop of blood, in which he most truly rejoices, and for the present will be considered as governor of the Territory.

Given at Santa Fé, the capital of the Territory of New Mexico, this 22d day of August, 1846, and in the seventy-first year of the independence of the United States.

S. W. KEARNY,
Brigadier General United States Army.

By the governor:
JUAN BAUTISTA VIGIL Y ALARID.

THE UNITED STATES OF AMERICA, *Territory of New Mexico:*

I, Alexander M. Jackson, secretary of said Territory, do hereby certify that the within and foregoing three pages contain a full, true, and perfect copy of the original proclamation of Brigadier General S. W. Kearny on file in my office. In testimony whereof, I have hereunto set my hand and seal of office this 20th day of June, A. D. 1859.
[L. S.] A. M. JACKSON,
Secretary of the Territory of New Mexico.

SURVEYOR GENERAL'S OFFICE, SANTA FÉ,
New Mexico, August 31, 1859.

The foregoing is a correct copy of the original on file in this office.

WM. PELHAM,
Surveyor General.

TESTIMONY.

Jornado del Muerto.

GASPER ORTIZ Y ALARID sworn:
Question. Have you any interest in this case?
Answer. I have none.
Question. How old are you?
Answer. I am thirty-four years old.
Question. What position did you hold under the departmental government of New Mexico when it was in existence?
Answer. I was an officer of the army.
Question. Did you know General Armijo?
Answer. I did. He was commander-in-chief and governor of the department.
Question Do you know his signature when you see it?
Answer. I do.
Question. Is the signature on folio 3 of the document [shown to him] Armijo's genuine signature?
Answer. It is his signature and rubric?
Question. Did you know José Albino Chacon, and what position did he hold?
Answer. I did. He was judge of original jurisdiction. Both of the above officers were in office in 1846.

Question. Do you know the signature of Albino Chacon?
Answer. I do. He was writing with me for one year. His signature on folios 5 and 7 are genuine.

Cross-examined by attorney for the United States.

Question. Do you know the Jornado del Muerto?
Answer. I do.
Question. Have you passed over it since 1846; and if so, how often?
Answer. I have passed over it, I believe, twelve times.
Question. Have you ever seen any wells or conveniences for water, or other improvements, put upon any part of the land?
Answer. I have seen none.
Question. Have you ever seen any person in possession of the land embraced within the Ojo del Muerto and Roblero at any time since 1846?
Answer. I have not.
Question. Do you know the Mesa del Contadero and Roblero?
Answer. I do. I believe the distance to be no less than thirty-five leagues.
Question. How far is it from the Rio del Norte to the mountains, to the east?
Answer. I believe it to be not less than ten leagues

GASPER ORTIZ.

Sworn and subscribed before me this 16th day of June, 1859.
WM. PELHAM,
Surveyor General.

MIGUEL E. PINO sworn:

Question. Have you any interest in this case?
Answer. None.
Question. What office did you hold under the Mexican government in the year 1846?
Answer. In the month of January I was chief clerk in the secretary's office.
Question. Is your signature on folio 3 of the document genuine?
Answer. It is.
Question. Did you know José Manuel Gallegos, and what position did he hold on January 12, 1846?
Answer. I did. He was member of the departmental assembly.
Question. Did you know Nicholas Quintana y Rosas, and what office did he hold?
Answer. I did. He was secretary of the assembly.
Question. Are the signatures of the above individuals on folios 1 and 4 genuine?
Answer. They are. I know them to be such.
Question. Did you know José Chaves, and what was his position in January, 1846?
Answer. I did. He was a member of departmental assembly; he

was the senior member and governor by the ministration of the law. His signature on folio 4 is genuine.

Question. Did you know Santiago Abreú, and what office did he hold in 1832?

Answer. I did. About that time he was political chief. Teodosis Quintana was his secretary. Their signatures on folio 8 are genuine.

MIGUEL E. PINO.

Sworn and subscribed before me this 16th day of June, 1859.
WM. PELHAM,
Surveyor General.

CHARLES BLUMNER sworn:

Question. Have you any interest in the case now pending?
Answer. I have not.
Question. Do you know the Jornado del Muerto?
Answer. I do.
Question. Do you know the Mesa del Contadero and Roblero?
Answer. I do.
Question. What is the distance between the Mesa del Contadero and Roblero?
Answer. I have always understood it to be about 100 miles.
Question. How far is it from the Rio del Norte to the mountains in the east?
Answer. I have no idea. It is a long distance—say from 60 to 100 miles.
Question. Have you ever seen any wells or other improvements on the land?
Answer. I have neither seen wells nor any other improvement of any description up to the last time I passed over them, in the fall of 1856.
Question. Were you in Santa Fé in 1846 when General Kearny arrived?
Answer. I was. He arrived here in August, 1846.
Question. When General Kearny took possession of the country did the Mexican authorities continue to exist or not?
Answer. They all ceased, with the exception of one or two who were reappointed. The governor was not here; he left before General Kearny arrived.

CHARLES BLUMNER.

Sworn and subscribed before me this 16th day of June, 1859.
WM. PELHAM,
Surveyor General.

DONACIAUS VIGIL sworn:

Question. Have you any interest in this case?
Answer. None.
Question. What position did you hold under the American government in September, 1846?

Answer. On the 22d September I was appointed secretary of the territory.

Question. What position did you hold under the Mexican government previous to the 18th August, 1846?

Answer. I was secretary to the military commander, and during that period was several times acting secretary of state.

Question. Did the prefects and other subordinate civil officers hold over under the American government by the sanction of General Kearney until the 22d September of the same year?

Answer. They did.

Question. What office did Juan Bautista Vigil hold during that period?

Answer. He was secretary of state at the time of the arrival of General Kearney; from that time to the 22d September he was acting governor.

Question. Do you know the signature of Juan Bautista Vigil y Alarid?

Answer. I do. The signature to the letter accepting the resignation of the first justice of Santa Fé is genuine.

Question. Did you know Nicolas Quintana, and what was his occupation in February, 1846?

Answer. I did. He was first clerk in the secretary's office. I know his signature. His signature to the order directed to the first justice of Santa Fé is genuine.

Question. What position did José Albino Chacon hold from August 18 to September 22, 1846?

Answer. He was an alcalde, acting as senior judge of the jurisdiction.

Question. Under what sanction did he exercise those functions?

Answer. By virtue of the proclamation of General Kearney, continuing in office all the civil employés until competent laws were promulgated.

Question. Do you know Albino Chacon's signature and rubric?

Answer. I do; his signature and rubric, on the reverse of folio 7, are genuine.

Question. Under the Spanish and Mexican government, would an addition to a legal proceeding, executed by the same officer, and his rubric only attached, be considered as valid, and hold good in law?

Answer. Official proceedings or agreements, written immediately after a judicial act, were considered to be sufficiently authenticated, and were held good in law, if rubricked only by the proper officer.

Cross-examined by United States.

Question. Did the officers of the Mexican government, in executing official documents and attaching their signatures thereto, ever place their rubric alone without their name?

Answer. It was the legal practice under the government of Spain and Mexico, and is the practice up to the present time, that when the two parties were not present, or when only one was present, that the judge or justice taking cognizance of the case, would simply make a memorandum or note, affixing his rubric only; this memorandum served as a notice or summons to the absent party.

Question. Did the justices of the peace under the Spanish and Mexican governments have the power and authority to alter or amend the acts of the governor in making grants, or suspend the compliance of conditions specified therein?

Answer. They did not.

Re-examined by counsel for claimants.

Question. If the justice of the peace, in giving judicial possession of lands granted by due course of law, ascertained, while complying with his duty, that the lands so granted encroached upon lands already granted in this case, did he not have the right to suspend further proceedings in the case, until the boundaries in dispute were settled?

Answer. If, while possession was being given, a claim was made against the grant so made, then all further proceedings were stopped until information was conveyed to the proper authorities, and the question in dispute was settled. He had the authority to give notice of the suspension until the matter was settled, or that the reasons why he did not comply with the instructions given him in the premises.

D. VIGIL.

Sworn and subscribed before me this 18th day of June, 1859.

WM. PELHAM,
Surveyor General.

Surveyor General's Office,
Santa Fé, New Mexico, August 31, 1859.

The foregoing is a true copy of the original record of evidence on file in this office.

WM. PELHAM,
Surveyor General.

Report.

Juan Bautista Vigil y Alarid *vs.* The United States.

Surveyor General's Office,
Santa Fé, New Mexico, August 29, 1859.

This case came on to be heard on the 16th of July, 1859, and continued until the 18th of July, when it was finally submitted by counsel.

On the 28th day of December, 1845, Antonio José Rivéra, for his patrons Juan Bautista Vigil y Alarid and José Miguel Houck, petitioned the governor of the department of New Mexico for a tract of land known as the Jornado del Muerto, with the boundaries therein set forth, solemnly binding themselves, upon receiving the grant and being placed in possession of the land, to commence the construction of two wells at the most central points on the Jornado for the purpose of supplying water to travellers and stock, and also to establish two factories of utility to the department. These factories were to be supplied with modern improved machinery, and the whole to be concluded within five years. They were also to have two cannons and a sufficient number of fire-arms to repel any attack from hostile Indians.

On the 10th day of January, 1846, Manuel Armijo, the governor of the department, referred the petition to the departmental assembly, recommending that the grant be made, if the propositions made by the applicants in the form of conditions were deemed to be of sufficient benefit to the country, and calling their attention to the nature of those conditions, which at that time was a novel undertaking in the department. On the same day the departmental assembly granted the land known as the Jornado del Muerto to Antonio José Rivéra and Juan Bautista Vigil y Alarid, for the purpose of opening wells and cultivating as much land as their means would allow, excluding Michael Houck from any participation in the grant on account of the prohibition contained in article 9th of the law of March 11, 1842, which forbids foreigners from acquiring lands in the frontier departments, without the previous knowledge of the supreme government.

On the 4th day of February, 1846, Nicholas Quentana, acting secretary by direction of the governor, ordered the justice of the peace of Santa Fé to place the grantees in possession of the land, and also directs an equal interest to be given to Houck upon the presentation of his naturalization papers.

On the 5th day of March, 1846, José Albino Chacon, first justice of Santa Fé, certifies that he placed Antonio José Rivéra and Juan Bautista Vigil in possession of the land granted them.

On the 16th day of September, 1846, the same José Albino Chacon declares José Miguel Solomon Houck as a party to said grant, he having filed the required naturalization papers.

Immediately after this statement, made after the sovereignty of the country had changed, there appears a memorandum or note, without any written signature, but merely a rubric, to the effect that as Manuel Amendaris, a resident of the department of Chihuahua, claimed a portion of the land embraced within the grant to the Jornada del Muerto, the grantees were forbidden to prosecute the work until a certain suit pending between the said Amendaris and the heirs of Francisco Xavier Chaves should be decided, and the period of five years, given for the conclusion of the work, was to commence from the time of the termination of said suit, by which the northern boundary would be determined.

Immediately thereafter follows the original certificate of naturalization declaring José Miguel Houck a citizen of the republic of Mexico.

The parties also file the original letter from José Manuel Gallegas, the president of the departmental assembly, returning the petition of the grantees, with the action had thereon. The original order to Albino Chacon, directing him to place the parties in possession, is also filed, as well as the acceptation of the resignation of Albino Chacon, by Juan Bautista Vigil y Alarid, acting governor on the 21st September, 1846. An agreement is also filed, dated May 3, 1859, between

Juan Bautista Vigil y Alarid and associates, of the first part, and Albino Chacon, of the second part, by which a one-fourth interest is conveyed to the said Albino Chacon, in consideration of the services rendered by him in placing the parties in possession of the grant.

A certified copy of the proclamation of Brigadier General S. W. Kearney, to the people of New Mexico, upon taking possession of the country in the name of the United States, on the 18th day of August, 1846, also accompanies the papers in the case.

The name of José Albino Chacon appears signed to the original petition, asking for the grant, but as his name does not appear in the granting decree, and as he was directed to place the parties in possession, which would not have been done were he an interested party, it is believed he attached his name thereto at a very recent date, long after the transaction in the case took place, and it has so been admitted by one of the grantees.

The papers acted upon are the originals filed by the claimants.

This is one of the most important cases that has been filed in this office for adjudication, embracing, as it does, an area of nearly two and one-half millions of acres of land, a large portion of which has been subdivided, and is now ready to be brought into market, and has received my most careful attention and close examination.

The parties claim a confirmation of their grant for the following reasons:

1. On account of the originality and genuineness of the documents.
2. That the grant was made in due accordance with the laws and customs in force at that time.
3. That the parties were forbidden from taking any further steps towards the construction of the wells and the establishment of the factories until a certain suit between Pedro Armendaris and the heirs of Francisco Xavier Chaves should be decided, and by which the northern boundary of the grant in question would be determined.
4. That the non-compliance of the conditions of the grant under the late government does not forfeit their rights under the government of the United States.

It is not necessary to dwell on the first and second points submitted in the brief of the claimants, as the originality and genuineness of the documents are not questioned and are fully proven in evidence.

The petition made by the parties asking for the grant solemnly bind themselves, upon being placed in possession of the land, to commence the construction of wells and the establishment of certain factories.

This possession, as will be seen by the certificate of the justice, was given on the fifteenth day of March, 1846.

And no further action is shown to have taken place in the matter until the twenty-first of September, 1846, when Houck is declared to be a party interested in the grant, having presented his naturalization papers, although the departmental assembly positively refuses to grant him an interest in the grant on account of being forbidden by law to hold land in the frontier departments without the previous knowledge of the general government; and, although it is contended that at that time Armijo was invested with extraordinary powers, his action in this case was in direct violation of law, and as no consent of the general government is recorded, or even contended for, the order of the governor to make him an equal participant upon the presentation of the necessary document, was null and void, and could not convey to him an interest which the law expressly forbids. After the execution of this document declaring Houck a participant in the grant made on the twenty-first day of September, 1846, over one month after the United States took possession of the country, and the laws of the United States extended over it by the proclamation of the conqueror, General Kearney, upon which so much stress is laid by the claimants, the order requiring the suspension of the construction of the wells, &c., is recorded. By reference to the original documents, it will be seen that this note or *razon* immediately follows the declaration in favor of Houck, and as Chacon's resignation was accepted on the twenty-first day of September, 1846, both must have been made upon the same day. It is true that the laws of Mexico were declared to be in force in the land, except where they conflicted with the Constitution or laws of the United States. In this case there was a conflict, for no other power than the Congress of the United States can alter or suspend the compliance of conditions in regard to severance of land from the public domain. The order was therefore valueless from want of authority in the officer directing the work to be suspended, and could not relinquish them from the compliance of their obligations.

The testimony of Donaciano Vigil, as well as the letter accepting the resignation of Chacon, shows that Juan Bautista Vigil y Alarid was the governor of New Mexico at the time the order is purported to have been issued. And to whom was the order issued? To himself, the principal grantee, and his associate, Rivera, which, to say the least, was very inappropriate and indelicate.

Admitting for a moment that the governor had the authority to issue such an order, and that it was proper, what were the parties doing from March, when they were placed in possession, until September, when the governor issued the order to himself to suspend any work upon the land?

No evidence has been introduced by the parties that any obstacle was thrown in their way, or that they had undertaken to commence the compliance of the conditions which were to give them a good title to the land. They do not show that they commenced digging wells, or had taken any steps to erect suitable buildings on the premises for the establishment of the factories that were to be of so much benefit and utility to the department, nor that they had broken up or planted the land their means allowed them to do. On the contrary, it is shown in evidence that no improvements had been placed upon the land, neither did they attempt any, and the Jornado del Muerto, to which the parties claim a title in fee, is the same, and has been since the grant was made as it was when Mexico declared her independence—the dead man's journey.

The fourth point made by the claimants requires but a passing notice. In the adjudication of the private land claims in New Mexico, the government of the United States is expected to act in the same manner as the government of Mexico would have acted under similar circumstances, to do what that government would do, and no more.

The granting decree of the departmental assembly clearly states that the land is given to them for the purpose of opening wells and cultivating the soil as far as their means would permit.

This is unmistakably a conditional grant, requiring the commissioners to comply with certain obligations which, when finished, would entitle them to the land asked for. The case is parallel to one arising under the donation laws of this Territory, where four years' occupation and cultivation are required to entitle the party to a patent to the land. If the occupation and cultivation does not take place, the land does not become severed from the public domain. The same process of reasoning applies to the case under consideration. As no wells have been dug, no factories established, and no land brought under cultivation, the grant is void.

By reference to the petition filed by the parties, they admit their willingness to concede any northern boundary which may be adjudged to the contending parties, and relinquish all claim to as much as is in dispute. If that concession is made now, it is reasonable to suppose that they were willing to make it when the claim was first made; and the order of Governor Vigil, requiring himself and associates to suspend the work was, therefore, useless and unnecessary.

There are other very objectionable points in the case which it is unnecessary to dwell upon.

This case is deemed to be entirely void of merit, and the land claimed believed to belong rightfully to the public domain of the United States. It is, therefore, rejected, and ordered to be transmitted to Congress for its action in the premises.

WILLIAM PELHAM,
Surveyor General.

Surveyor General's Office,
Santa Fé, New Mexico, August 31, 1859.

The foregoing transcript is a true copy of the original decision now on file in this office.

WILLIAM PELHAM,
Surveyor General.

NOTICE OF APPEAL.

Santa Fé, New Mexico,
July 25, 1859.

Sir: Your communication of the 6th of July, 1859, informing us that our grant, for various reasons, had been decided adversely to us, has been received.

It is our wish to appeal from your decision to that of Congress, and we feel competent in being able to establish that the grant is in form and valid in all respects, and that the non-compliance with the conditions subsequently annexed to said grant incurs no forfeiture of our rights, for the reason that the action of the constituted authorities of the country prevented the compliance upon our part with the conditions of the grant, and hence no fault attaches to us.

JUAN BAUTISTA VIGIL Y ALARID & CO.
By HOUGHTON, WATTS & JACKSON,
Attorneys.

Hon. WILLIAM PELHAM,
    Surveyor General.

SURVEYOR GENERAL'S OFFICE,
Santa Fé, New Mexico, August 31, 1859.

The foregoing is a true copy of the original on file in this office.

WILLIAM PELHAM,
Surveyor General.

CLAIM NO. 27.

TOWN OF LAS TRAMPAS.

Schedule of documents composing claim No. 27.

1. Notice—Spanish.
2. Notice—Translation.
3. Grant—Spanish.
4. Grant—Translation.
5. Testimony.
6. Report.

NOTICE—SPANISH.

Al Agrimensor General de Nuevo Mejico:

"Se le avisa por el presente que bajo las proviciones de la segunda seccion del Decreto del Congreso, aprobado el dia 22 de Julio de 1854, Titulado un Decreto para crear los destinos de Agrimensor General del Nuevo Mexico, Kansas y Nebraska, para conceder donaciones á los pobladores actuales en dichos Territorios y para otros fines."

Yo Cristobal Romero, del Condado de Taos, uno de los jueces de paz por el dicho condado, en el precinto del Chamisal, Territorio de Nuevo Mejico, reclamo el sitio ó porcion de terreno perteneciente á las plazas de las Trampas Chamisal y Balle que es una cierta porcion de terreno bajo los limites y linderos del Cajoncîto del Rito de San Leonardo á la sierra por el oriente: de la angostura del rio adonde baja un arrolla del lado Sur, y otro del Norte al rio, por el poniente: del lindero de la legua de los indios de Pueblo del Pecuriz, por el Norte: la ceja ó alto que divide las cañadas de las entrañas, y ojo Sarco llamado alto del ojo Sarco, por el Sur. Dicho terreno tiene 2 leguas 3,300 varas algo mas ó menos de Norte á Sur y de oriente á poniente se carcula que tendra poco mas á menos 4 y ½ leguas. El dicho terreno es reclamado en virtud de una dona hecha el dia primero de Julio de 1751, por Sebastian Martin, y de una merced del Gobierno de España concedida el dia 15 de Julio del dicho año por el Gobernador Tomas Velez á Juan de Arguello, Melchor Rodriguez, Antonio Dominguez, Pedro Felipe Rodriguez, Eusebio de Leyba, Luis de Leyba, Juan José Arguello, Juan Garcia, Salvador Baca, Ygnacio Vargas, Biciente Lucero, y José de Aragon; a quienes puso en posesion del dicho terreno el Alcaldé Juan Jose Lovato, el dia —— de Julio de 1751, y de quienes ahora los actuales posedores, que ocupamos el dicho terreno semos unos herederos y asignados, y otros compradores con traspasos y desendientes del donante finado Sebastian Martin.

Al lado del poniente del dicho terreno, se haya ahora pendiente ante la corte do Distrito del Condado del Rio Arriba, el choque del reclamo de una parte del terreno que á los actuales posedores hace Mariano Sanchez, con apariencia y sin probar legalmente que el es un heredero forzoso del donante arriba dicho; Sebastian Martin. Santa Fé, Junio 21, de 1859.

JUAN CRISTOBAL ROMERO,
Juez de Paz.

Surveyor General's Office, Translator's Department,
Santa Fé, New Mexico, August 29, 1859.

The above is a true copy of the original on file in this office.

DAVID B. WHITING,
Translator.

NOTICE—TRANSLATION.

Santa Fé, *June* 21, 1859.

The surveyor general of New Mexico is hereby notified that, under the provisions of the second section of the act of Congress, approved July 22, 1854, entitled an act to establish the office of the surveyor general of New Mexico, Kansas, and Nebraska, to grant donations to actual settlers therein and for other purposes.

I, Cristobal Romeo, of the county of Taos, one of the justices of the peace within said county, at the precinct of Chamisal, Territory of New Mexico, claim the site or tract of land belonging to the towns of Las Trampas, Chamisal, and Valle, which is a certain tract of land within the following metes and bounds from the Cajoncito del Rito de San Leonardo to the mountain on the east. The narrows in the river where a creek runs in on the south side and one on the north; on the west, from the termination of the league of the Ricuris Indians; on the north, the ridge or divide between the cañons of Los Entrances and Sarco spring, called the Ojo Sarco ridge, on the south. Said land contains 2 leagues 3,300 varas, more or less, from north to south and from east to west; it is believed to contain $4\frac{1}{2}$ leagues, more or less. The land is claimed by virtue of a donation made on the 1st day of July, 1751, by Sebastian Martin, and a grant from the government of Spain, made on the 15th of July of the same year, by Governor Thomas Velez to Juan de Arguello, Melchor Rodrigues, Antonio Dominguez, Pedro Felipe Rodrigues, Eusebio de Leyba, Luis de Leyba, Juan Jose Arguello, Juan Garcia, Salvador Baca, Ygnacio Vargas, Vicente Lucero, and Jose de Aragon, who were placed in possession of the land by Alcalde Juan Jose Lobato on the —— day of July, 1751, and whose heirs and assigns, and other purchasers, by deed, and descendants of the late Sebastian Martin, are now the actual possessors.

A contest is now pending between the actual claimants and Mariano Sanchez, before the district court for the county of Rio Arriba, in regard to the western boundary of said land, without proving legally that the said Mariano Sanchez is a legal heir of the said grantor, Sebastian Martin.

JUAN CRISTOBAL ROMERO,
Justice of the Peace.

Surveyor General's Office, Translator's Department,
Santa Fé, New Mexico, July 20, 1859.

The above is a correct translation of the original on file in this office.

DAVID V. WHITING,
Translator.

Surveyor General's Office,
Santa Fé, New Mexico, August 10, 1859.

The above is a true copy of the original on file in this office.

WM. PELHAM,
Surveyor General.

GRANT—SPANISH.

En el puesto de Nuestra Señora de la Soledad de el Rio Arriba en primero de Julio de mil setecientos y cinquinta y un años, Ante mi el Capitan Juan Joseph Lovato Alcalde mayor y Capitan á Guerra de toda esta jurisdiccion, comparecio el Capitan Sebastian Martin vecino de dicho puesto y dijo; que por cuanto tiene cierta noticia que el Señor Don Thomas Velez Cachupin Gobernador y Capitan General de este Reyno intenta por lignea de buen gobierno poblar el sitio de Santo Thomas Apostol de el Rio de las Trampas con doce familias que son las de los siguentes vecinos, Juan de Arguello, Melchor Rodriguez, Antonio Dominguez, Pedro Ph° Rodrigues, Eusevio de Leyba, Luis de Leiba, Juan Joseph de Arguello, Juan Garcia, Salvador Baca, Ygnacio Vargas, Vicente Lucero, y Joseph de Aragon, y que atento á que la dicha poblazon redundará en servicio de su magestad (que Dios guarde) y bien publico, sede, doná a traspasa, conforme á derecho en los espresados vecinos un pedazo de tierra de este su sitio, que linda con dicha poblazon, para que esta tenga estencion para sus labores de una y otra banda de dicho rio de las Trampas, que desde el peñasco del cañonsito al camino real medido dicho pedazo de tierra, importan un mil seiscientas y cuarenta varas, y á su respetive el terreno correspondiente á lignea recta de sur á norte, para que las gosen usen y cultiven por si sus hijos herederos y subsesores, y puedan cambiarlas venderlas ó enagenarlas que para ello sede y traspassa en los espresados vicinos la ancion real y personal que á dichas tierras tenia, dandoselas asi mismo libres de senso tributo hypoteca ú otra enagenacion, sobre que no les pasara pleito demanda ni contradicion por si sus hijos herederos y subsesores, y que si acaso se lo pusieren no sean vidos en juicio ni fuera de el por ser donado dicho pedazo de tierra espontanea y libremente por los justissimos fines que espresados lleva por lo que renuncia su propio fuero domicilio y vecindad cola ley sic benet y la general de el derecho, dando por buena y as * * [torn] * * esta escritura sin que por falta de circunstancia que aqui no se esprese deje de valer y valga; y para su mayor fuerza y validacion me suplico á mi el espresado Alcalde, mayor interpusiese mi decreto judicial que doy fe interpongo actuando como juez Reseptor con dos testigos de asistencia por no haber escribanos real ni publico en las distancias que el derecho previene y no firmo dicho otorgante por estar impedido de la vista, y es ficha en este dicho puesto dicho dia mes y año ut supra que de todo doy fe.

Esta-Duplicado vale.

JUAN JOSEPH LOVATO,
Juez Receptor.

De asistencia:
JUAN MANUEL LOVATO.

En la villa de Santa Fé, en quince dias del mes de Julio de mil setecientos cinquenta y un años. Don Thomas Velez Cachupin Gobernador de este reino del Nuevo Mejico y castellano de su real presidio: Dige que por curanto en la visita general que hize, en conformidad de reales rescriptos en todo el contenido de este dicho reino, como consta de diferentes autos; parece por ellos haberse multiplicado en gran copia los vecinos de esta dicha villa, en que ai muchos en la edad de jubentud, de manera que no hay ya tierras ni aguas para su mantencion, ni tienen otro modo de trato, oficios ni comercios que la agricultura, y cria de ganados ya que entre los parajes realengos y valdios, se hallan unas tierras hasta dora incultas y que ofrecen comodidad con su beneficio, y que podran hacer y fundar en ellos los personas de esta villa valdias y desocupadas que se nominaren en los lugares que asi se les asignaren: Y que demas de este beneficio se seguira el que por ellos no transiten los enemigos barbaros y sea reparo de sus entradas á ostilizar lo interior de las demas poblazones: Atento á lo cual y á que uno de dichos parages es el nombrado Santo Thomas Apostol del rio de las Trampas, situado en las cercanias de la poblazon de Santa Barbara: Por el presente asigno y señalo dicho sitio en la forma y en las personas siguientes:

A Juan de Arquello, ciento by ochenta varas de tierra pan llevar, con sus aguas pastos y arrebaderos, con entradas y salidas sin perjuicio de tercero.

A Melchor Rodriguaz, las mismas ciento y ochenta varas de tierra como su antecedente.

A Antonio Domingues, la misma cantidad y numero de tierra como sus antecedentes.

A Pedro Ph°. Rodriguez, las mismas ciento y ochenta varas sin bariacion.

A Eusebio de Leyba, tambien se le asignan la misma cantidad de tierras con las propias espresiones.

A Luis de Leyba, se le iguala con los otros en tierras y medidas.

A Juan Joseph de Arguello, asi mismo se le asigna la misma cantidad y con las calidades presitadas.

A Juan Garcia, se le señala las propias ciento y ochenta varas.

A Salvador Vaca se le hace la misma merced de tierras con la mensura y calidades exprasadas.

A Ygnacio Vargas, en la misma forma, se le adjudican ciento y ochenta varas de tierra.

A Vicente Lucero, se le dan en la misma conformidad que los antecedentes.

A Joseph de Aragon, que es el ultimo cabeza de las doce familias, la misma cantidad de tierras en la misma conformidad que á los antecedentes quo van nominados, á quienes por los motivos expresados en nombre de S. M. (que Dios guarde) hago merced de dos mil ciento y sesenta varas de tierras utiles todas de regadio y de pan llevar en la cañada y riveras del asio de las Tampas que corre de oriente á poniente, para ellos sus hijos subsesores y demas que fueren, partes lexitimas para que las gosen, cultiven y se aprovechen sus frutos cosechas y demas utilidades sin perjuicio de tercero, y considerando no ser suficiente esta porcion de tierras de pan llebar por la multiplicacion de estas familias respecto de que en la cañada ó parage de su ubicacion de oriente á poniente no hay otras de riego en que puedan estenderse, y haviendo dos cañadas nombradas las de los Alamos, y Ojo Sarco, que estan al sur de las del rio de las Trampas, aunque son de temporal pingues umedas, y de vuena calidad, les hago igualmente merced de ellas por iguales partes en la misma conformidad que las dos mil ciento y sesenta varas, señalandoles por linderos un cajoncito que hace el rio inmediato á la sierra por la parte de el oriente. Por el poniente la angostura de el rio hasta donde les dono Sebastian Martin, y tirando una linea recta desde la angostura para el sur, hasta el alto de la cañada del Ojo Sarco, por el norte el lindero del Pueblo de Pecuries. Y con la condicion de que no han de poder vender, ceder, ni traspasar, ni en otra manera enagenar el todo ni parte de dichas tierras, hasta que no á ran pasado los cuatro años del derecho, ni á personas eclesiasticas, combentos, colegios, ni otras comunidades: Y el alcalde mayor que lo es de la villa de la cañada Don Juan Joseph Lovato, dara posesion real y personal á todos juntos y en particular en su pertenencia, y para ello y lo de mas anexo y concerniente con los instrumentos autenticos que les correspondan, se le da comision quanto de derecho se requiere, y que fechas todas las diligencias y autos, necesarios los remitira integros á esta gobernacion. Otro si respeto de haber Sebastian Martin. * * * * * * * * *•
Soledad hecho donacion de un pedazo de tierra * * * *

con las que ban espresadas aprueba dicha do   *   *   *   *
ó interpongo mi autoridad y judicial D   *   *   *   *   *
á ella incluyendose en las dos mil ciento y sesenta varas con la cual donacion se completan, todo lo cual yo dicho gobernador he determinado con premeditado acuerdo deseando el servicio del Rey y beneficio publico. Y asi lo mande y firme actuando can dos testigos de mi asistencia á falta de de escribano publico ni real que no lo hay en este reino, de todo doy fe.

THOMAS VELEZ CACHUPIN,
THOMAS DE ALVEAR Y COLLADO.

Torivio Ortiz.

En este paraje de Santo Thomas Apostol de el Rio de las Trampas, yo Juan Joseph Lovato, alcade mayor y capitan á guerra de la villa nueva de Santa Cruz y sus distritos, por la comision que me es conferida por el Señor Don Thomas Velez Cachupin, gobernador y capitan general de este reino de la Nuevo Mejico. En conformidad de lo que su señoria me ordena puse en posesion real y personal á los espresados vecinos en el contenido de el auto de suso haviendo precedido todas las ceremonias dispuestas por reales ordenanzas, siendo presentes y por testigos instrumentales Joseph Zamora, Manuel Martin, y Juan Fresqui sitados por mi para dicho fin, siendo la ubicacion   *   *   *
ntro y linderos, en la forma y manera siguiente.

   *   *   *   *   á la vivienda y havitacion de las doce familias se señalaron por   *   *   *   ada viento sincuenta y siete y media varas dejando para chorreras corrales, caballerizas y demas urgencias de esta naturaliza quince   *   *   *   *   *   *   *
por el Pos   *   *   *   *   *   *   *   *
no real q   *   *   *   *   *   *   *   *
comun de cor   *   *   *   *   *   *   *
y en las tierras de su   *   *   *   *   *   *   *
rreno haviendo disp   *   *   *   *   *   *   *
calidad y cantidad   *   *   *   *   *   *   *
te y sesenta varas de tie   *   *   *   *   *   *
nio Dominguez otras   *   *   *   *   *   *
A Luis de Leyba otras ciento   *   *   *   *   *   *
das sin embargo de que   *   *   *   *   *   *
nos el ambito referido pa   *   *   *   *   *   *
setenta y dos y media var   *   *   *   *   *   *
la vivienda hasta el Rio   *   *   *   *   *   *
vados Vaca les señale á es   *   *   *   *   *   *
tas y sesenta y una baras por yguales partes desde la boca del Cañonsito, y siguiendo las medidas por la banda del Sur, le pertenecen á Juan de Arguello ciento y ochenta varas—á Eusebio de Leyba ciento y ochenta varas, á Vicente Lucero otras ciento y ochenta varas de tierra—á Juan Garcia las mismas ciento y ochenta varas de tierra—á Joseph Aragon otras ciento y ochenta varas de tierra—á Juan Joseph de Arguello, asi mismo le cupieron ciento y ochenta varas dichas—á Melchor Roderiguez, las propias ciento y ochenta varas de tierra—

á Pedro Phelipe Roderiguez otras ciento y ochenta varas de tierra—á Salvador Vaca respeto de haber angostado la tierra de labor á la entrada de en cañonsito desde á donde les dono el Capitan Sebastian Martin, se le señalaron docientas varas de tierra, y atendiendo á que un arroyo en la labor por la parte del norte impide el * * * gualen en las mismas ciento y ochenta varas que es * * * res recibieron de posesion hechando linderos á lignea recta de commenos varas quedaron ási mismo apocecio * * * á espresada vanda de el norte, haciendo divie * * * * * *

*	*	*	*	*	*	*	ando fixen de Poi	
*	*	*	*	*	*	*	señalados pena	
*	*	*	*	*	*	carcel alque no lo execu-		
*	*	*	*	*:	*	ntorio de cuarenta dias in		
*	*	*	*	*		tarlo se esperimentan perni-		
*	*	*	*	*		linderos de esta poblazon por el		
*	*	*	*	*		mediato á la sierra por el ponien		
*	*	*	*	*		mismo rio desde donde les dono		
*	*	*	*	*	Martin por el sur alto de la cañada			
*	*	*	*	*	Norte el lindero del pueblo de Pe-			
*	*	*	*	*	lo conste firme esta real posesion yo			
*	*	*	*	*	ayor actuando por receptioria con			
los	*	*	*	os á falta de escribanos real y publico				

y es fecho en este dicho parage de Santo Thomas Apostol en veinte dias de el mes de Julio de mil setecientos y cinquenta y un anos que de todo doy fe.

JUAN JOSEPH LOVATO,
Juez Receptor.
FRANCO. ZISNEROS,

ANTONIO JOSEPH LOVATO.

Note.—The original grant is very much torn and eaten by mice.
TRANSLATOR.

SURVEYOR GENERAL'S OFFICE, TRANSLATOR'S DEPARTMENT,
Santa Fé, *New Mexico, August* 29, 1859.

The above is a true copy of the original on file in this department.
DAVID V. WHITING, *Translator.*

GRANT—TRANSLATION.

Year 1751. No. 380.

Grant, and royal possession, and donation of Sebastian Martin, in favor of the resident settlers, included herein at the new settlement of the place called "Santo Tomas del Rio de Las Trampas."

At the town of Nuestra Señora de la Soledad del Rio Arriba, on the first of July, in the year one thousand seven hundred and fifty-one, before me, Captain Juan José Lovato, chief justice and war captain of all this jurisdiction, appeared Captain Sebastian Martin, resident of said town, and declared: That, whereas he has reliable information that Don Thomas Velez Cachupin, governor and captain general of this kingdom, intends, as good governments should do, to settle the place called Santo Tomas Apostol del Rio de las Trampas, with twelve families, consisting of the following named citizens: Juan de Arguello, Melchor Rodrigues, Antonio Dominguez, Pedro Felipe Rodrigues, Eusebio de Leyva, Luis de Leyva, Juan Jose de Arguello, Juan Garcia, Salvador Baca, Ygnacio Vargas, Vicente Lucero, and José de Aragon, and considering that said settlement will redound to the service of his Majesty (whom may God preserve,) and to the public weal, he grants, donates, and conveys, according to law, to the above mencitizens, a piece of land from his possession, which adjoins said settlement, in order that it may have sufficient land for cultivation on both sides of the Trampas river; that from the Peñasco del Cañoncito to the main road said piece of land, on being measured, contains one thousand six hundred and forty varas, and in proportion the proper amount of land in a direct line from south to north, to have, use, and cultivate it for themselves, their children, heirs, and successors, and barter, sell, or dispose of the same, for which purpose he assigns and transfers to the aforesaid citizens all the royal and personal title he had to said lands, granting the same to them free of all tax, tribute, mortgage, or other encumbrance, for which neither himself, his children, heirs, or successors will enter suit, dispute, or complaint against them, and if he should do so he requests not to be heard in court or out of court, as said land is donated freely and voluntarily, for the just ends above expressed, and for which he resigns his own rights, residence, and vicinity, under the law "*cit combenerit*," and the general law in reference to the matter, acknowledging this deed to be good, and (valid) any want of form to the contrary notwithstanding, and for its greater force and validity, he requested me, the aforesaid senior justice, to interpose my judicial decree, which I certify to have interposed, acting as appointed judge, with two attending witnesses, in the absence of public or royal notaries, within the limits provided by law; said conveyor did not sign this document, as he has an impediment in his sight, and it is executed at the aforesaid town on the day and date above mentioned, to all of which I certify.

Este—duplicate—valid.

JUAN JOSE LOVATO.

Acting Judge—attending:
  JUAN DOMINGO LOVATO.

In the city of Santa Fé, on the fifteenth day of the month of July, one thousand seven hundred and fifty-one, I, Don Thomas Velez Cachupin, governor of this kingdom of New Mexico and castillian of its royal garrison, stated: That whereas, in the general visit made by me, in conformity with royal orders throughout the entire extent of this kingdom, as will appear by reference to several decrees, it appears that the inhabitants of this said city have increased to a great extent, many of whom are yet of a youthful age, consequently there is not land or water sufficient for their support, neither have they any other occupation, trades, or means of traffic, excepting agriculture and the raising of stock; and whereas, in the King's domains which are unoccupied, there are lands which up to this time are uncultivated, and which will yield comforts to those who cultivate them, and where such persons as shall be named in this town, who have no occupation or employment, can settle upon and cultivate such lands as shall be assigned to them, from which the further benefit will result that the hostile Indians will not travel over them, and will serve as a barrier against their entrance to despoil the interior settlements. In view of all which, and whereas one of the said sites is called Santo Thomas Apostol del Rio de las Trampas, situate in the vicinity of the settlement of Santa Barbara, therefore, I hereby assign and distribute said site in the manner and to the persons following:

To Juan de Arguello, one hundred and eighty varas of wheat-growing land, with corresponding water, pastures, and watering places, entrances and exits, without injury to third parties.

To Melchor Rodriguez, the same hundred and eighty varas as the foregoing.

To Antonio Dominguez, the same amount and number of varas as the preceding one.

To Pedro Felipe Rodriguez, the same, one hundred and eighty varas, without variation.

To Eusebio de Leyva is assigned the same amount of land, under the same conditions.

Luis de Leyva is placed on an equality with the others in lands and measurements.

To Juan José de Arguello is assigned the same quantity, with the conditions above prescribed.

To Juan Garcia is assigned the same amount of one hundred and eighty varas.

To Salvador Vaca a like grant of land is made, with the measurements and conditions above-mentioned.

To Ygnacio Vargas, in the same manner, are assigned one hundred and eighty varas of land.

To Vicente Lucero will be given the same amount, in conformity with the above.

To Joseph de Arragon, who is the last of the twelve heads of families, the same amount of land, in conformity with the conditions imposed on the balance, above described.

To whom, for the reasons above stated, I grant, in the name of his Majesty, (whom may God preserve,) two thousand one hundred and sixty varas of arable land, all of which are wheat-growing and under irrigation, in the cañon and streams of the Trampas river, which runs from east to west, for themselves, their children, successors, and other legal—[torn;] to have, cultivate, and reap the benefits of its fruits, crops, and other profits, without injury to third parties; and considering that this quantity of wheat-growing land will not be sufficient, on account of the increase of their families, and as in the cañon or place where they are to settle, from east to west, there are no other lands under irrigation that they can use, and whereas there are two cañons, called De los Alamos and Ojo Sarco, south of the Trampas river, which, although not susceptible of irrigation, are most fertile, and of good quality, I also grant them to the above-mentioned persons, to be equally divided between them, in the same manner as the two thousand one hundred and sixty varas, assigning them as boundaries a narrow made by the river, where it joins the mountain, on the east; on the west the narrows (Angostura) of the river, to where the grant made to Sebastian Martin terminates, and drawing a straight line from the Angostura towards the south to the summit of the Cañada del Ojo Sarco; on the north, the boundary of the Pueblo of Picuris; and on condition that they shall not sell, transfer or convey, or in other manner dispose of all or a portion of said lands, until the expiration of the four years provided by law, and not even then to ecclesiastics, convents, colleges, or other communites. And Juan Joseph Lovato, the chief justice of the town of Cañada, will give the royal and personal possession to all in common, and to each one in particular, of their respective tracts; and for that purpose and the other purposes herein mentioned, and concerning the authentic documents thereunto appertaining, he is hereby commissioned as the law requires, and after having executed all the necessary acts and decrees in the premises, he will return them complete to this government.

Further, in regard to Sebastian Martin having [torn] made a donation of a piece of land, with what has been before stated, I approve said (donation,) and interpose my authority and judicial (decree,) including them in the two thousand one hundred and sixty varas, with which they will have sufficient. All of which I, the said governor, have determined, after mature deliberation, desiring the service of the King and the public good. And I so ordered and signed, acting with two attending witnesses, in the absence of a public or royal notary, there being none in this kingdom. To all of which I certify.

THOMAS VELEZ CACHUPIN.

THOMAS DE ALVEAR Y COLLADO.
THORIBIO ORTIZ.

At this place of Santo Thomas Apostol del rio de las Trampas, I, Juan Joseph Lovato, chief justice and war captain of the new city of Santa Cruz and its districts, by virtue of the commission conferred upon me by Don Thomas Velez Cachupin, governor and captain general of this kingdom of New Mexico, and in conformity with the directions therein contained, I placed the aforementioned citizens in royal and personal possession, according to the decree of his excellency, after having performed all the ceremonies directed by the royal ordinances. Joseph Zamora, Manuel Martin, and Juan Fresque, being present and acting as instrumental witnesses, having been summoned by me for that purpose, the distribution, centre, and boundaries being as follows [torn:] The residences and dwellings of the twelve families, fifty-seven and one-half varas, were set aside towards (the four points of the compass) leaving for drippings, enclosures, stables, and other objects of that nature [the following fifteen lines in the original are so much torn as to be unintelligible] sixty-one varas in equal parts from the mouth of the little cañon, and continuing the measurement on the southern side, one hundred and eight varas belong to Juan de Arguello; one hundred and eighty varas to Eusebio de Leyba; to Vicente Lucero another hundred and eighty varas of land; to Juan Garcia a like one hundred and eighty varas of land; to José Aragon another hundred and eighty varas of land; Juan Joseph Arguello also received one hundred and eighty varas of land; to Melchior Rodriguez the same, one hundred and eighty varas of land; to Pedro Phelipe Rodriguez another one hundred and eighty varas of land; to Salvador Baca, in consequence of the arable land having become narrower as it entered the cañon, were assigned two hundred varas of land; and considering that a gulch in the centre of the fields prevents [torn] the same amount of one hundred and eighty varas which is [torn] received in possession, establishing the boundaries in direct lines, [the remaining portion of the original document, with the exception of the last four lines, is torn in half and illegible,] in the absence of a royal or public notary, and it is done at the aforesaid place of Santa Thomas Apostol, on the twentieth day of the month of July, in the year one thousand seven hundred and fifty one, to all of which I certify.

JUAN JOSEPH LOVATO,
Acting Judge.
FRANCISCO ZISNEROS.
ANTONIO JOSEPH LOVATO.

NOTE.—The portions of the above translation included in brackets are torn out in the original, and substituted to complete the sentence.
—TRANSLATOR.

SURVEYOR GENERAL'S OFFICE,
Translator's Department, Santa Fé, N. M., July 28, 1859.

The foregoing is a translation of the original on file in this office.
DAVID V. WHITING,
Translator.

SURVEYOR GENERAL'S OFFICE,
Santa Fé, New Mexico, July 28, 1859.

The above is a true copy of the original on file in this office.
WILLIAM PELHAM,
Surveyor General.

TESTIMONY.

MARIANO SANCHEZ sworn:

Question. What is your age, and how long have you known the town of Las Trampas?

Answer. I am about 67 years old; have known the town of Las Trampas since I was five years old.

Question. Has the town been occupied by the settlers and their descendants from that time up to the present?

Answer. It has.

MARIANO SANCHEZ.

Sworn and subscribed before me this 21st day of June, 1859.
WILLIAM PELHAM, *Surveyor General.*

JUAN LORENZO ARMIJO sworn:
Question. How old are you?
Answer. 59 years old.
Question. How long have you known the town of Las Trampas, and was it in existence in the year 1846?
Answer. About 30 years; it was in existence in 1846, and has been in continued existence from the time I first knew it until now.
Question. What is the population of Las Trampas?
Answer. About 200 souls.

JUAN LORENZO + ARMIJO.
his
mark.

Sworn and subscribed before me this 21st day of June, 1859.
WILLIAM PELHAM *Surveyor General.*

SURVEYOR GENERAL'S OFFICE,
Santa Fé, New Mexico, August 15, 1859.
The above is a true copy of the original on file in this office.
WILLIAM PELHAM, *Surveyor General.*

REPORT.

TOWN OF LAS TRAMPAS *vs.* THE UNITED STATES.

This case was set for trial on the 21st of July, 1859.

The parties claim a perfect title to the land embraced within the limits set forth therein, by virtue of a grant made to twelve families residing at Santa Fé by Governor Thomas Velez Cachupin on the 17th day of the month of July, in the year 1751, and also a donation of 1,620 varas made to the same persons by Sebastian Martin, being a portion of a grant made to him by the royal authorities in 1712.

It has been proven in evidence that the town has been in existence for a number of years, and is in existence at the present time. The papers acted upon are the original grant and subsequent proceedings had thereon, which was selected from the archives of the Territory, and are on file in this office.

The town having been in existence from the time the grant was made, and the grant having been made according to law, the claim is confirmed to the legal representatives of the original grantees, and is ordered to be transmitted to Congress for its action in the premises.

WILLIAM PELHAM, *Surveyor General.*
SANTA FÉ, *New Mexico, August* 1, 1859.

SURVEYOR GENERAL'S OFFICE,
Santa Fé, New Mexico, August 20, 1859.
The above is a true copy of the original on file in this office.
WILLIAM PELHAM, *Surveyor General.*

CLAIM No. 28.

HEIRS OF SEBASTIAN MARTIN.

Documents composing claim No. 28.

1. Notice.
2. Grant—Spanish.
3. Grant—translation.
4. Report.

NOTICE.

UNITED STATES OF AMERICA, }
Territory of New Mexico: }

To the Surveyor General of New Mexico:

Mariano Sanches, a citizen of the United States and resident of the Territory of New Mexico, respectfully represents that he is the claimant and legal owner in fee of a certain tract of land lying and being situate in the county of Rio Arriba, in said Territory of New Mexico, and bounded and described as follows, to wit: The boundaries assigned and measured by Lieutenant General Juan Paez Hurtada, who run the line from the pueblo of San Juan to a point where a cross was placed, and from thence up the river to the cañon which reaches the El Embrudo, and on the east by the road which leads from Chemago to the pueblo of Picuris, and on the west by the table land on the other side of the Rio del Norte; all of which points and boundaries are well-known landmarks in the said county of Rio Arriba, and the said Mariano Sanches, the present claimant, claims a perfect title to the said land as descendant and legal representative of Sebastian Martin, to whom the original grant was made, in the year one thousand seven hundred and twelve, on the 23d day of May of said year, by Don Joseph Chucon Medina Salasar y Villasuir, gentleman of the order of Santiago, Marques of Peguela, governor and captain general of New Mexico; which said grant was made as aforesaid by authority of the laws, usages, and customs of the then Spanish provinces at that time in force, for which power and authority see the collection of the decrees and orders of the courts of Spain, published by Mantano Galvan.

The said Mariano Sanches, claimant, cannot show the quantity of land claimed by him except as set forth in said grant as within the above well-described metes and bounds, nor can he furnish a plat of survey, as no survey has ever been executed. Your claimant knows of no other claimant to said grant; and that, by virtue of said grant, the said original grantee was legally put in possession of said lands, and that the same has been, either by him or his descendants, occupied from the date of said grant down to the present time. The original grant, marked A, is herewith filed and made a part of this his claim. Claimant files this his said claim before you under the 8th section of the act of Congress approved July 22, A. D. 1854, entitled "An act to establish the offices of surveyor general of New Mexico, Kansas, and

Nebraska, to grant donations to actual settlers therein, and for other purposes," and respectfully asks confirmation by you of this his said claim.

MARIANO SANCHES,
By M. ASHURST,
His Attorney.

Surveyor General's Office,
Santa Fé, New Mexico, June 22, 1859.

The foregoing is a true copy of the original on file in this office.
WILLIAM PELHAM, <i>Surveyor General.</i>

GRANT—SPANISH.

Sr. Marques de la Penuela, Gobernado y Capitan General:

El Cap^n. Sebastian Martin vecino de la jurisdiccion de la villa de Santa Cruz, paresco ante la grandeza de V.S. con profundo rendimiento, en la mejor forma que el derecho me concede, y digo que por cuanto el año de mil setecientos y tres, registre y hirze denunciacion yo y Antonio Martin unanimes y conformes para ambos, un sitio heriaso yermo y despoblado, que es en el Rio Arriva, [torn] pocomas del pueblo de San Juan presente reino el cual tenian registrado muchos años, antes Joseph Garcia Jurado, Sebastian de Vargas, y Sebastian de Polonia, y quienes nunca lo poblaron, por cuya razon perdieron el derecho y accion á dicho sitio como su [torn] que Dios guarde lo previene y dispone en su [torn] leyes, cuyo registro y denunciacion que hisimos [torn] sentamos ante el Sor. Marques de la Naba [torn] Brasinas Gobernador y Capitan General de este reino y [torn] quien en vista de el fue servido de hacernos dicha merced en nombre de Su Magestad, declarando por no partes á los dichos primeros registrantes arreglandose á dichas reales leyes para que por ninguna via pudieran pretender derecho á dicho sitio y en cuya [torn] se me dio la posesion real que aprendi quieta y pacificamente sin contradicion alguna, la cual me do el Sargento Mayor Juan de Ulibarri en virtua de comision que para ello le dio el General Don Francisco Cuerbo y Valdez desde cuyo tiempo y año referido lo poble y he susistido en dicho sitio, asi yo como cinco hermanos mios, he abierto tierras sacado sequia madre del Rio del Norte, para el riego de la labor, fabricado una casa con cuatro cuarteles y dos torreones fuertes para la defensa de los enemigos que quisieren invadir por ser fronteriso, y la parte del sitio que pertenecia á dicho Antonio Sisneros lo compre en venta real á Joseph Lujan vecino del dicho Antonio Sisneros, cuya escritura se celebro y paso ante el Capitan Antonio Montoya alcalde ordinario que entonces era; y porgue todos los dichos instrumentos titulos y escritura pertenecientes á dicho sitio y tierras se han perdido y no he podido hallarlos por diligencias que tengo hechas y para poderlos tener sin embargo de las leyes que me favorecen de ser poseedor de buena fee en caso de que yo no hubiera registrado se ha de servir V.S. justicia mediante, en vista de esta mi relacion de hacerme merced en nombre de S. M. del dicho sitio y tierras de labor y para crias de ganados y de caballada, con las aquas pastos montes y abrevaderos segun y como se dio dicha posesion real y hasta el lindero que señalo y midio el The General Juan Paez Hurtado, que hacho el cordel desae dicho Pueblo de San Juan hasta donde esta una cruz, que mando poner en señal de lindera y las demas Rio Arriva hasta la Cañada que llega al Embudo, y por la parte del oriente hasta el Pueblo de Pecuries, y por la del Poniente hasta la mesa de la otra banda del Rio del Norte, que de todo ello se me disposesion real por dicho Sargento Mayor como lleva dicho. Para todo lo cual se ha de sirvir V.S. de mandar se me ruelva á dar dicha real posesion y que en todo tiempo conste ser legitimamente mio dicho sitio de tierras, declarando V.S. por nopartes los dichos primeros registrantes por se en algun tiempo pretendieren maliciosamente tener derecho á dicho sitio, por todo lo, cual y lo mas que, [torn.]

A V.S. pido y suplico con la veneracion y respeto que debo sea servido de mandar hacer lo que lleva pedido en este mi escrito que asi lo espero de lan gran justificacion de V.S. y que tanto atiende a'los vasallos de S. M. en la buena y recta administracion de justicia la cual pido y juro en forma no ser de malicia y en lo necesaria, &c.

Otro si represento á la grandeza de V.S. que desde dicho año de setecientos y tres hasta el presente, me he mantenido en dicho sitio y frontera, aunque ha havido muchisimo riesgo de los enemigos Apaches que suelen dar sus emboscadas, como á V.S. le consta que desde que entro á gobernor este Reyno siempre me ha conocido vivor en dicho sitio por lo que se ha de servir declararlo asi por [torn] que es de justicia que pido, ut supra.

SEBASTIAN MARTIN.

En la villa cabesera de este reino y Provincia de la Nueva Mejico en veinte y tres dias del mes de Mayo de mil setecientos y dose años ante mi el Almirante Don José Chacon Medina Salasar y Villasñor, caballero de la orden de Santiago Marques de la Peñuela gobernador y capitan general de este dicho Reyno sus Provincias y Castellano de sus fuerzas y Presidios por su Magestad se presento esta peticion por el en ella contenido y por mi vista la hube por presentada en cuanto á lugar en derecho y atendiendo á su contexto y las razones con que justifica su pedimento le concedo la muva merced segun y como la tenia y la ha gosado y praierdo como consta por su pedimento de que lo declaro por parte legitima de dicho sitio apartando de cualquiera derecho que malicios amente pretendan dichos vecinos á dichas tierras á quines desde ahora para entonces no seran vidos en juicio ni fuera de el y ruego y encargo á los Senores y mis subsesores asi le guarden la justicia que tan notoná le asiste pues en el tiempo de mi gobierna le he conocido por legitimo dueño [torn] como es voz publica declarando como declaro por no partes legitimas al que con danada intencion denunciare dicho sitio á demandare contra el suplicante con algun fin particular y con siniestro informe contra el sus odiecho Sebastian Martin en cuya virtud y por el presente rebalido y reitero esta merced segun y como la pide para que libremente la gose el sus hijos herederos y susesores sin perjuicio de su persona dando como doy por nulas y de ningun valor ni efecto otros cualesquiera instrumentos [torn] averlo poblado como su Magestad ordena y el susodicho Sebastian Martin haverse mantenido en ella con el manifiesto riesgo de la vida que pudieran executar los enemigos comunes por ser fronteriso dicho sitio donde ha presistido hasta el dia de hoy, y ordeno á mi Secretario de Governacion y Guerra el Sargento Cristobal de Gongora pase a dicho sitio y deje á dicho Sebastian Martin en quieta y pacifica posesion señalandole los linderos segun y como lo pide y que este auto le sirva de bastante titulo y merced y para que conste asi lo provei mande y firme con el susodicho mi Secretario de Gobernacion y Guerra, á quien cause poner el sello de mis armas en dicho dia, ut supra.

EL MARQUES DE LA PENUELA.

Ante mi CRISTOBAL DE GONGORA,
    Secretario de Govon. y Gur'a.

SURVEYOR GENERAL'S OFFICE, TRANSLATOR'S DEPARTMENT,
    Sante Fé, New Mexico, September 10, 1859.

The above is a true copy of the original on file in this office.

DAVID V. WHITING,
Translator.

GRANT—TRANSLATION.

To the Marquis de la Pezuela, governor and captain general.

Captain Sebastian Martin, resident of the jurisdiction of the city of Santa Cruz, appears before the greatness of your excellency with profound submission, and in the most approved manner the law allows me, and state, that whereas in the year seventeen hundred and three Antonio Martin and myself registered and denounced for both of us a vacant, uncultivated, and unoccupied tract of land in Rio Arriba, [torn,] a short distance from the pueblo of San Juan, [torn,] present year, which many years ago was registered by Joseph Garcia Jurado, Sebastian de Varges, and Sebastian de Polonia, who never occupied it, for which reason they lost all rights and title to it as his Majesty (whom may God preserve) has ordered and directed in his royal laws, which registration and denouncement was made by us before the Marquis de la Naba de Brazinos, governor and captain general of this kingdom, who by virtue thereof was pleased to confer the grant upon us in the name of his Majesty, declaring the first parties without any right according to the royal laws, in order that they should never lay any claim to said tract, and therefore royal possession was given to me by Sergeant Major Juan de Ulibarri, by virtue of a commission given to him for that purpose by General Don Francisco Cuvero y Valdes, which I took quietly and peaceably, without any opposition whatever; and myself as well as five of my brothers have resided upon and possessed the same from that time. I have broken up lands, opened a main ditch from the Del Norte river for irrigating the land, built a house with four rooms, and two strong towers for defence against the enemy in case of an invasion, being on the frontier; and the portion belonging to Antonio Zisnero was bought by me at royal sale from Josefa Lajan, widow of the said Antonio Zisnero, which sale was effected and took place before Captain Antonio Montoya, who at that time was judge of first instance; and whereas all the said instruments, deeds, and titles belonging to said tract and lands have been lost and have not been able to find them, although I have diligently sought for them, and although the laws would protect me in holding them, being a possession in good faith, in case I had not registered them, however justice intervening, your excellency will be pleased, in view of what I have stated, to grant to me, in the name of his Majesty, the said tract and arable land, also for raising cattle and horses, with waters, pastures, woodland, and watering places, in the manner in which said royal possession was given to me, and to the boundary assigned and measured by Lieutenant General Juan Paez Hurtado, who ran the line from the said pueblo of San Juan to where he ordered a cross to be placed as proof of a boundary, and the others up the river to the cañon which reaches to the El Embudo, and on the east to the river which leads from Chimayo to the pueblo of Picuris, and on the west to a table land on the other side of the Del Norte river; all of which was given to me in royal possession by the said sergeant major, as above stated.

Therefore, in view of all that has been stated, your excellency will be pleased to direct that royal possession be given to me again, so that in all time to come it may appear that said tract and lands are lawfully mine, and to declare as forfeited the right of the first parties who registered and who at some future time may maliciously set up a claim against said tract; in consideration of all which [torn] I pray and request your excellency, with all due veneration and respect, to be pleased to direct this my petition to be complied with, which I expect from your excellency's great justice, who so faithfully attends to the wants of the subjects of his Majesty in the good and impartial administration of justice, which I solicit; and I swear that this is not done through malice, and whatever may be necessary, &c. I further state before the greatness of your excellency that from the said year seventeen hundred and three up to this time I have resided upon said land, which is on the frontier, notwithstanding the great risks to be encountered from the Apache enemy, who occasionally make their descents upon us, as your excellency is well aware, from the time you entered upon the government of this kingdom, that I have always resided there. Therefore your excellency will be pleased to decree in my favor, justice being what I sue for. Ut supra, &c.

SEBASTIAN MARTIN.

In the capital city of this kingdom and province of New Mexico, on the twenty-third day of the month of May, in the year one thousand seven hundred and twelve, the foregoing petition was presented before me, Admiral Don Joseph Chacon Medina Salazar y Villasenor, gentleman of the order of Santiago, Marques of Pezuela, governor and captain general of the said kingdom, its provinces, and Castillan of its forces and garrisons by his Majesty, the contents whereof having been seen by me, I considered it presented as the law requires; and in consideration of its contents and the reasons upon which he bases his petition, I confer upon him the new grant as he has held, enjoyed, and possessed it, as appears by his petition, and of which I declare him to be the lawful owner, notwithstanding any right which said citizens may claim to said lands, who now or hereafter shall be heard in court or out of court; and I pray and enjoin upon my successors to protect him in the rights he is so justly entitled to, as during the time of my government I have known him to be the lawful owner thereof, as is well known, declaring, as I do declare, without any legal right any person who with evil intentions shall denounce said land, or who shall enter suit against the petitioner for any private end or any sinister representation, against the said Sabastian Martin; and by virtue thereof I hereby revalidate and confirm this grant, as he requests, in order that he may enjoy the same for himself, his children, heirs, and successors, without injury to his person, declaring, as I do declare, as null and void any other instrument, [with which an adverse claim may be set up against him,] the said Sebastian Martin having occupied the land as his Majesty directs, and having remained there at the imminent risk of his losing his life by the hands of the common enemy, said tract being situated on the frontier, where he has persisted in remaining up to this day; and I direct my secretary of government and war, Sergeant Cristobal de Gingora, to proceed to said tract of land and leave the said Sebastian Martin in quiet and peaceable possession, assigning him the boundaries he asks for; and in order that this decree may be to him a sufficient title and grant, and as a matter of record, I so provided, ordered, and signed with my aforesaid secretary of government and war, [whom I directed to attach hereto] the seal of my arms on said date, *ut supra.*

EL MARGUES DE LA PEZUELA.

Before me—

XPTTOBAL DE GONGNA,
Secretary of Government and War.

NOTE.—The original document is so much torn and rubbed that portions of it are entirely obliterated. Those sentences enclosed in brackets convey the meaning intended, as ascertained by the context.

TRANSLATOR.

SURVEYOR GENERAL'S OFFICE, TRANSLATOR'S DEPARTMENT,
Santa Fé, New Mexico, June 8, 1859.

The foregoing is a translation of the original on file in this office.

DAVID V. WHITING,
Translator.

SURVEYOR GENERAL'S OFFICE,
Santa Fé, New Mexico, June 22, 1859.

The foregoing is a true copy of the original on file in this office.

WILLIAM PELHAM,
Surveyor General.

REPORT.

The Legal Representatives of Sebastian Martin, deceased, *vs.* The United States.

This case was set for trial on the 19th June.

This claim is made by Mariano Sanchez, present claimant, as the heir and legal representative of Sebastian Martin.

From the documents filed in the case, it appears that in the year 1703 the original grantee, in company with others, registered a tract of land in what is now known as Rio Arriba county, which was granted to them by due course of law. All of the parties to whom the grant was made, with the exception of the petitioner, failed to occupy or improve the land, he alone having remained upon it. He therefore petitioned the governor, Marquis de la Pezuela, governor and captain general of the kingdom of New Mexico, asking that the grant be made to him alone, and that the other parties who had forfeited their claim should be declared without any right or interest in it. This petition bears no date.

On the 23d May, 1712, after reviewing the case, the governor and captain general granted the request of the petitioner, and confirmed the land to him alone, declaring the rights of the other parties forfeited, and null and void, and directs his secretary of government and war to leave the said Sebastian Martin in quiet and peaceable possession of the land. The document filed is signed by the governor and his secretary, and sealed with the governor's coat of arms, and is believed to be genuine.

The case has been duly advertised, and no one has appeared to contest the claimant's right to the land, except a portion which was donated to the town of Las Trampas by the said Sebastian Martin, as will appear by the papers in that case.

The present claimant has not shown a perfect chain of title from the original grantee. The grant was made and occupied so long since that it reaches beyond that point whereof the memory of man runneth not to the contrary, and as there is no contest in the case, the grant is deemed to be a good and valid one, and the land embraced within the metes and bounds set forth legally severed from the crown lands of the King of Spain. It is therefore approved and ordered to be transmitted to Congress, with the request that, excepting the portion donated to the town of Las Trampas, it be confirmed to the legal representatives of Sebastian Martin, deceased.

WILLIAM PELHAM,
Surveyor General.

Surveyor General's Office,
Santa Fé, New Mexico, July 25, 1859.

Surveyor General's Office,
Santa Fé, New Mexico, August 25, 1859.

The above is a true copy of the original on file in this office.

WILLIAM PELHAM,
Surveyor General.

CLAIM No. 29.

TOWN OF ANTON CHICO.

Documents composing claim No. 29.

1. Notice.
2. Grant—Spanish.
3. Grant—translation.
4. Testimony.
5. Report.
6. Notice of appeal.

NOTICE.

UNITED STATES OF AMERICA,
Territory of New Mexico, County of San Miguel, } *sct.*

To the Hon. William Pelham, surveyor general of the Territory of New Mexico.

Your petitioners, David Stewart, for himself and in behalf of the heirs and legal representatives of the original grantees and the present inhabitants of the town of Anton Chico, respectfully represent that they claim a certain piece of land lying in the county of San Miguel, in the Territory of New Mexico; that said grant was made by Facundo Melgares, civil and military governor of New Mexico, on the thirteenth day of February, A. D. 1822, to Salvador Tapia, Francisco Baca, Rafael Duran, and others, whose names appear in the documents herewith presented, marked A, B, and C; that they possessed and cultivated the said tract and erected dwellings thereon, which same now compose the town of Anton Chico. Said grant has never been surveyed or regularly laid out, or a map or plat made of the same. Petitioners, therefore, refer to the accompanying documents, A, B, and C, for a description of the extent of said grant of land, which is situated in said county of San Miguel, on El Rio Pecos, about thirty miles south of the town of San Miguel del Bado; that said town and settlement existed and was about the same as at present in August, A. D. 1846, when possession was taken of New Mexico by the authorities of the United States.

The town of Anton Chico is not an incorporated town; but the heirs of the original grantees and the present "lot holders" know of no adverse claim to them, and respectfully pray to be confirmed in their present possessions and enjoyments. The said claimants say that the grantors had full power and authority to make said grant by virtue of the laws, customs, and usages in force at the time of said grant, and by authority of the various colonization acts of the Mexi-

PRIVATE LAND CLAIMS IN NEW MEXICO. 139

can government up to the colonization acts of the Mexican Congress of August 18, 1824. All of which is respectfully submitted.

J. HOUGHTON,
Attorney for the inhabitants of Anton Chico.

Surveyor General's Office,
Santa Fé, New Mexico, August 25, 1859.

The foregoing is a copy of the original on file in this office.

———————————,
Surveyor General.

GRANT—SPANISH.

Señor Presidente y respectivo tribunal de Independencia, &c. :
El vecino Salbador Tapia, cuidadano de esta jurisdiccion del ilustre cargo de V.V. a las venerables plantas : Se presente en la mejor forma que es debida y conlada sumission, y en compania de 18 hombres digo que hallandonos sumamente cortos de recientes de tierra para el sartenimiento de nuertras familias y hallandonos con cartante amorosidad y animo de que implicamos no vean con mejor caridad que ari lo esperamos de V.V. favoreciendonos en nombre de S.M. y de la nacion de la monarquia y soberano corte Mejicana, con na pedaga de tierra en este Rio en donde le nombran Anton Chico, lo que fuere bastante para el mantenimiento de nuestras familias siendo el todo objeto esto que a V.S.S. inpetramos esta infelises, que son los menciona, dos que referira el marzen no siendo otras las inconitos mas esperamos gosar del mayor afecto y felicidad de V.S.S. y su inacta piedad esperamos el gozo en nuestra pretencion, recibiendo todo merced y gracia.

SALBADOR + TAPIA.
Bado, *Enero de* 24 *de* 1822.

Los 17 que se refieren ir voluntarios en mi compania, san los siguente.

Salbador Tapia.
Francisca Baca.
Rafael Duran.
Juan Sebastian Duran.
Diego Antonio Tapia.
Bernardo Ulibarri.
Felipe Valencia.
Luis Gonzales.
Juan Cristobal Garcia.

Tomas Martin.
Juan José Martin.
Miguel Martin.
José Medina.
Simon Estrada.
Lorenzo Tapia.
Mariano Aragon.
José Duran.

Sin embargo de conveer la necesidad y derecho que tienen las representantes á que seles confiera lo que solicitan nome resuelvo á ello porno ser comprencibo el territorio que solicitan por estar fuera de la merced de este partido y avi para al Señor Gobernador para que con su anuencia si lo tirbiera á bien se haya como lo piden y de no queden los interesados entendidos.

ENERO 25 *de* 1822.
MANUEL BACA.

Corresponde que se estienda la representacion en papel corriente; que el ayuntamiento instruya el expediente y lo dirigo á la Exma. Junta de Provincia para su aprobacion é ratificacion.

SANTA FÉ, *Febrero* 13, *de* 1822.
MELGARES.

Segundo de la independencia de este Imp'o: Enterados de la representacion que antecede y con el pleno conocimiento de la necesidad que tienen los individuos representantes para que seles confiera su soliertad, no nos resolvemos por noser comprencibo el terreno que solicitan a la merced de esto partido. Bajo este supuesto pase a la Exma. Diputacion de Prova. para que interado de ella resuelva lo que hallaré por de justicia.

Yo el Gobernador D. Facundo Melgares, caballero de la orden de San Exmeregildo, Gobernador politica y militar de dicho Reyno, Inspector de la tropa reglada enel, é Inspector de malicias por S. M. Q. D. G.

Bisto el presente escrito y su pedimiento del V. Manuel Herera por sixen vay de trienta y seis hombres y mande el alcalde constitucional de la jurisdiccion de San Miguel del Bavol y primero comandante de armas Don Manuel Baca, los panga en posecion de la dicha merced que piden los suplicantes para que por si, los hipos y sulsesores la tengan y posecion en nombre de S.M. observando en su docta todas las circumstancios y requisitos que en semijantes cosas je deben practicar y en particular lo que sita perjuicio. An lo provec, mande y firme con los testigos demi aristencia con quien Antonio de Escribano, publico ni real que no la hay en el citado reyno y en este papel comun por no haberlo de ningan Sello de que day fe. En 2 de Mayo de mil ochocientos veinte y dos.

MELGARES.

Assa. JOAQUIN MADRID.
BADO, *N. de N. de* 1822.

Yo el Alcalde constitucional, Commandante de las armes Don Manuel Baca, en complimiento de la mandado por el Señor Gobernador Don Facundo Melgares, Caballero de la orden de San Exmeregildo, Gobernador Politico y militar de este regno antes de pasar yo dicho, Alcalde al puerto de la Sangre de Cristo, que vulgarmente le llaman Anton Chico, en campania de dos regidores que la fueran. Don Bontura Frugilla, 2° Regidor, y Don Miguel Sisneros, 3° Regidor: estando presentes los 36 presentantes les hire contender la peticion que hafien degnardar y complir en toda forma de derecho las condiciones signientes Primeramente: que el parifi prefigado hade ser comme no solo ellos sino á todos los vecimos que se puedon y congregando en lo succesion.

Segundo. Que respecta alo aresgado del parase deberan mantenerse equipados de armas defuego y flechas deque seles hade pasar mestra tanto en su entrada como en qualquier tiempo quele tuviera conveniente el alcalde queles mandare.

Tercero. Que ari las maniobras desu plaza, como sacas de asequias y todos cuantas mani, obras se les afrescan hacer para su bien, para su bien comun las hun de ejecutar todos, y demas le encargo a todos, y cado uno har si dela sitas yo referidas en su canformidad respondieron deman comun quedar impuertos enterados delos que les adviertes en consequencia delo qual les tome par la mano y dije en voz clara, intelegible vazes que in nombre de et nerbra Independencin que dias guarda perjucio desu real haber in el, V. los pasie por di chas tierras arrancundo sacate tirando piedras dieran voges diciendo: viva la Independencia tamando posecion de dehs téerras y pacificamente sin contradicion alguna San Calandoles los linderos que San Porel Norte cunel lindero de Don Antonio Ortiz, ponel sur la Seja dela Piedra pintada y la mesita de Guadalupe; por el Oriente el ajo del Sabino. Can el alto delos Esteros adonde encanona el Rio Abajo donde mataron a los hombres y por el poniente la cuerta y el Serrito de Bernal, que es el lindero del Bado, advirtiendo quelos pastos y abrevanderos quelos pastos y abrevanderos son comunes sin perjuicio de tercera. Y para que entodo impro consta la firmo con mi secretario de cabaldo hay en 2 de Mayo de 1822, degneday fé.

MANUEL BACA,
Presidente.
JOSÉ MIGUEL SANCHEZ,
Secretario.

En El Pueblo de Anton Chico litubado nuevamente cun el Novembre y Abogacion de Atro Sor. y Sangre de Cristo, alos ocho dias del mes de marro de mil ocho cientos treinta y cuatro por orden verbal del sor alcalde constitucional C. Juan Fou Cabeza de Baca sobre quela jeute, &c., hallaba es cara de tierras de labranza para ju subsistencia y estar eula totalidad valdios las tierras de Anton Chico jin cultivo porsus legitimos a quienes deles tenia duado hasta el tiempo de siete o'ocho años y que en la actual los tensas abando nados causa las naciones que porsus ataques i incursiones desproblaron el mencionado parage y quehay para el cabrismiento delos necessidades manifestados delos cuidadanos desacomodados de terenos y aumento ala agricultura cosa de tanto interes para la subsistencia desus habitantes, pasase a entregar sus legistimidades alos que los reclamara y repartiera tado lo antes donado a manos vivos y laboriosos que los quieran posear la que verifique en el dia dicha arriba entregando y donando alos nuevamente agraciados en dicho terreno poniendo procecivnados y donando lasobrante a nombre de los leges quenos rigen alos que quinisieran ser agraciados que san los ciquientes.

Biterva Sandoval antes donado la punta del ancon sin variar.
Bisente Legino donado con ....100 vs.
Miguel Jaramilla en compra...100 vs.

Pablo Ortiz donado con...100 vs.
Janasio Aragon donado...125 vs.
Santiago Aragon donado. .... 75 vs.
Julian Garcia donado..100 vs.
Bartolo Ocaña donado con...100 vs.
Miguelito Duran antes donado..200 vs.
José Antonio Duran donado...100 vs.
José de Jesus Duran...100 vs.
 Y el sobrante en el arroyo.
José Antonio el mudo donado...100 vs.
Francisco Sandoval con..100 vs.
Gertrudes Mestas donado... 50 vs.

 La que en cumpliments denu encargo y como actual rejidor y alcalde constitucional accidental les agracio, dono a nombre de los leges que obedecemos para que los gosen cultivando los y no en agenando los hasta que por el legal tiempo de posesion tengan dorecha para hacerlo, guardando los fuerot, circumstancias y ejerciones que debe guardar tado poblador, en cargandoles principalmente mantengan las correspondientes armas trabajando nuidos y pacificos para que en ningun tiempo jean sorprehendidos de los carbaros y para su debida constancia la firmo en el dicho punto en dicho dia mes y año con dos testigos que actua en la forma ordinaria que day fé.

JUAN MARTIN.

De asst'a, MIGUEL SISNEROS.
   MANUEL RIVERA.

 SURVEYOR GENERAL'S OFFICE, TRANSLATOR'S DEPARTMENT,
    Santa Fé, New Mexico, August 25, 1859.
 The foregoing is a true copy of the original on file in this office.
DAVID V. WHITING,
Translator.

GRANT—TRANSLATION.

To the president and respective tribunal of independence, &c. :

 Citizen Salvador Tapia, resident of this jurisdiction, under the charge of your excellencies, presents himself at your feet in the most approved manner required, and with due submission, and in company with seventeen men, state that having an exceedingly small amount of land with which to support our families, and very much reduced, we pray you to look upon us with the greatest charity, and we expect that your excellencies will so do, favoring us, in the name of his Majesty and the nation of the monarchy, and the sovereign Mexican court, with a tract of land on this river called Anton Chico, a sufficient amount thereof for the support of our families, this being the only object for which the unfortunates contained in the list on the margin petition your excellencies. There being no other petitioners we therefore expect more clemency and attention from your excel--

lencies; and from your known generosity we fully expect a favorable answer to our petition, receiving thereby grace and favor.

SALVADOR TAPIA.

Bado, *January* 24, 1822.

The seventeen referred to who volunteer to accompany me are as follows:

Salvador Tapia.
Francisco Baca.
Rafael Duran.
Juan Sebastian Duran.
Diego Antonio Tapia.
Bernardo Ulibarri.
Felipe Valencia.
Luiz Gonzales.
Juan Cristobal Garcia.

Tomas Martin.
Juan José Martin.
Miguel Martin.
José Medina.
Simon Estrada.
Lorenzo Tapia.
Mariano Aragon.
José Duran.

Notwithstanding the fact of the right and necessities of the petitioners favoring the granting of their request, I cannot determine to do so, as it is beyond the limits of the grant to this place; therefore it is referred to his excellency the governor, who will, if he deems proper, comply with their request, and if not the parties will be informed.

MANUEL BACA.

January 25, 1822.

It is proper that the representation be made on ordinary paper, that the corporation initiate the proper proceedings, and transmit the same to the provincial assembly for its approval or consent.

MELGARES.

Santa Fé, *February* 13, 1822.

Bado, N. of N., 1814. Second of the independence of this empire.

Informed of the foregoing representation, and fully knowing the necessity requiring the request of the petitioners to be complied with, we will not resolve in the matter, as the land they solicit is not embraced within the limits of this district. Such being the case, it is referred to the most excellent provincial deputation, in order that it may resolve as it may deem just, upon being informed of the matter.

I, Governor Facundo Melgares, gentleman of the order of San Ermeregildo, military and political governor of said kingdom, inspector of the standing army therein, and inspector of the militia for his Majesty, whom may God preserve.

Having seen the present document and the petition of citizen Manuel Rivera, for himself and in the name of thirty-six men, I direct Manuel Baca, constitutional justice of the jurisdiction of San Miguel del Bado, and first commander of arms, to place the parties in possession of the grant they ask for, in order that they, their children, heirs, and successors, may hold and possess them in the name of his Majesty, observing, in so doing, all the circumstances and requirements which should be practiced in similar cases, and particularly the one citing injury. I so provided, ordered, and signed, with my attending witnesses with whom I act, there being no public or royal notary within this kingdom, and on this ordinary paper, there being none of the stamped, to which I certify.

MELGARES.

Attending:
JOAQUIN ALARID.

On the 2d day of May, 1822.

I, Manuel Baca, constitutional justice and commander of arms, in compliance with the directions of Governor Don Facundo Melgares, gentleman of the order of San Ermeregildo, political and military governor of this kingdom, before proceeding to the Sangre de Christo, vulgarly called Anton Chico, in the presence of two aldermen, who were Don Ventura Trufillo, 2d alderman, and Don Miguel Cisneros, 3d alderman, the 36 petitioners being present, I read the petition to them, and gave them to understand that they were to comply with, and perform according to law, the following conditions:

First. That the place selected should be common, not only for themselves, but also for all those citizens who in the future should remove to and settle there.

Second. That, concerning the arrangements of the place, they shall be equipped with fire-arms and arrows, and they shall pass muster upon entering upon the land, and whenever the justice sent to them shall deem proper.

Third. That the labors of the town, such as digging of ditches, and as many other works as may be necessary to be performed for the common good, shall be performed by all other town-charge, each one for himself.

In regard to their compliance with the foregoing conditions, they unanimously answered that they understood them, and were acquainted with the conditions I had imposed upon them, in consequence of which I took them by the hand and stated, in a clear, intelligible voice, that in the name of our independence, which may God preserve without injury to its royal credit nor the 4th. I walked with them over the lands; they pulled up grass, throwing stones, and crying aloud, saying, long life to the independence, taking possession of said lands quietly and peaceably, without any opposition, assigning them their boundaries, which are: On the north, the boundary of Don Antonio Ortiz; on the south, the ridge of the Piedra Pintada and the little table land of Guadalupe; on the east, the Salino Spring, with the Alto de los Esteros, where the river forms a cañon below, where the men were killed; and on the west, the Cuesta and the little Bernal Hill, which is the boundary of El Bado, with the understanding that the pastures and watering places are common, without injury to third parties.

And in order that it may be on record at all times, I signed, with my town clerk, this 2d day of May, 1822, to which I certify.

MANUEL BACA, *President.*
JOSÉ MIGUEL BACA,
Secretary.

At the town of Anton Chico, newly called by the name of "The Avocation of our Lord and Sangre de Christo," on the 8th day of the month of March, one thousand eight hundred and thirty-four, by verbal orders from citizen Juan José Cabeza de Baca, constitutional justice, in regard to the fact that there was a scarcity of land for the people to cultivate, and the lands of Anton Chico being entirely vacant, without being cultivated by the legitimate individuals to whom it had been given seven or eight years previously, and that they are now entirely abandoned, because the Indians had attacked them so often that they had depopulated the place, and that now, in order to administer to the necessities above mentioned of the unoccupied citizens having no lands, and for the encouragement of agriculture, a matter of so much interest for the support of its inhabitants, I was directed to deliver the land to those who should claim it, and distribute what had been before granted to available and laborious hands, which I did on the above-mentioned day, delivering and donating to those newly applying for lands and reinstating those to whom land had been formerly granted, and donating the surplus, in the name of the laws governing us, to whomsoever wished for lands, who are as follows:

To Biteroo Sandoval, former grantee, the point of the valley, without measurement; Vicente Legino, donated, 100 varas; Miguel Jaramillo, by purchase, 100 varas; Pablo Ortiz, donated, 100 varas; Ignacio Aragon, donated, 125 varas; Santiago Aragon, donated, 75 varas; Julian Garcia, donated, 100 varas, and a strip; Bartolo Ocoña, donated, 100 varas; Miguel Duran, former grantee, 200 varas; José de Jesus Duran, 100 varas, and the remainder of the arroyo; José Antonio, the dumb, 100 varas; Francisco Sandoval, 100 varas; Gertrudis Mertas, 50 varas.

Which, in fulfilment of my trust, and as actual alderman, and acting constitutional justice, I grant and donate to them in the name of the laws we obey, in order that they may hold the same, and not dispose of them until they are authorized to do so within the period required by law, and complying with the conditions, rights, and requirements exacted from all settlers, enjoining upon them particularly that they be always provided with arms, laboring together peaceably and friendly, so as not to be surprised by the savages. And in testimony thereof I signed, at the afore-mentioned place, on the said day, month, and year, with two witnesses, with whom I act in the ordinary way, to which I certify.

JUAN MARTIN.

Attending: MIGUEL SISNEROS,
MANUEL RIVERA.

SURVEYOR GENERAL'S OFFICE, TRANSLATOR'S DEPARTMENT,
Santa Fé, New Mexico, June 16, 1859.

The foregoing is a translation of the original on file in this office.

DAVID V. WHITING,
Translator.

SURVEYOR GENERAL'S OFFICE,
Santa Fé, New Mexico, September 10, 1859.
The foregoing is a correct copy of the original on file in this office.
WM. PELHAM,
Surveyor General.

TESTIMONY.

JUAN BAUTISTE VIGIL sworn:
Question. Have you any interest in this case?
Answer. I have none.
Question. How old are you?
Answer. I am sixty-six years old.
Question. Did you know Facundo Melgares; and, if so, what office did he hold in New Mexico in the year 1822?
Answer. I did; he was political chief of the Territory of New Mexico in that year.
Question. Do you know his signature, and have you seen him write?
Answer. I do; have seen him write. His signature on document "A" is genuine.
Question. Did you know Manuel Baca, of El Bado, in 1822?
Answer. I did know him, and his son also; the elder one was called Corporal Baca.
Question. Do you know his signature?
Answer. I do; his signature on document "A" is genuine; the one on document "B" is also genuine; that of José Miguel Sanchez, secretary of the corporation, on the same document, is also genuine.
Question. Do you know the town of Anton Chico; if so, how often have you visited it, and when did you first know it?
Answer. I do; I have been there twice. I was there in 1839 and 1841, when the Texans came in.
Question. Do you remember who were the original settlers at that time, and were their heirs in occupation when you were there?
Answer. The Martinez and Flores. I don't know if their heirs were in possession when I was there. The Cisneros were also among the original settlers.
Question. What was the population of Anton Chico in 1841?
Answer. About six hundred souls.

Cross-examined.

Question. Did you ever see Governor Melgares sign his name?
Answer. I have seen him do it frequently. He held the office of political and military chief under the Spanish government, and subject to the control of the headquarters at Chihuahua.
Question. Look upon document "B," and see if you see Melgares' signature on it.
Answer. There is no original signature of Melgares on that docu-

ment; it is a copy only, signed by Baca and Sanchez, whose signatures are genuine.

Question. Do you know, from your own knowledge, that such an original document ever existed as this purports to be a copy from?

Answer. I do not.

Question. Do you state that it is a copy from the appearance of the document, or from any other knowledge you may have in regard to it?

Answer. I know that it is a copy only from the signatures of Baca and Sanchez, and from no other knowledge.

Question. What was the date of the declaration of the independence of Mexico?

Answer. In 1822; don't remember the date. When Melgares executed the document in question the country was under the government of Spain.

Question. Did Governor Melgares ever hold office under the Mexican government?

Answer. I believe not; Vizcarra proclaimed the independence here.

Question. What office did Manuel Baca hold when this grant was made?

Answer. He was justice of the peace and president of the corporation of El Bado.

Question. Under the Mexican government after the revolution who had the authority to make grants of land?

Answer. The provincial deputation created by the laws of Spain.

Question. Do you recollect whether Melgares ever attempted to enforce his office after the declaration, or endeavored to exercise his functions after that time?

Answer. I do not know. The provincial deputation was the only one that had any authority to dispose of the public domain after the declaration of independence. I was the senior member of the first assembly that met here after the independence.

Re-examined by counsel for claimants.

Question. Was Melgares relieved by Vizcarra or Bartolome Baca?

Answer. He was relieved by Vizcarra, who was appointed by virtue of a petition of the citizens of New Mexico requesting Melgares' removal.

Question. After the declaration of independence, and under the plan of Iguala, did not the old officers under the Spanish government hold office until the officers under the new constitution were regularly installed?

Answer. Under the plan of Iguala all of the old authorities were relieved by the new officers.

JUAN BAUTISTA VIGIL Y ALARID.

Sworn to and subscribed before me this 27th day of June, 1859.

WILLIAM PELHAM,
Surveyor General.

DONACIANO VIGIL sworn:

Question. Have you any interest in this case?

Answer. I have not.

Question. How old are you?
Answer. I am fifty-seven years old.
Question. Did you know Facundo Melgares, and what office did he hold in 1822?
Answer. I did. He was political and military governor of New Mexico.
Question. Do you know his signature, and have you seen him write?
Answer. I know his signature, having seen it often on documents filed in the archives. I have not seen him write. His signature on document "A" appears to be genuine.
Question. Did you know Manuel Baca and José Miguel Sanchez, and what offices did they hold in 1822?
Answer. I knew Manuel Baca slightly; Sanchez I knew well. I cannot say that I know Baca's signature; Sanchez's I do. Sanchez's signature on document "B" is genuine.
Question. Do you know when Melgares was relieved by Vizcarra as governor?
Answer. On the 21st December, 1822.
Question. From the 1st January, 1822, up to December, 1822, who was the political and military governor of New Mexico?
Answer. Facundo Melgares.
Question. Do you know the town of Anton Chico?
Answer. Slightly; I was there in 1827. There was a small settlement there then; I have not been there since.

Cross-examined.

Question Was it the practice, under the Mexican government after the independence, to allow the authorities under the government of Spain to exercise their duties in any governmental affairs?
Answer. The public affairs were conducted entirely under the Spanish laws until the adoption of the constitution in 1824. In Mexico the officers were changed immediately after the declaration of independence, but no change was made here, owing to the absence of mail facilities, until the 21st of December, 1822.
Question. Did the government of Mexico, after its independence, recognize any act or officer as emanating from the crown of Spain or from the new government established by the declaration?
Answer. They did recognize the laws of Spain as approved or sanctioned by the new government under the declaration of independence.
Question. Did not the validity of the acts of the officers of Spain who held office under the new government depend entirely upon the authority of the Mexican revolutionary government, and not upon the authority of the former government of Spain?
Answer. Up to the 22d of December, 1822 nothing was known here of the declaration of independence, and the same order of things existed, and all the authorities exercised their duties under the Spanish government. After the declaration was promulgated here the general government of Mexico approved of all the public acts done by the officers of this country from the date of the declaration up to th

time it was published here; or, in other words, they canonized them. There was no statute declaring their approval, but none of their acts were disapproved.

Question. Do you know if the grant in question was brought to the knowledge of the central government of Mexico?

Answer. I do not know.

Question. Subsequent to the Mexican authorities going into full operation here, who had the authority to declare which was public land and subject to grant, or which was private land, and not subject to grant?

Answer. The governors, upon a report from the provincial deputation created by the authority of the decrees of the cortes of Spain of 1811.

Question. If the governor and provincial deputation made a grant of land which conflicted with a grant previously made under the laws of Spain, which of the two prevailed?

Answer. The previous one had preference.

Question. Who had the final jurisdiction to dispose of the validity of a grant?

Answer. The matter was firstly investigated by the governor, and the case was referred to the chief commander of the department who held final jurisdiction in the matter, and a final appeal was had from him to the audience at Guadalajara.

Question. From what time did New Mexico date its independence from the crown of Spain?

Answer. On the 21st of December, 1822.

Question. How is it that the legal documents in this case are dated the second year of the independence?

Answer. I do not know.

Question. Was not the declaration of independence recognized here as having gone into effect on the date it was promulgated in Mexico; and did not New Mexico date her independence from that time, that is, the 27th of September, 1821?

Answer. The people of New Mexico considered themselves as separated from the crown of Spain from the date of the declaration of independence, on the 27th of September, 1821.

D. VIGIL.

Sworn and subscribed before me this 27th of June, 1859.
WM. PELHAM,
Surveyor General.

SURVEYOR GENERAL'S OFFICE,
Santa Fé, New Mexico, August 25, 1859.

The foregoing is a true copy of the original on file in this office.
WM. PELHAM,
Surveyor General.

Town of Anton Chico.

ALEXANDER DUVALL sworn:

Question. Have you any interest in this case?
Answer. I have not.
Question. Do you know the town of Anton Chico, situated in the county of San Miguel; and if so, when were you there?
Answer. I do. I was there in March, 1847.
Question. When you were there in 1847, was there a settlement there?
Answer. It was a settled town, with about thirty or forty houses.
Question. At that time, did the town have the appearance of a newly built town?
Answer. It appeared as if it had been built for some time past; the houses did not look as if they were new.
Question. How far below the town of San Miguel, on the Pecos river, is it situated?
Answer. About thirty-five miles.

ALEX. DUVALL.

Sworn and subscribed before me this 30th day of June, 1859.
WM. PELHAM,
Surveyor General.

SURVEYOR GENERAL'S OFFICE,
Santa Fé, New Mexico, August 25, 1859.

The foregoing is a true copy of the original on file in this office.
WM. PELHAM,
Surveyor General.

REPORT.

TOWN OF ANTON CHICO, *vs.* THE UNITED STATES.

This case was set for trial on the 27th day of June, 1859.
On the 24th day of January, 1822, Salvador Tapia, for himself and sixteen others, petitioned the tribunal of Independence, supposed to be the corporation of the town of San Miguel, for a tract of land known as Anton Chico, on the Pecos river. The president of that corporation for the want of power, the land asked for being beyond the jurisdiction of that body, referred the petition to the governor for his action in the premises. Melgares, the governor, on the 13th February of the same year, remanded the paper back to the corporation, with instructions to make application to the provincial deputation for its approval.

The corporation of San Miguel, repeating its want of jurisdiction in the matter, on the 9th November referred the matter to the provincial deputation.

No further action appears to have been taken in the matter until the 2d of May, 1822, when Governor Melgares is purported to have granted the land to Manuel Rivera and thirty-six men, and directed Manuel Baca, the constitutional justice of El Bado, to place the parties in possession, which was done on the 2d day of May of the same year.

The claimants file a third document, dated March 8, 1834, purporting to be a distribution of the Anton Chico lands by Juan Martin, under verbal authority from Juan José Cabeza de Baca, constitutional justice of El Bado.

It is stated in this document that the original grantees were compelled to leave the land on account of having been driven off by the Indians. Under this distribution fourteen persons are placed in possession of a certain amount of arable land, varying from fifty to one hundred varas, and among them there are two of the former grantees.

This document is considered as entirely superfluous, and has no bearing whatever on the case.

The documents marked A and C are original. Document B contains a copy of the grant made by Governor Melgares, and certified to by Manuel Baca, the justice aforesaid. The documents filed are all disconnected, and appear to bear no relation to each other.

Evidence has been introduced by the claimants, proving the town to have been in existence since 1839.

This claim is contested by the heirs of Preston Beck, deceased, so far as it conflicts with the grant made to Juan E. Pino, of which they are the assigns.

The grant made by Melgares on the 2d May, 1822, severed the land from the public domain, and placed it beyond the further reach and control of the government. The instructions to this office provide that the existence of a town when the United States took possession of the country being proven, is to be taken as *prima facie* evidence of a grant to said town; and as it is proven to have been in existence in 1839, and up to 1846, with the knowledge and tacit consent of the Mexican government, and was recognized as a town by that government, it is believed to be a good and valid grant, and the land claimed severed from the public domain. It is therefore approved, and ordered to be transmitted to Congress for its action in the premises.

WM. PELHAM,
Surveyor General.

SURVEYOR GENERAL'S OFFICE,
 Santa Fé, New Mexico, *July* 15, 1859.

SURVEYOR GENERAL'S OFFICE,
 Santa Fé, New Mexico, *August* 25, 1859.

The foregoing is a true copy of the original on file in this office.

WM. PELHAM,
Surveyor General.

NOTICE OF APPEAL.

IN THE MATTER OF THE CLAIM OF THE INHABITANTS OF ANTON CHICO.

To the Surveyor General of New Mexico:

The heirs of Preston Beck, jr., deceased, and Hugh N. Smith, as claimants and owners of the tract of land originally granted to Juan Esteran Pino, and confirmed to Preston Beck, jr., deceased, in his lifetime, appear to contest said claim of the inhabitants of Anton Chico, or so much thereof as conflicts with or encroaches upon the said grant to Juan Esteran Pino, and confirmed to Preston Beck, jr.

A. M. JACKSON,
Attorney for Preston Beck, jr.

SURVEYOR GENERAL'S OFFICE,
Santa Fé, New Mexico, August 25, 1859.

The foregoing is a true copy of the original on file in this office.

WM. PELHAM,
Surveyor General.

CLAIM NO. 30.

INDIANS OF LAGUNA.

Documents composing claim No. 30.

1. Notice.
2. Grant, No. 1—Spanish.
3. Grant, No. 1—translation.
4. Grant, No. 2—Spanish.
5. Grant, No. 2—translation.
6. Conveyance—Spanish.
7. Conveyance—translation.
8. Testimony.
9. Report.

NOTICE.

To the Hon. Wm. Pelham, surveyor general of the Territory of New Mexico:

The petition of certain Pueblo Indians, occupying, constituting, and known as the pueblo of Laguna, in said Territory, respectfully represents to you that the said pueblo of Laguna is the claimant and legal owner of certain tracts and parcels of land lying in the vicinity of their said original pueblo grant, and in the county of Valencia, in the Territory of New Mexico aforesaid.

Your petitioner, the pueblo aforesaid, proceeds to describe the said several parcels as follows:

1st. The rancho called Pagnate situated to the north and adjoining the site of Cebolleta, distant three leagues from the said pueblo of Laguna.

This rancho became the property of your petitioners by purchase from Pascual Pagarito, Vicente Pagarito, Antonio Pagnati, and Miguel Mognino, who were the original grantees of the same, and for the validity of the original grant of the same, and of the purchase thereof by your petitioner, reference is hereby made to the document A, on file, executed by Manuel Aragan, chief justice and war chief of the pueblos of Acama, Laguna, &c., in the year 1813, and approved by Narbona, civil and military governor of the Territory of New Mexico, on the 28th day of August, 1826.

2d. The rancho called "E. Rito," lying to the east of the pueblo; your petitioner, the pueblo aforesaid, claims to be owner of this rancho by virtue of the original grant to them, and as enclosed within the the same, which original grant is now on file in your office for separate proceedings thereupon; but your petitioner also claims the said rancho by virtue of the recognition of its title thereto contained in the said document marked A, above referred to, and also by virtue of the purchase of the pretended right and title of the heirs of the original grantee, for the evidence of which purchase your petitioner refers to the deed or document, on file, marked C, and for information as to the pretended title so purchased to the document marked C.

Your petitioner claims confirmation of its title to this rancho as well by virtue of the documents here referred to as by virtue of its inclusion within their said original grant.

3d. A certain tract of land known as the Gigante Cañon, lying eastwardly from the said pueblo to the ajo del chamiso, and for the title of your petitioner thereto, reference is made to the said document marked A, and above referred to, whereby the same is fully recognized and confirmed.

4th. The rancho commonly called San Juan, lying eastwardly from said pueblo, and for the title thereto your petitioner also makes reference to said document A.

5th. The site known as Cubero, lying westwards from said pueblo, with the asequia and privileges appertaining thereto, to which their title also will appear upon reference to the said document marked A.

6th. The rancho called Santa Ana, lying westwardly from the said pueblo one mile, more or less, and for their title thereto the petitioner refers to the said document A, whereby the same is recognized and confirmed; and for a further recognition of the right and title of your petitioner to the said several parcels of land, reference is further made to the document marked B No. 2, whereby the metes and bounds are more specifically set forth and defined, and which document was approved by the said Narbona, civil and military governor as aforesaid, on the 26th August, 1826.

Your petitioner states that those documents here referred to contain the best written evidence of their right and title to the above-mentioned property, which is in existence so far as your petitioner knows and believes. That your petitioner is not able to produce the original documents referred to by the said document so filed, because the same are so lost or destroyed that your petitioner is unable to procure and present the same.

But your petitioner is prepared and now offers to prove its continued possession and enjoyment of the said several tracts of land by virtue of its rights and title thereto, hereby advanced.

Your petitioner, the pueblo of Laguna aforesaid, prays confirmation of its said claim and title to the said several tracts or parcels of land.

J. S. WATTS,
Attorney for Petitioner.

SURVEYORS GENERAL'S OFFICE,
Santa Fé, New Mexico, August, 25, 1859.

The foregoing is a true copy of the original on file in this office.

WM. PELHAM,
Surveyor General.

GRANT NO. 1.—SPANISH.

Don José Manuel Aragon, Alcalde mayor y capitan de guerra de estas Pueblos de Acoma, Laguna Poblacion de Seballeta y sus dertritos.

En atencian a tener hecho renuncia al superior gobierno me exono rare de ese empleo, el que hase el tiempo de veinte años sirbe en esta pantera se me presento José Alarrigna, gubernador de este Pueblo de San José de la Laguna y las cabecillas de el can su interprete Antonio Herrera pidiendome les depase un Estado de gobierno y ordenes mandadas por las señores gobernadores de esta Provincia, supli candome encaresi damente a ver si pur esta medida se podian libertar de las desardenes y gravamenes que sufrio el pueblo antervormente en las mudadas de alcaldes y ministros de el, precabiendo estas que eulo sucesiro noles su ceda otro tanto ensupobre Puebla.

Y atendiendo a esta justa supesca les estendi en este papel este instrumento declaratorio diciendo coma digo, que hallandome presente en los visitas generales que han hecho en este Pueblo los señores gobernadores Don Fernando Chacan, Don Alberto Maynes y Don José Manuri ques cancediendale a estos indias se estenduran en hacer sus siembras, amas de la segua que el Rey los libro la que pudieran (le) sembrar para po precisca mantencian y alimento de sus famolias, por estar el Pueblo resentardo en parte que no tienen ni padran tener la suficienta labor dentro de la legua que el Rey libro y padeciendo este Pueblo des de anteriormente esta necessidad de tierra para sembrar en trempo que gobernaba esta Provincia Don Tomas Veles Cachupin, compraran estos indios el rancho que llaman de Pagnate. Don al Norte Conlindantes con el citeo de Sebolleto dutante de aste Pueblo tres legnas. Este dicha Rancho fire dado por merced anterior meate a Pascual Pagerito, Vicente Pagerito, Antonio Pagnate y a Miguel Mognino, y habiend le estos poseado treinte anos jelo vendieran al

Pueblo y habiendo pretendido y solicitado algunos vecinos resentarse en el, nolo han pudido consegoir canel superior gobierno a causa de ser compra hecha por el Pueblo y tener un instrumento autorisardo por el Alcalde que fue de este Pueblo Don Antonio Sedillos; por lague miro el lado del oriente selos ha cancedido a sembrar en el rancho que llaman del Rito, y porlo consiguiente la cañado delos gigantes, puntamente con el rancho que llaman de San Juan hasta el ajo del chamiro para parteaderos de su caballado por ser esta una frontera tan espuerta y ur poder aventurarla en otro rumbo: Parel poniente tienen el sitio que llaman de Cubero, en donde tienen Siembras y seguia propria y riegan con la mismo agna que paso por este Pueblo, y al mismo rumbo de el poniente á distancéa de una Legua de dicho Pueblo esta el rancho que llaman de Santa Ana en donde tienea sembra en man comun.

Porla que mira el Alcalde que sucediera en este Pueblo segun los ordenes superiores yu notiene que servirse del trabajo de los Indios para nado mas de solo pagando les justamente su trabajo, siendo estos libres en adelante ni tampoco pundo nombrar es caltas para negocios particulares solo que sea llamado porel gobernador para tratar asuntas del Real Servicio Porlogne mira al Padre que ministra, dehe estar en los mismos terminos que el Alcalde sui tener facultad de gravar al Pueblo ni á los Indios en trabajo de su servicio mas de solo mi sacristan para que toque la campana y mi cabello que le debe mantener el Pueblo para cuando se le opresca ir á una confession.

Este es el metodo establecido porlos Señores Gobernadoes para el buen Gobierno de estes Pueblas, el que naprosediendo de ningune malicia dejo a pedimiento de los hipos de este Puebla de la Laguna y la firme a veinte y cinco de marzo de mil acho ciento trese.

JOSÉ MANUEL ARAGON.

SANTA FÉ, *Augusto* 28 *de* 1826.

Aprabado este documento a cuanto toca a este gobierno por legal, por el merito y formalidad can que a parece.

NARBONA.

Marginal notes.

Este documento ha deparar en pader de Don Juan Miguel, casique y en falleciendoel en sus day lupas Catarina y Josefa, quienes tienen el mirmo derecho y an sian al potio juntamente cantodos los hipos del Pueblo en compania de Don Vicente Romero, comprehendido en la misma ausian.

Prubrica el cetio que cito el celio de Cuberio que cita este documento y la agua que por este rio corre es la unica que estos Indios disfrutan, pones esta demana del ajo del Gallo desuerte que llegadore a poblar dicho ajo perecian estos probres Indios porser la misma agua que llega harta el Pueblo y don acredores estos naturales por en antignedad por pobladores de buena fe demas de cien años.

SURVEYOR GENERAL'S OFFICE, TRANSLATOR'S DEPARTMENT,
Santa Fé, New Mexico, August 25, 1859.

The foregoing is a true copy of the original on file in this office.

DAVID V. WHITING,
Translator.

GRANT NO. 1—TRANSLATION.

Don José Manuel Aragan, chief justice and war captain of these pueblos of Acoma, Laguna, settlement of Ceballeta, and its districts.

In view of the resignation I have tendered of the office I have held on this frontier for the period of over twenty years, José Alarrigua, governor of this pueblo of San José de la Laguna, and the chiefs thereof, together with their interpreter, Antonio Herrera, appeared before me, asking me to leave them a statement of the government and orders given by the honorable governors of this province, urgently requesting me to see if by this means they could be relieved from the disorders and grievances the pueblo formerly suffered in the changes of justices and ministers, and providing against a recurrence of the same thing in the future ; and, in compliance with this just demand, I have executed on this paper this declaratory statement, saying, as I do say, that being present at the general visits made to this pueblo by Governors Don Fernando Chacon, Don Joaquin del Real Alencaster, Don Alberto Maynes, and Don José Manriques, authorizing these Indians to extend their fields beyond the league granted to them by the king as far as they could plant, for the actual support and maintenance of their families. The pueblo being situated in such a locality as not to afford them a sufficient quantity of arable land within the league allowed them by the king, and this pueblo having formerly suffered this scarcity of land for cultivation when this province was governed by Don Thomas Veles Cachupin, these Indians purchased the rancho called Pagnati, situated to the north and adjoining the site of Ceballeta, distant three leagues from this pueblo. This rancho was formerly granted to Pasual Pagarito, Vicente Pagarito, Antonio Pagnati, and Miguel Magnino, and having possessed it for thirty years, they sold it to the pueblo ; and certain citizens having petitioned and asked for permission to settle there they have not been allowed to do so by the superior government, as it was a purchase made by the Indians, who held a deed authorized by the former justice of the peace of this pueblo, Don Antonio Sedillo.

In regard to the land towards the east, they have been allowed to plant on the rancho known as el Rito, and therefore also the gigante cañon to the ajo del Chamiso, together with the rancho commonly called San Juan, for pasture lands for their animals, the frontier being so much exposed that they cannot risk them in any other direction. On the west they have the site known as Cubero, where they have fields under cultivation and an asequia of their own, and they irrigate with the same water that passes through this pueblo ; and in the same westerly direction, distant a mile from said pueblo, in the rancho called Santa Ana, where they hold lands for cultivation in common, as far as the alcalde is concerned, who is to reside in this pueblo, he is forbidden by superior orders from availing himself of the labor of the Indians for any purpose except by paying them the just value of their labor ; neither can he compel them to serve on escorts for private individuals unless required by the government to treat upon subjects connected with the royal service.

As far as the officiating minister is concerned, he is placed upon the same terms as the justice, without any authority to tax the pueblo or any Indian with their services excepting a sexton to ring the bell and the feed of a horse, which is to be furnished by the pueblo in case it should be necessary for him to hear a confession. This is the method established by the government for the good government of these Pueblos, and having no private malice to accomplish, and at the request of the Indians of the pueblo of Laguna, I leave this statement, which I signed on the 25th day of March, 1813.

MANUEL ARAGON.

SANTA FÉ, *August* 28, 1826.

Approved so far as this government is concerned, and legal and formal in its contents.

N. ARBONA.

Marginal Notes.

This document is to remain in the hands of Don Juan Miguel Casique, and at his death in those of his two daughters, Catarina and Josefa, who have the same right and interest in the site together with Don Vicente Romero, included in the same interest.

[Rubric.]

The site of Cubero, mentioned in this document, and the water running through it, is the only water these Indians have the use of, as this proceeds from the Gallo spring; therefore if the said spring is settled, these poor Indians would perish, as it is the same water that reaches to the pueblo and these Indians are entitled to it, being old settlers in good faith for more than one hundred years.

[Rubric.]

SURVEYOR GENERAL'S OFFICE, TRANSLATOR'S DEPARTMENT,
Santa Fé, New Mexico, June 29, 1859.

The above is a translation of the original on file in this office.

DAVID V. WHITING,
Translator.

SURVEYOR GENERAL'S OFFICE,
Santa Fé, New Mexico, August 25, 1859.

The foregoing is a true copy of the original on file in this office.

WM. PELHAM,
Surveyor General.

GRANT NO. 2—SPANISH.

En este año de mil ocho cientos venite D. Inacio Sanches Vergara, protector general de Indios de esta provincia del Narevo Mexico, &c., lebro un documento arreglado al instrumento antorisado por D. Antonio Sedillo, desde el año de mil Sietecientas Sesenta y unebe y por falta dela citacion de tres linderos que decho Protector no menciono en su documento me suplicaron los mencionadas en dicho documento sacara un tanto y mencionara los linderos que en el rancho de Paguasti se anotan; cuyo documento es del tenor si guiente.

En este Pueblo de Xemes en primero de Junio del año de mil achocientos veinte serne presento un documento instruido por el Alcalde que fue del pueblo de la Laguna por los Indios naturales de dicho Pueblo Lorenso y Alonso Santiago Segundo Alonso, Toribio y Rito para que me hisiera cargo del derecho que representaban al rancho (pag) Nombrado del paguasti; y habiendolo registrado, encuentro que decho Alcalde en aquel tiempo Don Antonio Tedillo, entendiendo en el litis que promovieran Juan Paguati y Pasenal Pajarito amboy vesinos del estado Pueblo, se dispuso que darn cado uno en quieto en lo suyo sin perjudicarse en tal cunsepto y como Protector de Indios por la Real Andiencia de Guadalajara a quien corresponde representar privativamenti por las Indios en comun y en particular si san perjudicado en alguna manera ó si les falta tierra de la que las leyes les consede ó que por derecho hayan adquerido y en virtud de la antigna posesion de que hacen referencia los dichas naturales alcitado terreno, nombrado el rancho de Pagnasti por justo titulo adquerido, y que la uneba poblacion dela Sebolleta cansediela de merced a los vecinas porel Señor Gobernador Don Farnando Chacon, y posecian dada por el Alcalde Don José Manuel Aragon cun las formalidades que prescribe la ley de posecian y asiento y habiendo señalado linderos quedo libre con sus antignedade, el mencionado rancho y sus linderos por rumbo de Sebolleta hasta la mesa del gabilan porel sur hasta la cuesta, por el poniente hasta el rito de San José y porel oriente hasta el cañoncito del cajo. Los unebos Calonos Sebolletanos quedaron conformes con su lindero a la mesa del gavilan, conlindantes, canlos pociadores de buena fe.

Es de consideracion la necesidad que tienen estos naturales de terreno y que salo el citis de Pahuati en algun mado mitiga sus miserias en las escases siembras y aunque en sus principios gozaban de mayor estencion ampliandore hasta el rito, ruas replegando los Don Joaquin Pino a un terreno yuntil pordados rumbos con haberles privado del citado sitio por derecho que represento de merced a tudifunto padre, pero abandonada mas de trémta años se le con sedio y quedaron tan estrechos que sola les queda el auxilio del pahuati en que los principales dueñños hacen siembras de commidad canel pueblo y quedan Sacorridos los mas que no tienen terreno para sus labores y susistencia.

Todo esto bien premeditado y considerado deberare representar siempre que se les quierra perjudicar con quererlos privar de la antigua posecion del referido Paguati que ocurriendo a la superioridad por si a por el protector acompanando el documento de que se hase referencia hecho por el Alcalde Don Antonio Sedillo como queda dicho no dejara duda que penetrado de las poderosas rasones espuertos quedaran sasegados y disfrutaran de loque estan justo y por tanto derecho suyo e sin disputa.

En virtud de tado y en cumplimiento de mi encargo tan repetido por las reales leyes de la recopilacion de Indias le day este documento pare su resignardo como protector de Indios y que tanto me lo recomienda el Senor fiscal protector general de Indios y la su debido complimiento la firme para la constancia en dicho dia mes y ano.

Firme este tanto como testigo de la como dicho protector lo dise.

ENSEBIO ARAGON.

Santa Fé, *Augusto* 28 *de* 1826.

Aprovado este documento en cuanto a este gobierno y segun el merito y formalidad con que aparece.

NARBONA.

Surveyor General's Office, Translator's Department,
Santa Fé, New Mexico, August 25, 1859.

The foregoing is a true copy of the original on file in this office.

DAVID V. WHITING,
Translator.

GRANT NO. 2.—TRANSLATION.

In this year one thousand eight hundred and twenty, Don Ignatio Sanches Vergara, protector general of the Indians of this province of New Mexico, executed a document alike to the instrument authorized by Don Antonio Tedillo, in the year one thousand seven hundred and sixty-nine; and for not stating three boundaries which said protector did not mention in his document, the parties mentioned in said document requested me to make a copy thereof, stating the boundaries to which the rancho of Pagnasti is entitled, which document is of the tenor following:

For this pueblo of Jemes, on the 1st day of June, in the year one thousand eight hundred and twenty, a document authorized by the former alcalde of the pueblo of Laguna was presented to me by Lorenzo and Alonzo Santiago, Alonzo the second, Torribio and Rita, native Indians of said pueblo, requesting me to take charge of the interests they represented in the rancho called Pagnasti; and having registered it, I find that Don Antonio Sedillo, the said alcalde at that time, took cognizance of a suit brought by Juan Pagnasti and Pascual Pagarito, both residents of said pueblo, and it was ordered that each one should quietly remain upon his own property, without disturbing each other.

Such being the case, and as protector of the Indians for the royal audience of Guadalajara, to whom alone it is proper for the Indians to refer matters of a common or private nature if they are in any way aggrieved, or if they have not a sufficient amount of land with that the law allows them or that they may have legally acquired, and by virtue of the ancient possession of said land to which the said natives refer, called the rancho of Pagnasti, acquired by a legal title, and that the new settlement of Ceballeta, granted by Governor Don Fernando Chacon to certain citizens, and possession given by the Alcalde Don José Manuel Aragon, with the formalities required by the laws of possession and settlement, the boundaries having been marked out. The aforesaid ranch and its boundaries in the direction of Ceballeta remained free with its ancient appurtenances as far as the table-land of El Gabilan, on the south to La Cuesta, on the west to the Rito de San José, and on the east to the Cañoncito del Cajo.

The new settlers of Ceballeta were satisfied with their boundaries at the table-land of El Gabilan, adjoining the holders in good faith.

The want of land by these Indians is to be taken in consideration, and that the tract of Pagnasti is the only one that in a measure aids them with a scant produce in their misery; and although at the commencement they had more land extending as far as El Rite, they were restricted by Don Joaquin Pino to a tract of waste land, he having deprived them of the said land by virtue of a right to it held by his late father, whom he represents, but which land had been abandoned for more than thirty years. Nevertheless, his title was recognized, and they are so much reduced that the only aid they received is from Pagnasti, where the principal owners cultivate the soil in common with the Pueblo, and those who have no lands to cultivate for their support are in a measure relieved.

All of which has been well premeditated and considered, and will be shown whenever an effort is made to injure them by depriving them of the ancient possession of Pagnasti. There is no doubt that, presenting themselves in person or through their protector to the Superior Audience, they will be allowed to remain in peace, in the enjoyment of what is unquestionably theirs. In testimony whereof, and in compliance with the duties so repeatedly enjoined upon me by the royal laws of the recopilation of the Indies, I executed this document for their protection, as protector of the Indians who are so highly recommended to me by the attorney, protector general of the Indians, and for its due authenticity I signed on this said day, month, and year.

I signed this as a witness to the truth of the statement made by the protector.

ENSEBIO ARAGON.

SANTA FÉ, *August* 28, 1826.

This document is approved so far as this government is concerned, and according to the merit and formality in which it appears.

NARBONA.

SURVEYOR GENERAL'S OFFICE, TRANLATOR'S DEPARTMENT,
Santa Fé, New Mexico, June 29, 1859.

The above is a translation of the original on file in this office.

DAVID V. WHITING,
Translator.

SURVEYOR GENERAL'S OFFICE,
Santa Fé, New Mexico, August 25, 1859.

The foregoing is a true copy of the original on file in this office.

WM. PELHAM,
Surveyor General.

CONVEYANCE—SPANISH.

En la jurisdiction de la Laguna a los 23 dias del mes de Agosto de 1843, ante mi, el Cuidadano Juan Garcia, Juez de Paz de dicha jurisdiction comparecieron presentes por sus propias personas los C. C. Don José Francisco Chaves y Baca, vecino de la jurisdiction de Belen y Juan Inacio Chaves, gobernador del pueblo de la Laguna, y Luis Saracino, natural del mismo pueblo, á quienes doy fe conosco y dijo el primero que como apoderado de su padre politico Don José Ant° Pino, vecino del Sabinal y por si mismo vendio y enefecto vendio á los segundos como apoderados del pueblo de la Laguna todas las tierras de labor que tiene en el rancho del Rito, como tambien las de la misma clase que tenia Don José Antonio Pino, con mas la ancion que como herederos legitimos tienen al dicho rancho, por el precio y cantidad de setenta y siete carneros cien pielas de marka de toda clase y seis reses de la siguientes clases ; Dos bueyes, una baca, dos toros y una ternera, la quese obligan dichos apoderados a entregar a Chaves y Baca lo antes possible a su satisfacion con lo que se da y se dio dicho vendedor por satis fecho y pagado y si mas vale ó valer puedan dichas tierras a ansiones de la demasia le hace gracia y donacion al referido pueblo para que las goze por si mismo y sus herederos y sucessores, sin que para el uso libre de dichas tierras de labor y merica al referido rancho les sen puesto pleito ni demanda alguna ni por si sus hijos herederos ó sucessores y por lo mismo los de su citado padre politico pues desde de ahora para cuando suceda remoncio al fuero y derecho en favor de los compradores suplicando a los justicias nacionales en donde se presenten no sean didos en juicio ni fuera de el a mayor Abundamiento dijo que dichas ansiones y tierras de labor las daba libre de senso y tributo ni otra enajenacion, como posedores que habian sido de ellas de una y otra parte como herederos, legitimos de Don Mateo José de el Pino, sin perjuicio de los demas herederos a dicho rancho con sola la condicion que las cosechas de este año corriente san del vendedor que dando las tierras de labor y ansiones de ahora por legitima propiedad de los compradores a cujo efecto renuncio sus propios derechos y los de su poderdante, en favor de dicha Pueblo de la Laguna domicilio y vecinduo sin que queda en favor de dicho vendedor y su poderdante en el referido rancho del rito mas que las casas de sus habitaciones con loque les es anexio y a al sans ámiento de esta escritura, obligo dicho vendedor sus bienes muebles habidos y por haber con poderio y sumission a los justicias nacionales para que a su cumplimiento le compelen y aprisman por ria ejecutiva como por sentencia pasada de cosa juzgada consentida y na apelada, dada por juez competente y enel presente papel comun por no haber en esta demarcacion de sello que corresponda que dandolos interesados con la obligacion de agregarlo arpiado cuando lo encuentren y para que tenga la fuerza y validez que por derecho se requiera me suplicaba y implico dicho vendedor enter pussiera mi autoridad y decreto judicial y yo el referidor juez dijo que la interponia y interfenso con los testigos de mi assistencia con quienes autuo por resetoria a falta del escribano publico que de todo dai fé en dicho dia mes y año.

JUAN GARCIA.

Derechos, 3 pesos.
Assⁿ: Florentine Castillo,
Jesus Ma. Beitin.

Surveyor General's Office, Translator's Department,
Santa Fé, New Mexico, August 25, 1859.

The foregoing is a true copy of the original on file in this office.

DAVID V. WHITING,
Translator.

CONVEYANCE—TRANSLATION.

In the jurisdiction of Laguna, on the 23d day of the month of August, 1843, before me, citizen Juan Garcia, justice of the peace of said jurisdiction, appeared before me in their own proper persons, citizens Don José Francisco Chaves y Baca, resident of the jurisdiction of Belen, and Juan Ignasio Chaves, governor of the pueblo of Laguna, and Luis Sarracino, a native of said pueblo, whom I certify are known to me; and the first party stated that, as the agent of his father-in-law, Don José Antonio Pino, resident of Sabinal, and for himself, he sold, and in effect did sell, to the parties of the second part, as representatives of the pueblo of Laguna, all the arable lands he owns in the rancho of El Rito, as well as those of the same kind owned by Don José Antonio Pino; also their interest as legal heirs in said rancho, for the value and sum of seventy-five sheep, one hundred skins of the standard quality of all classes, and six horned cattle, as follows: two oxen, one cow, two bulls, and one heifer; all of which the said representatives promised to deliver to Chaves y Baca as soon as possible, to his satisfaction; at which the vendor expressed himself, and does express himself, as satisfied and paid. And if said lands are or should be worth more, he donates and cedes the remainder to the aforesaid pueblo, to hold them for themselves, their children, heirs, and successors, in the free enjoyment of said arable lands, and no suit or litigation shall be commenced against them for said rancho, by themselves, their children, heirs, or successors, nor those of his father-in-law, as they now and forever renounce all their right and titles to said lands in favor of the purchasers, requesting the national justices to whom they may present themselves not to hear them either in court or out of court; and he further stated that he conveyed said arable lands and interests, free from all tax, tribute, or other incumbrance, being the lawful possessor of the same, as the legal heirs of Don Mateo José de el Pino, and without injury to the remaining heirs to said rancho, with the only condition that the crops for the present year shall belong to the vendor, the arable lands and interests being from this time the lawful property of the purchasers, for which object he relinquished his rights, as well as those of his client, in favor of the said pueblo of Laguna, as also his residence and vicinity, the vendor retaining no further interest in the rancho del Rito excepting the houses where they reside, situate thereupon. And for the fulfillment of this instrument the vendor pledged his personal property now held or in future acquired, with power and authority to the national justices to compel and require the fulfillment thereof in a summary manner, as by judgment, rendered by competent authority in a case duly tried, confessed, and not appealed, and on the present common paper, there being none of the proper stamp in this jurisdiction, the parties interested binding themselves to attach it hereto whenever they procure it. And in order that it may have the force and validity required by law, the said purchaser requested me to interpose my authority and judicial decree; and I, the aforesaid justice, stated that I would, and did interpose it with my attending witnesses, with whom I act by appointment in the absence of a notary public. To all of which I certify on said day, month, and year.

JUAN GARCIA.

Attending, FLORENTINE CASTILLO, JESUS M. BEITIN.

SURVEYOR GENERAL'S OFFICE, TRANSLATOR'S DEPARTMENT,
Santa Fé, New Mexico, June 29, 1859.

The above is a translation of the original on file in this office.

DAVID V. WHITING,
Translator.

SURVEYOR GENERAL'S OFFICE,
Santa Fé, New Mexico, August 25, 1859.

The foregoing is a true copy of the original on file in this office.

WM. PELHAM,
Surveyor General.

TESTIMONY.

JOSÉ GONZALES, sworn:

Question. Have you any interest in this case?
Answer. I have none.
Question. How old are you?
Answer. I believe I am forty years of age.
Question. Do you know the rancho called Palmate, adjoining Cebolleta; and how long have you known it?
Answer. I have known it since 1833.
Question. Who have possessed it from that time up to the present?
Answer. I am satisfied that it has never been occupied by any others than the Indians of Palmate, who are the same Indians residing at Laguna.
Question. Have the Indians held undisputed and undisturbed possession of it from the time you knew the land?
Answer. The right to it has never been disputed to my knowledge?
Question. Do you know the rancho called "El Rito"?

Answer. I have known it since 1842.

Question. Are the Laguna Indians in possession of that rancho; and for how long?

Answer. I know that they purchased in 1842 from the former settlers, and that they have been in possession from that time to this. I was also informed by the old settlers of Cebolleta that the Rito belonged formerly to Laguna, but that the Pinos had usurped their rights; and that the Indians had purchased what was actually their own before.

Question. Do you know the tract of the Gigante Cañon; and who has been in possession of it since you have known it?

Answer. I have known it since 1833; but I don't know who owns it. The land is used for pasture by the people of Laguna and Cebolleta.

Question. Do you know the rancho called "San Juan;" and who is in possession of it?

Answer. I have known it since 1833; it has always been in the possession of the Laguna Indians.

Question. Do you know the rancho of Santa Ana?

Answer. I have known it since 1842; it is occupied in whole or in part by the Laguna Indians; I do not know which is the line between the Acoma and Laguna Indians; both are upon the land; when I first knew the rancho the Laguna Indians alone held possession.

Question. Have you lived in the immediate vicinity of the lands since you have known them?

Answer. I have lived at the Cebolleta for five years; and previous to my removing to Cebolleta I lived at Ranchos. I am a Mexican citizen by birth.

The above testimony was taken in the presence of Col. I. L. Collins, superintendent of Indian affairs.

JOSÉ GONZALES.

Sworn and subscribed before me this 30th day of June, 1859.
WM. PELHAM,
Surveyor General.

JOSÉ FRANCISCO ARAGON, sworn:

Question. Have you any interest in this case?
Answer. I have none; I reside at Cebolleta.
Question. How old are you?
Answer. Forty-nine years old.
Question. Do you know the rancho of Palmate; and who has possession of it?

Answer. I have known it since 1820; the Pueblo of Laguna has held undisputed possession up to this time.

Question. Do you know the rancho of El Rito? who has occupied it?

Answer. I have known it since 1820; it was first owned by the Riteños, and afterwards purchased by the Laguna Indians, who have held undisputed possession from that time to this. I do not know its boundaries.

Question. Do you know the Gigante Cañon?
Answer. I do; it is used by the whole neighborhood for pasture ground.
Question. Do you know the rancho of San Juan?
Answer. I have known it since 1820; it has been held by the Laguna Indians since that time; I do not know its boundaries.
Question. Do you know the rancho of Santa Ana?
Answer. I have known it for the same period of time; it has always been occupied by the Laguna Indians.

JOSÉ FRANCISCO ARAGON.

Sworn and subscribed before me this 30th day of June, 1859.
WM. PELHAM,
Surveyor General.

Rev. SAMUEL GORMAN, sworn:
Question. Do you know the rancho of Palmate? if so, state its limits to the best of your knowledge.
Answer. I do; on the north a little mountain called the Gabitan; on the east the Cap Cañon; on the south the Old Spring, the boundary of the pueblo; on the west the Rito of San José.
Question. What are the boundaries of El Rito?
Answer. I do not know.

SAM. GORMAN.

Sworn and subscribed before me this 30th day of June, 1859.
WM. PELHAM,
Surveyor General.

SURVEYOR GENERAL'S OFFICE,
Santa Fé, New Mexico, August 28, 1859.

The foregoing is a true copy of the original on file in this office.
WM. PELHAM,
Surveyor General.

REPORT.

The Pueblo of Laguna vs. The United States.

SURVEYOR GENERAL'S OFFICE,
Santa Fé, New Mexico, July 10, 1859.

This case was set for trial on the 30th day of June, 1859.

The Indians of the Pueblo of Laguna claim title to certain tracts of land, in the vicinity and adjoining the league granted them by order of the King of Spain in 1689. One of these tracts was acquired by grant and purchase, and for the others they claim a possessory title.

Document A, filed by the claimants, is a statement, made at the request of the Indians of Laguna, by José Manuel Aragon, chief justice and war captain of the Pueblos of Acoma, Laguna, Cebolleta, and its districts, upon his resignation of the above office, which he had held for twenty years, to the effect that he was present during the several visits made by the governors of the province to said Pueblo, and that in consequence of the scarcity of lands within their league they were allowed to extend their fields as far as they could plant, for their maintenance. The land which they were allowed to cultivate, as above-mentioned, is known as the rancho of Pagnaste, and purchased by them subsequently from José Francisco Chaves y Baca, his own share, and of his father-in-law, José Antonio Pino, as will appear by document C; and also states that the Indians occupied the tract known as El Rito, and also the rancho known as San Juan, for pasture lands. On the west they also had the rancho of Cabero, which they used in common with the residents of that town; and a mile distant from the Pueblo, in a westwardly direction, they also occupied a rancho known as Santa Ana. This document bears date the 25th of March, 1813. On the 28th of August, 1826, it was approved and made legal and formal by Governor Narbona, as will appear by his certificate attached to document A.

Document B purports to be a statement made by Eusebio Aragon, to the effect that he was a witness to the establishment of certain boundaries of the Pagnasti rancho, by Ignasio Sanches Virgan, protector of the Indians, in 1820, which boundaries had been omitted in the deed made in 1769. Also that the Indians had been deprived of the best lands within that tract by Juan Pino, as the legal representative of his grandfather, to whom the land had been granted, but which had been abandoned for over thirty years.

This document also bears the confirmation of Governor Narbona, and is declared legal and formal, and bears the same date as the confirmation of document A.

Document C is the conveyance of the interest of Juan Pino, in the Pagnasti rancho, to the Indians, as above stated.

Evidence has been produced by the claimants to prove their quiet and undisturbed possession of the land, from the year 1820 up to the present time.

The papers acted upon by this office are the originals, filed by the claimants.

In the absence of any conflicting grant or claims to the land claimed by the Indians, the approval of Governor Narbona to the statements made in documents A and B, and their legalization by him, is deemed to be equivalent to a grant made to said Indians; and, although it is not in exact accordance with the usages and customs of the time, it is believed that the Indians have a good and equitable claim to the land, which is sustained by the fact of their having been in the uninterrupted possession of it for the period of forty years, as well as the fact of the boundary of Cebolleta, the site of which was granted in 1800, being the same as the one claimed by the Indians, showing conclusively that their claim was recognized as good by the government at that time.

The tracts known as the rancho of Pagnaste, rancho of El Rito, the tract known as the Gigante Cañon, and the rancho of San Juan and

PRIVATE LAND CLAIMS IN NEW MEXICO.   167

Santa Ana, are deemed to be severed from the public domain, and are therefore approved to the Indian Pueblo of Laguna, and ordered to be transmitted to Congress for its action in the premises.

WM. PELHAM,
Surveyor General.

Surveyor General's Office,
Santa Fé, New Mexico, August 25, 1859.

The foregoing is a true copy of the original, on file in this office.

WM. PELHAM,
Surveyor General.

GRANT—SPANISH.

En el Pueblo de Nuestra Sna. de Guadalupe del Passo del Pro. del Norte en veinte y cinco dias del mes de Setiembre de mil seiscientos y ochenta y nueve años, ante mi el Señor governador y capitan general Don Domingo Jironza y Petroz de Cruzate dijo, que por cuanto en el alcanze de su facultad que tiene en el de la Nueva Mexico y el poder en los Indios Queres y los Apostatas y los Teguas y de la nacion Thanos, y que despues de haber peleado con todos los demas Indios de todos Pueblos, un Indio llamado Bartolome de Ojeda que fue el que mas se senalo ele la batalla acudiendo a todas partes se rindio viendose herido de un balaso y un flechaso y lla baldadi le mandaron prender ehize le curazen con mucho cuydado para que sea examinado y diga en su confesion, el estado en que   *   *   *   *   *
demas Apostatas de aquel reyno y por que el Indio es ladino en lengua castellana y capaz y ge save leer y escriber y que fue el habia entrado en aquel Pres. el Gen. Don Pedro Penero de Possada y viniendo ya de vuelta para este paraje y estando en la casa del Miso. de campo Baningnas Mendoza lla viniendo de regreso del Pres. lo Alcanzo Bartolome de Ojeda pues lla dho Indio es puesto en mi presencia y que debajo de juramento declare como se llama.

Preguntado que si esta en disposicion de conferar la verdad en lo que supiere que le fuere preguntado   *   *   *   *

Preguntado como se llama, de donde es natural que edad y oficio tiene y que diga como se alla la Laguna; y dijo el confesante que se llama Bartolomo de Ojeda y que es natural de la provincia de la Neuva Mexico en el pubo. de Zeá y que tendra de edad de veinte y como a veinte y dos años poco mas, poco menos y que no ha tenido mas oficio que el ejercicio de la ga. y que save como se alla la laguna y que fue que fue apostata en el reyno de la Nueva Mexico y esto responde preguntado que de ha donde eran los lagunas que vecinos del Puo. de Acoma se allan y que compromiso tubieron; y dize el comfesante que eran de todos pueblos pero que la mayor parte eran de la nacion queres y que en el alzamiento ya hacin algunos años que estaba poblandose, pera que el pueblo de acoma   *   *   *   m   *   cho poblado primero la laguna—y este responde.   *   *   *   *

Preguntado que si este Puo. volvera en algun tiempo á apostatarse, como ha sido costumbre entre ellos y dize el confesante que no, que ya muy metido en temor que aunque estaban los Indios mui abilantado y habia sido un Pueblo mui revelde, pero que con lo que les havia susedido en el Pueblo de Zia el año pasado jusgaba que era un imposible que no dieron la obediencia, y esto responde.

Preguntado si tiene mas que decir del Pueblo de Laguna que vecino se alla del Pueblo de Acoma y dize el confesante, que tiene dicho es la verdad que á el mismo se lo habian contado ambos das Pueblos el de Acoma y el de Laguna y que todo el manejo y costumbre no lo ignoraba y esto responde.

Preguntado cuales son los linderos que consta tener la Laguna y á donde se sugetaron las Indios cuando se agregaron al Pueblo de Acoma y dice el confesante que la Laguna quedo sujeto al norte al ojo de la agua fria y que ha este ojo le llamaban Paguate, y al oriente la mesita Colorada que da virtu á donde el sol sale y a la mesita Piedras de á molar y que al poniente tiene la cañada ancha que reclama al norte cuando llueve que al sur leagua que queda de bajo de una peña y este responde.

Preguntado que si sabe mas de la que ha dicho; y dize el confesante que no, que lo que tiene dicho es la verdad por el juramente que tiene echo en que se afirmo y ratifico por muchas veces y siendole leida y dada á entender esta merced y lo firmo * * * * * * mi el presente * * * de Gov. y guerra que de ello doy fe.

BARTOLOME DE OJEDA.

DOMINGO JIRONZA,
P. Strar de Cruzate.

Ante mi,
DON PEDRO LANDRON DE GUITARA.
Seo. Degn. y Gura.

SURVEYOR GENERAL'S OFFICE, TRANSLATOR'S DEPARTMENT,
Santa Fé, New Mexico, August 25, 1859.

The foregoing is a true copy of the original on file in this office.
DAVID V. WHITING,
Translator.

GRANT—TRANSLATION.

Year 1689.—At the town of our lady of Guadalupe del Paso del Rio del Norte, on the twenty-fifth day of the month of September, one thousand six hundred and eighty-nine, before me, Don Domingo Jironza y Petroz de Cruzate, governor and captain general, stated that whereas, by virtue of the authority vested in him over New Mexico, and power of the Queres Indians, and the Apostates and the Teguas, and those of the Thanos nation, and that after having fought with all the other Indians of all the Pueblos, an Indian named Bartolome de Ojeda, who distinguished himself the most in the battle, lending his aid everywhere, surrendered, having been wounded with a ball and an arrow, and after being wounded he was ordered to be seized, and I caused him to be healed with much care, so that he could be examined, and could state in his confession the condition [torn] and other apostates of that kingdom, and because the Indian is well versed in the Spanish language and apt, and understands how to read and write, and the same who conducted General Don Pedro Venero de Passada to that pueblo, who being on his return to this place, and having stopped at the house of Field Marshal Barengues, Mendoza Bartolome de Ojeda overtook him. Said Indian having now been brought before me, he was ordered to state under oath what his name was.

Questioned. If he is disposed to confess the truth in what he knows and should be asked?

Questioned. What is his name? where he is a native of? what age, and what is his occupation? and to state what is the condition of Laguna.

And the deponent answered: That his name is Bartolome de Ojeda; that he is a native of the pueblo of Zia, in the province of New Mexico; that he is twenty-one or twenty-two years of age; that he has never had any other occupation than that of a warrior; that he knows the condition of Laguna, that apostatized in the kingdom of New Mexico; and this is his answer.

Questioned. Where the Lagunas came from? who are the neighbors of the Acomas, and what compromise took place between them?

And the deponent answered: That they were from all pueblos, but that the greater portion were of the Queres nation; and that in the rebellion which occurred several years previous, that it was becoming inhabited, but that the pueblo of Acoma had settled upon it some time before; and this is his answer.

Questioned. If this pueblo will at any future time rebel again, as it was customary for them to do?

The deponent answered: That they would not, that they are very much intimidated; that although they were a very haughty people, and had been a very rebellious people, but that with what had happened to the pueblo of Zia during the year previous he judged that it would be impossible for them to fail in giving their allegiance; and this is his answer.

Questioned. If he has anything further to say in regard to Laguna, which is near the pueblo of Acoma?

And the deponent answered: That what he stated was the truth; that he himself had been so informed by both pueblos, those of Acoma as well as those of Laguna, and that he was not ignorant of the arrangement and the custom; and this is his answer.

Questioned. Which are the known boundaries of Laguna, and what bounds did they retain when they joined the pueblo of Acoma?

And the deponent answered: That Laguna was restricted on the north to the Agua Fria spring, and that spring is called Pagnaste; and to the east the Mesita Colorado, towards the rising of the sun, and to the little table land of Piedras de Armolar; and that towards the west they have to the Cañada Ancha, which empties towards the north when it rains, and on the south to a water which is under a rock; and this is his answer.

Questioned. If he knows more than what he has stated?

And the deponent answered: That he did not; that what he has stated is the truth, under the oath which he has taken, which he affirmed and ratified several times.

And this grant having been read and explained to him, [torn] me, the present secretary of government and war, to which I certify.

DOMINGO JIRONZA PETROZ DE CRUZATE.

BARTOLOME DE OJEDA.

Before me,
DON PEDRO LADRON DE GUITARA,
Secretary of Government and War.

SURVEYOR GENERAL'S OFFICE, TRANSLATOR'S DEPARTMENT,
Santa Fé, New Mexico, August 1, 1859.

The foregoing is a translation of the original on file in this office.
DAVID V. WHITING,
Translator.

SURVEYOR GENERAL'S OFFICE,
Santa Fé, New Mexico, August 31, 1859.

The above is a true copy of the original on file in this office.
WM. PELHAM,
Surveyor General.

CLAIM NO. 31.

GASPAR ORTIZ.

Schedule of Documents comprising Claim No. 31.

1. Notice.
2. Grant—Spanish.
3. Grant—translation.
4. Testimony.
5. Report.

NOTICE.

UNITED STATES OF AMERICA, } ss:
Territory of New Mexico. }

To the Surveyor General of New Mexico:

Gaspar Ortiz, a citizen of the United States and resident of the county of Santa Fé, New Mexico, respectfully represents that he is the claimant and legal owner in fee of a certain tract of land lying and being situate in the county of Santa Fé, in said Territory, and known and bounded as follows, to wit: lying east of the pueblo of Nambe, and bounded on the north by an arroyo seco, (dry run,) on the south by the lands of Bernardo de Sena, on the east by a mountain, on the west by the lands of the Indian pueblo of Nambe; and the said Gaspar Ortiz, the present claimant, claims a perfect title to said land by virtue of a grant made on the twenty-fifth of September, A. D. 1739, by Gaspar Domingo y Mendoza, governor and captain general of the Spanish province of New Mexico, which said grant was made as aforesaid by authority of the laws, usages and customs of the then Spanish province; for which power and authority see collection of the decrees and orders of the Cortes of Spain, published in Mexico by Martino Galvan, in 1829, page 56, and from page 91 to 101. The said Gaspar Ortiz, claimant, further states that he cannot show the quantity of land claimed by him except as set forth in said grant, as within the above described well known metes and boundaries, nor can he furnish a plat of the survey, as no survey has ever been executed. Claimant knows of no adverse claimant to said land; claimant further states that by virtue of said grant Vicente Duran y Armijo was lawfully put in possession of said tract of land by competent authority, and said Vicente Duran de Armijo retained and occupied said lands until about the year A. D. — he sold and disposed of the same to Gaspar Ortiz, the grandfather of the present claimant, under whom your present claims. The claimant further states that the deed or document from the said Vicente Duran y Armijo to the said Gaspar Ortiz has been lost or destroyed. Claimant files this his said claim before you under the 8th section of the act of Congress approved 22d July, 1854, entitled "An act to establish the offices of Surveyor General of New Mexico, Kansas, and Nebraska, to grant donations to actual settlers therein and for other purposes," and respectfully asks confirmation by you of his said claim.

M. ASHURST,
Attorney for Claimant.

SURVEYOR GENERAL'S OFFICE,
Santa Fé, New Mexico, September 10, 1859.

The above is a true copy of the original on file in this office.

WM. PELHAM, *Surveyor General.*

GRANT—SPANISH.

Señor Gobernador y Capitan General:

Bisente Duran de Armijo, vecino de la villa de Santa Fé, poblador y conquistador de este reyno de la Nueva Mejico, puesto a los pies de Vssa. en tuda forma quel derecho me permite, y digo que habiendo experimentado inumerables trabajos y desdichas dehambres y desnuderes y otros menos cabas que hemos padecido en este probre reyno por ocasion de perder nuestro personal trabajo en nuestros sembrados

de trigos y maises canque poder mantener nuestras obligaciones causado en algunos años de la falta de agua no . . . .
dicha vilta por no llover á tiempo donde no tenemos el afan nuestro personal trabajor y hallandome en este reyno de poblador desde el año de noventa y cuatro, siempre ha prontado de todas armas y caballos á mi costa para las campañas y albaros que se han ofresido como leal vasallo de su Mgtd. que Dios guarde, este Señor, ha sido asi siempre en merito de haber seguido al ejercito que ha salido á dichas campañas y albaros que se han dado a las barbaras naciones que habitan por estas partes de este reyno oy Señor con me deligencia tengo algun corriente con salir á la tierra afuera, aunque con bastante peligro de la vida, donde me reo con algun ganado mayor y este no tenerlo seguro de las naciones barbaras que habitan en algunas ocasiones por donde suele comer dicho ganado y es carmentado de dos bacas greel enemigo me mato este presente año, he tenido por bien de haber registrado nu pedago de tierras que san sobras de los Indios Amigos de el pueblo de Nambe no estorbando los partos ni aguas para que á parte la caballada de este real presidio, ni menos para las bestias, de los dichos Indios ni para ninguna persona que dicho, pedazo de tierras, en el cabra seis fanegas de trigo y dos de mais y sus linderos san los siguientes. Por el Norte linda con una allo seco, por el sur con tierras de Bernardo de Zena por el oriente con una sierra, por el poniente con tierras de los dichos Indios de Nambe. Este pedazo de tierras en nombre del Rey nuestro Señor que Dios guarde . . . .
cuatro familias que tengo mansipadas hijos mi os que en el pedazo de tierras que en esta dicha villa tengo no es suficiente para todos que de consederme dicho pedazo de tierras padremas lagrar nuestro trabajo y tendre mi ganado seguro de el enemigo y que sea con partas y abrevaderos y se me de posecion real en nombre de su Majestad y juro en debida forma no ser de malisin este mi escripto, &c.

BISENTE DURAN DE ARMIJO.

Posecion real.

En la villa de Santa Fé, cabezera de este reyno de la Nueva Mexico en veinte y cinco dias del mes de Setiembre de mil sietecientos treinta y nueve, yo Don Gaspar Domingo de Mendoza, gobernador y capitan general de dicho reyno, por su Magd., que Dios le gde., visto este lo hube por presentado y en atencion á su contenido mande de se le de la posecion de tierras que pide el suplicante, no obstante de este no debe ser las que sisstan en el escripto, por haber habido oposicion en los Indios del pueblo inmediato a las tierras que pide, sin embargo de haber hecho venir á mi presencia á los Indios de dicho pueblo, los que se conformaran delante del suplicante y á vista de que eran gustosos se le diesen las tierras en aquellas cercanias de sa pueblo en donde dixeran no recibir ningun perjuicio por lo que ordeno y mando al alcalde mayor de la jurisdicion, en donde corresponde, pare á darle posecion de dichos tierras en nombre de su Magd. para que las pueble, cultivo, y beneficie como previenen las reales ordenes, para si, sus hijos herederos subsesores y quien mas derecho tenga, formandole estos linderos con todas las circunstancias que se requieren en lo tocante á las mercedes reales, para que precediendo estas circunstancias se obien todas las inconvenientes que en lo futuro pueden afreserse. Asi lo prove y firme y mande con los testigos de mi assistencia actuando por receptoria á falta de Gorio. real y publico que no hay en este reyno, y en el papel comun por no correr el sellado, &c.

DON GASPAR DOMINGO DE MENDOZA.

Testigos : DIEGO DE VAGARETE.
JOSEPH DE TERRUS.

En cinco dias del mes de Octubre de este presento año de mil siete cientas treinta y nueve, yo el alcalde mayor y capitan de guerra de la villa Nueva de Santa Cruz y sus distritos en cumplimiento del auto del Señor Gobernador y Capitan General Don Gaspar Domingo de Mendoza pasé el Pueblo de Nambe pertenesiente á esta mi jurisdicion tlevando en mi compania cinco testigos para que la fuesen y sirviesen los tres de instrumentales y los dos de mi assa. Con quienes actue y presentes estos con las, Ptes. de Bizente Duran de Armijo el Casique y viejos naturales del dicho Pueblo con el Gobernador y de mas justicias del espresado Pueblo de Nambe les lei el escripto antecedente que presento, Bizente Duran de Armijo y asi mismo les lie en vozes altas éintelegibles el proveimto de dicho Señor Gobernador y Capitan General en que su Señoria determina y manda que se la de la posecion de tierras que pide el suplicante Pero despues attendiendo a que los Indios del referido pueblo hisseran aposicion, á que les hera la pueste de tierras que el suplicante pedia, de mucha perjuicio aunque no eran pertenentes á el pueblo, que de buena voluntad querian darle á dicho Bicente Duran de Armijo una pueste de tierras pr. el sus hijos herederos y subsessores de las mismos del pueblo pr. ó aquellas que pedia y que les fuese de menos contra peso ó perjuicio. En cuyo atentacion su Señoria prover no sean las que zita il dicho. pedimiento y di las que par convenio de dicho Indias se la señalaren. E yo dicho alcalde mayor como dicho dejo, juntos todos los hijos del referida pueblo y enterados del orden de su señoria y de todo lo que dejaran tratado con dicho Bicente en presencia de dicho Señor Gobernador y Capitan General dijeran que le señalaban como señalaran á dicho Vicente Duran de Armijo un pedazo de tierras al poniente de dicho pueblo de Nambe en los fines de sus tierras que por dicho viento poniente linda un pedazito con tierras del pueblo de Pujuaque cuyo lindero es un aroyo hondo que baja del Rio de Nambe este es de la Vanda del Sur de dicho Rio de Nambe y porel oriente con una majanera de piedras y un Sabino mediano que es division de las tierras del Pueblo y de derecho Bicente y por el norte linda este pedazito con dicha rio y por el sur con la zegnia que corre a el pie de unas lomas peladas que consta de tres cordeles de a cincuenta varas desde el referido rio a la dicha zegnia y el pedazo de tierra que lo dieron a dicho armijo que esta al norte de dicho rio consta de siete cientos y cuarenta varas de latitud las que seden a entender de oriente a poniente, y de norte a sur consta de quinientas y cincuenta varas cuyos linderos san por el norte unas majoneras de piedras que van por entre unas lomas peladas que van a dar y lindan con tierras del Gen. Don Juan Paez Hurtado y por el sur linda con el rio de dicho pueblo ; por el oriente es lindero una craz que esta a un lado del camino real y tierras de dichos Indios de el dicho pueblo y por el poniente linda con tierras del Gen. Don Juan Paez Hurtado, que quedaron senalados con varas montones de piedras y en uno de ellos una Santa Cruz que sera la division y lindero en cuyos dichas tierras de uno y otro pedazos de tierras le metí en posecion Real en Nombre de su magd. que Dios gde. y en señal de dicha posecion le caji por la mano, la pasée por dicho sitio, tiro piedras aranco zacate y dio voges apellidando. Viva el Rey en cuyo Nombre le deje en quieta y pacifica posecion y ofrecio cultivar y poblar segun manden las Rey Ordenes sola pena de perder el derecho a ellos como su magd. mande en sus Reales Ordenanza, y para que conste de dicha posecion y consentimiento y convenio que tubreran con dicho Bicente de Armijo los referidos Indios, doy fé haber pasado asi y lo firme con los testigos infra escriptos de mi assistencia, siendo los instrumentales Antonio Truzillo, Tomas Madrid y Gregorio Garduno, que fue el que elijieron el casique y justys del dicho pueblo para que a su ruego firmase para ellos por no saberlo hacer ninguno de los naturales, y como dicho es lo actuo y firme con los dichos de mi assistencia a falta del Srio. Publico ó Real que no le hay en este reyno, y en el presente papel comun por no correr en estas partes el sellado. De todo doy fé.

JUAN GARCIA DE MORA,
Juez Receptor.

Testigo: FRANCISCO GARDUÑO,
NICOLAS ORTIZ.

Aruego de los naturales de este pueblo de Nambe.
GREGORIO GARDUÑO.

Marginal note.

Santa Fé, cinco de Octbre de mil siete cientos treinta y nueva años. Queda cupiado en mi libro de gobierno que para en el archibo de esta capital a fin de que conste quando contienga, &c.
MENDOZA.

SURVEYOR GENERAL'S OFFICE,
Santa Fé, New Mexico, August 25, 1859.

The foregoing is a true copy of the original on file in this office.
DAVID V. WHITING,
Translator.

GRANT—TRANSLATION.

To His Excellency the Governor, Captain General:

Vincente Duran de Armijo, resident of the town of Santa Fé, and settler and conqueror of the kingdom of New Mexico, appears at your excellency's feet in the most approved manner the law allows, and states: That having experienced innumerable sufferings, and hunger, and nakedness, and other misfortunes we have undergone in this poor kingdom, on account of having lost our personal labor in our corn and wheat fields, with which we were to meet our obligations, owing to the scarcity of water in the river running through the city, which arises from the absence of rain for some time back, and our personal labor bestowed upon our grain crops being useless, as they have all failed; and having been one of the settlers of this kingdom from the year '94, and always ready armed and equipped at my own expense to go upon any campaign or expedition whenever required as a loyal subject of his Majesty, whom may God preserve; this, sir, has always been—[torn]—having been in the army which has gone on said campaigns and expeditions against the hostile Indians who inhabit these parts of this kingdom at this time. Sir, I have by my exertions accumulated a little capital with a great risk of my life, by making journeys to the outer country, and have become the owner of a certain amount of stock which is not secure from the hostile attacks of the Indians, who on certain occasions inhabit the country where my stock is pastured; and I have taken warning from two cows belonging to me which have been killed by the enemy during the present year. I have seen proper to register a piece of land which is a surplus beyond the lands of the friendly Indians of the Pueblo of Nambe, without disturbing the pastures or waters upon which the herds of this royal garrison or the animals of the aforesaid Indians are pastured, nor any other person that (uses) said lands. It contains about six fanegas of wheat and two of corn, and its boundaries are as follows: On the north it is bounded by a dry gulch, (arroya;) on the south by lands of Bernardo de Sena; on the east by a mountain; on the west by lands of the aforementioned Indians of Nambe. This piece of land in the name of the king, our sovereign, whom may God preserve—[torn]—four families whom I have emancipated—my children, that the piece of land in this city is not sufficient for all; and by granting us the aforesaid land we may receive some benefit from our labor, and my cattle will be secure from the enemy to be with pastures and watering places, and that royal permission be given to me in the name of his Majesty; and I swear in due form that this, my petition, is not made through malice, &c.

VICENTE DURAN DE ARMIJO.

Royal possession.

In the city of Santa Fé, capital of the kingdom of New Mexico, on the twenty-fifth day of September, in the year one thousand seven hundred and thirty-nine, I, Don Gaspar Domingo de Mendoza, governor and captain general of said kingdom by his Majesty, (whom may God preserve,) having seen the above, considered it as presented, and having ascertained its contents, I ordered that possession be given to the petitioner of the land he solicits. It is not, however, the lands he mentions in his petition, the Indians of the adjoining pueblo having objected to his having the land he asks for; although I caused the Indians of said pueblo to appear before me, who before the petitioner declared themselves pleased that the land should be given to him in the vicinity of their pueblo where no injury would result to them. Therefore, I order and direct the senior justice of the proper jurisdiction to proceed to place him in possession of said lands in the name of his Majesty, in order that he may settle upon, cultivate, and improve them according to the royal decrees, for himself, children, heirs, successors, and others having a better right thereto; establishing his boundaries with all the formalities required in royal grants, so that by virtue of these formalities all difficulties may be prevented in the future. I so provided, signed, and ordered with my attending witnesses, acting by appointment in the absence of a royal or public notary, there being none in this kingdom, and on this common paper, there being none stamped.

DON GASPAR DOMINGO DE MENDOZA.

Witnesses:
DIEGO DE UGARTE.
JOSEPH DE TERRUS.

On the fifth day of the month of October of the present year, one thousand seven hundred and thirty-nine, I, the senior justice and war captain of the new city of Santa Cruz and its districts, by virtue of the decree of his excellency the Governor and Captain General, Don Gaspar Domingo de Mendoza, I proceeded to the pueblo of Nambe, within my jurisdiction, taking with me five witnesses to act in that capacity, and three of whom were to act as instrumental and two as my attending witnesses with whom I acted, and these being present with the parties Vicente Duran de Armijo and the casique (war chief) and old men, natives of said pueblo, with the governor and other authorities of the aforesaid pueblo of Nambe, I read to them the foregoing document presented by Vicente Duran de Armijo. I also read to them, in a clear and audible voice, the provisions made by the said governor and captain general, where his excellency directs and orders that possession be given to him of the lands the petition asks for, but afterwards the Indians of the aforementioned pueblo, having made opposition on the ground that the granting of the land asked for by the petitioner would be a great injury to them, although it did not belong to the pueblo, they voluntarily agreed to give to the said Vicente Duran de Armijo a piece of land for himself, his children, heirs, and successors from the lands of the pueblo, in the place of that he asked for, and which would be so much to their injury. In view of which, his excellency provides that he shall not have the lands he asks for, but that which may be selected with the consent of said Indians, and I, the said senior justice, as aforesaid, all the natives of the aforesaid pueblo being present and informed of his excellency's order, and of all that had been agreed upon with the said Vicente in the presence of the said governor and captain general, they stated that they would assign, and did assign, to the said Vicente Duran de Armijo a piece of land to the west of said pueblo of Nambe, on the borders of their lands; that on the said western side a small portion is bounded by lands of the pueblo of Pajaoque, whose boundary is a dry gulch (arroyo) that runs into the Nambe river, that is on the southern side of said river of Nambe, and on the east by a stone mound and a medium sized cedar, which is the boundary between the pueblo and the said Vicente; and on the north this little piece is bounded by said river, and on the south by a ditch, (acequia,) which runs along the foot of some barren hills, the distance being cords of fifty varas each from the river aforesaid to the said acequia; and the large piece of land which they gave to the said Armijo, which is north of said river, contains seven hundred and forty varas in latitude, which is understood to be from east to west, and from north to south it contains five hundred and fifty varas; the boundaries of which are: on the north some stone mounds scattered along some barren hills, which form the boundary of the lands of General Don Juan Paez Hurtado, and on the south is bounded by the river of said pueblo; on the east the boundary is a cross, on the side of the main road and lands of the Indians of said town; and on the west lands of General Juan Paez de Hurtado, which boundaries were marked by several mounds of stone, and on one of them is a holy cross, which is to serve as a boundary and division, of which two pieces of land I gave him royal possession. I took him by the hand, and walked with him over said lands. He threw stones, pulled up grass, and cried aloud, saying long life to the king, in whose royal name I left him in quiet and peaceable possession; and he offered to cultivate and settle the same, as directed by royal decrees, under penalty of forfeiture, as directed by his Majesty in his royal orders; and in order that said possession and the consent and agreement had with the said Vicente de Armijo by the aforesaid Indians be placed upon record, I certify that such has been the case, and I signed, with my undersigned attending witnesses, Antonio Tullio, Thomas Madrid, and Gregorio Garduno, being instrumental; the last having been selected by the casique and authorities of the pueblo at their request to sign for them, name of the aforesaid Indians, knowing not how to do so themselves; and as aforestated I so acted, and signed with those in my attendance in the absence of a royal or public notary, there being none in this kingdom, and on this common paper, the stamp not being in use in these parts; to all of which I certify.

JUAN GARCIA DE MORA,
Acting Justice.

Witnesses:
NICOLAS ORTIZ.
FRANCO GARDUÑO.

At the request of the natives of the pueblo of Nambe.
GREGORIO GARDUÑO.

SURVEYOR GENERAL'S OFFICE,
Santa Fé, New Mexico, September 7, 1859.

The above is a true copy of the original on file in this office.
WM. PELHAM,
Surveyor General.

H. Ex. Doc. 14——12

TESTIMONY.

PEDRO RAFAEL TRUJILLO sworn:

Question. Have you any interest in this case?
Answer. I have none.
Question. How old are you?
Answer. I am eighty years old; was born in the year 1779.
Question. Did you know Vicente Duran de Armijo?
Answer. I did not.
Question. Did you know Gaspar Ortiz, the grandfather of the present claimant?
Answer. I did.
Question. Was the grandfather of Gaspar Ortiz, the present claimant, ever in possession of the land formerly owned by Vicente Duran de Armijo, and did he live upon it, and did he build there?
Answer. He lived there and built a house there; I knew it well; he also cultivated the land; he lived there from the year 1789 until 1824, when he died; it was always known as his property; it has been occupied by him and his heirs continuously up to the present time.
Question. Did you ever see a document in the possession of the grandfather of the present claimant, executed by Vicente Duran de Armijo, conveying the land he occupied?
Answer. I did not.

PEDRO RAFAEL TRUJILLO.

Sworn to and subscribed before me this 30th June, 1859.
WM. PELHAM,
Surveyor General.

ANTONIO QUINTANCE sworn:

Question. Have you any interest in this case?
Answer. None.
Question. How old are you?
Answer. I am in my 81st year.
Question. Did you know Vicente Duran de Armijo?
Answer. I did not know him.
Question. Did you know Gaspar Ortiz, the grandfather of the present claimant?
Answer. I knew him well.
Question. Do you know the land owned formerly by Vicente Duran de Armijo, and subsequently by the grandfather of the present claimant?
Answer. I do; it is adjoining the league of the pueblo of Nambe to the boundary of the Bernardin de Sena.
Question. Did the grandfather of the present claimant occupy the lands formerly owned by Vicente Duran, and how long did he occupy them continuously?
Answer. He did; I do not know how long; it has been in the continuous possession of the grandfather of the present claimant and his heirs up to the present time.

Question. Who were the heirs of Gaspar Ortiz, the present claimant?

Answer. Gaspar Ortiz, the late Nicolas Ortiz, his daughters who are dead, and Roman Sena, Faustin Ortiz, Juan Louis Ortiz, and many others.

Question. Did you ever have in your possession or see a deed executed by Vicente Duran, in favor of Gaspar Ortiz, for the lands now in question?

Answer. I have seen the deed; I believe the deed was made about seventy-five years ago; I have seen it several times.

Question. When did you last see the deed, and in whose hands was it?

Answer. I saw it in Gaspar Ortiz's hands about thirty years ago; Gaspar Ortiz called me to see his papers; I was induced to ask for a piece of land which the Indians claimed; in order to be certain that it was public land I examined Ortiz's papers, and found it was his land.

ANTONIO ^{his} ⋈ QUINTANCE.
mark.

This witness is so old he cannot see to write his name.

WHITING,
Clerk.

Sworn to and subscribed before me this 30th June, 1859.

WM. PELHAM,
Surveyor General.

SURVEYOR GENERAL'S OFFICE,
Santa Fé, New Mexico, September 9, 1859.

The above is a true copy of the original on file in this office.

WM. PELHAM,
Surveyor General.

REPORT.

GASPAR ORTIZ, PRESENT CLAIMANT, vs. THE UNITED STATES.

This case was set for trial on the 30th day of June, 1859.

Gaspar Ortiz claims a title to a tract of land, by virtue of an agreement made by Gaspar Domingo de Mendoza on the 25th September, 1739, to Vicente Duran de Armijo, and possession given by him on the fifth of October of the same year by Juan Garcia de Mora, senior justice and war captain of the town of Santa Cruz. It has been proven in evidence by the present claimant that his grandfather, Gaspar Ortiz, purchased the land claimed from Vicente Duran de Armijo, and that himself and his heirs have occupied the land continuously from the year 1789 up to the present time, and that the land was duly conveyed by an instrument in writing to the said Gaspar Ortiz, senior, and that the document has been lost or mislaid in such a manner as to prevent its being produced. The land has been quietly and peaceably held by the claimant and his ancestors, and is believed to be a good and valid grant; but as the chain of title from the original grantee to the present claimant, the claim *being* inchoate, it is approved to the legal representatives of Vicente Duran de Armijo, and ordered to be transmitted to Congress for its action in the premises.

WM. PELHAM,
Surveyor General.

SURVEYOR GENERAL'S OFFICE,
Santa Fé, New Mexico, July 2, 1859.

SURVEYOR GENERAL'S OFFICE,
Santa Fé, New Mexico, September 10, 1859.

The above is a true copy of the original on file in this office.

WM. PELHAM,
Surveyor General.

CLAIM No. 32.

TOWN OF MORA.

Documents composing claim No. 32.

1. Notice.
2. Grant, Spanish.
3. Grant, translation.
4. Receipt for deed, Spanish.
5. Receipt for deed, translation.
6. Testimony.
7. Report.

NOTICE.

UNITED STATES OF AMERICA,
Territory of New Mexico.

To the surveyor general of New Mexico:

José Ma. Valdez and Vincente Romero, on behalf of themselves and the other inhabitants, settlers of the valley of Mora, and those claiming under or deriving title under the original grant, respectfully represent to you that they are the claimants and legal owners in fee of a certain tract of land lying and being situate in the county of Taos, in said Territory of New Mexico, and known as the valley of Mora, and bounded on the north by the Rio de Ocate, on the east by the Aguage de la Llegua, on the south by the mouth of the Sapello, where it empties into the Rio de Mora, and on the west by the Estillero, all of which points and boundaries are well-known landmarks in the said county of Taos. And the said claimants claim a perfect title to said lands by virtue of a grant made on the twenty-eighth day of September, A. D. 1835, by Albino Peres, political chief of the Territory of New Mexico, but which said grant has been lost or destroyed, as also by virtue of being placed in actual legal possession of said lands, and occupying and cultivating said lands from said twenty-eighth day of September down to the present time, which said grant and occupation was made according to the laws, usages, and customs of the republic of Mexico, which were declared and recognized to be in force and effect at that time in the republic of Mexico, for which power and authority see Collection of the Decrees and Orders of the Cortes of Spain, published in Mexico by Martin Galvan, in 1829, page 56, and from pages 91 to 101; see also the decrees of Mexico of June 4 and September 18, 1823, pages 123 and 180 of 2d vol. of Galvan's Decrees; see Ordenanzas de Pierras y Aguas, and 8th Peters's Reports, 436, 15th Peters, 130, 1 Howard, 24, 6th Peters, 691, Holcomb's U. S. Digest, 358 to 363.

The present claimants cannot show the quantity of land embraced in the said grant except as therein set forth, as within the above well-known metes and boundaries, nor can they furnish a plat of survey, as no survey has ever been executed. Claimants know of no adverse claim to said grant, and further state that the original grantees, under whom the present claimants claim, were legally put in possession of said lands, and have held the undisturbed possession down to the present time.

Claimants file this their said claim under the 8th section of the act of Congress approved 22d July, 1854, entitled "An act to establish the offices of surveyor general of New Mexico, Kansas, and Nebraska, to grant donations to actual settlers therein, and for other purposes," and respectfully ask confirmation by you of this their said claim.

M. ASHURST,
Attorney for Claimants.
JACKSON, *for Claimants.*

NOTE.—The present claimants hereby relinquish all right and interest they may have in and to a grant made to John Scolly and others, made on the 7th day of May, 1846, and approved on the 15th of August, 1859, by the surveyor general of New Mexico, so far as the said grant conflicts with this grant.

M. ASHURST, *for Claimants.*
JACKSON, *for Claimants.*

SURVEYOR GENERAL'S OFFICE,
Santa Fé, New Mexico, August 20, 1859.
The above is a true copy of the original on file in this office.
WILLIAM PELHAM,
Surveyor General.

GRANT—SPANISH.

Sello Tercero. [SEAL.] Dos Reales.

Para los años de mil ochocientos cuarenta y mil ochocientos cuarenta y uno.

VALE UN PESO EL PLIEGO.

En veinte de Octubre de mil ochocientos treinta y cinco, yo Manuel Antonio Sanches alcalde constitucional de la jurisdiccion de San José de Las Trampas, con los testigos de mi asistencia con quienes actuo por receptoria; en cumplimiento al superior decreto del Sor. gefe politico del Territorio Don Albino Perez, fecha 28 de Septiembre de este mismo año, pase al punto de lo Demora jurisdiccion de mi cargo, con el fin de repartier este sitio baldio segun lo dispuesto en el referido superior decreto; y estando en el presentes los interesados pobladores que son en numero de setenta y seis cuidanos, se le puso por ubicacion al valle de abajo, valle de Santa Gertrudes, y al de arriba valle de San Antonio: y en el nombre de la nacion Mejicana y de esta municipalidad se brizo el señalamiento de plasas en uno y otros valles, siendo la de Santa Gertrudes de norte a sur al docientas varas, y de oriente a poniente ciento y cincuenta varas, dejando treinta varas afuera para chorreras y pisos de todos, y la veja para beneficio comun con sus entradas y salidas libres la plaza de San Antonio es de norte a sur de docientas varas, y de oriente a poniente ciento y cuicuenta varas quedando la cienega para beneficio comun de los pobladores, con las entradas y salidas por el norte la cañada de los Comanches, por el sur el Rio de la Casa y al valle de la Sebolla. En requida se procedio al repartiemento de tierra para labor, y tirado el cordel de oriente a poniente se midieran en el valle de Santa Gertrudes a la banda del sur, cuatro mil cien varas de tierra, y a la banda del norte que nirra al tulquillo, se midieron mil sebecientas varas de tierra, las cuales fueron repartidas a los agraciados pobladores por el orden que abajo quedan alistados. A continuacion el dia signiente pasamos al valle de San Antonio, yestando en el tirado el cordel de la orilla de la canega al rumbo del Poniente, se midieron y repartieron, segun el orden de la lista como dicho es, dos mil ochocientas varas de tierra en el valle; quinientas sesenta varas de tierra en la Lagunita: y dos cientas cincuenta varas de tierra enfrente de la plaza al sud—Veshe de ella, segun consta en la citada lista. Siendo los linderos generales de este sitio, para beneficio de los agraciados y pasteos comunes al ellos, por el norte el Rio de Ocate: por el sur donde desemboca el Rio del Sapelló, por el oriente el Aguaje de la Slequa, y por el poniente el Estillero. Y de haberze tomado esta posesion quieta pacificamente y sin contradicion de persona alguna, los agraciados de ella en demostraciones de alegria arrancaron yerbas, tiraron piedras, esparcieron puñadas de tierra, e hicieron otros actos posesorios dando vivas a dios ya la nacion.

En testimonia para constancia perpetua y obligatoria en todo tiempo de lo ahora estipulado, se estendio este titulo de mercenacion, y las particulares escrituras de cada uno, las cuales con este acto, la peticion, y superior decreto a ella estampado quedan protocoladas en el archivo de la gefactura politica en Santa Fé: y copia en esta de mi cargo de solo lo actuado por mi el citado alcalde.

La lista de los agraciados que se anotan y el numera de tierra que á cada uno toco es del tenor siguiente, valle de Santa Gertrudes, banda del sur, medida de oriente á Poniente; Jose Tapia, cien varas; Carmen Arce, ciento cincuenta varas; Juan Lorenzo Aliso, docientas varas; Juan Antonio Garcia, ciento cincuenta varas; Carlos Rinto, docientas varas; Mateo Ringinel, docientas varas; Manuel Suhazo, cien varas; Geronimo Martin, cien varas; Francisco Sandobal, cien varas; Francisco Loré, cien varas; Francisco Conen, docientas varas; José Mestas, cien varas; Ramon Archuleta, cien varas; Antonio Abá Trujillo, cien varas; Juan de Jesus Cruz, cien varas; Maria Dolores Romero, docientas varas; Faustin Mestas, cien varas; Maria Dolores Sanches, docientas varas; José Miguel Pacheco, cien varas; Yldefonso Pacheco, cien varas; Manuel Sanches, cien varas; Juan Trujillo, docientas varas; Felipe Carbajal, cien varas; José Maria Garcia, cien varas; Miguel Garcia, cien varas; Gabriel Lujan, cien varas; Manuel Arguello, cien varas; Ygnacio Gonzales, docientas varas; José Guadalupe Ortega, cien varas; Felipe Arguello, cien varas; Manuel Gregorio Martin, cien varas; Juan Cristobal Trujillo, cien varas; Banda del norte que mira al Tulquillo medida de oriente à Poniente; Tomas Encarnacion Garcia, ciento cincuenta varas; Carlos Salazar, ciento cincuenta varas; Francisco Arguello, cien varas; Francisco Sena, cien varas; José Ygnacio Madrid, cien varas; Miguel Paez, cien varas; Manuel Paez, cien varas; Miguel Mascareñas, docientas varas; Cecilio Montano, cincuenta varas; Cruz Medina, cien varas; Bernardo Martin, cien varas; Miguel Arguello, ciento cincuenta varas; Ramon Amado, ciento cincuenta varas; Pedro Aragon, ciento cincuenta varas; Esteban Valdez, cien varas.

Valle de San Antonio, banda del Sur medida de Oriente á Poniente, Manuel Sanches, cien varas; Juan Ygnacio Sanches, cien varas; Francisco Sarracino, cien varas; Albino Chacon, cien varas; Damasio Chacon, cien varas; Teodocio Quintana, cien varas; José Garcia, cien varas; Rafael Paez, cien varas; Nepomoceno Gurule, cien varas; José Vigil, cien varas; Nestor Armijo, trecientas varas; Andres Ornelas, cien varas; Mateo Montoya, cien varas; Juan de la Cruz Trujillo, cien varas; Juan de Jesus Lujan, cien varas; Francisco Trujillo, cien varas; Andres Trujillo, cien varas; Juan Andres Archuleta, cien varas; Ramon Abreu, cien varas; Jesus Maria Alarid, cien varas; Vicente Sanchez, cien varas; Mateo Sandobal, cien varas; Juan Lopez, cien varas; Pedro Chacon, cien varas; Miguel Antonio Mascareñas, cien varas; Antonio Arguello, cien varas; Lagunita de San Antonio, medida de Oriente á Poniente, José Silva, docientas ochenta varas; Juan José Vigil, docientas ochenta varas; Frente á la plaza de San Antonio punto al Serrito que divide á la Lagunita; Miguel Olguin, docientas cincuenta varas. Los individuos anotados han quedado unanimes conformes y posesionados del terreno de lo Demora, Valles de Santa Gertrudes y de San Antonio; á los que con el fin de que sepan lo que poseen y con quien lindan se les da copia de sus particulares escrituras, y hechoseles saber la estencion del terreno y sus egidos, segun la generalidad del sitio. Lo que para constancia perpetua de la legalidad de esta posesion, la antoriozo y firmo con los testigos referidos, de que doy fe. Manuel Antonio Sanchez. Ynstrumental, Teodocio Quintana. Ynstrumental, Nestor Armigo. Testigos de asistencia, Albino Chacon. Testigo de asistencia, Rafael Paez. Copiado, Agasto 12 de 1842.

Territorio de Nuevo Mejico, } *Condado de Taos.*

Yo Manuel Antonio Sanchez uno de los jueces de paz en y por el Condado de Taos. Certifico que un documento igual y conforme en todas sus partes al que antecede (y del que este es una correcta y legal copia) fue trabajado con autoridad competente en lo Demora los dias mes y año que en el mismo se mencionan y depositado entonces con los adjuntos documentos que se citan, en Santa Fé en el archivo del gefe politico. Y yo ademas certifico que el abajo subscrito juez de Paz ahora, fue en aquel tiempo el mismo alcalde que con autoridad de las leyes de Mejico actuo el dicho documento en todas sus partes.

Firmado y sellado de mimano y sello privado por no haberlo publico en el precinto del llano numero 7 en la oficina de mi despacho hoy 3 de Febrero, A. D. 1857.

MANUEL ANTONIO SANCHEZ, [L. S.]
Juez de Paz.

Surveyor General's Office, Translator's Department,
Santa Fé, New Mexico, September 10, 1859.

The above is a true copy of the original on file in this office.
DAVID V. WHITING, *Translator.*

GRANT—TRANSLATION.

Seal Third.   [SEAL.]   Two Reals.

For the years one thousand eight hundred and forty and one thousand eight hundred and forty-one.

[SEAL.]   Its value is one dollar per sheet.

On the 20th of October, one thousand eight hundred and thirty-five, I, Manuel Antonio Sanchez, constitutional justice of the jurisdiction of San José de las Trampas, with my attending witnesses, with whom I act by appointment, in compliance with the superior decree of Don Albino Perez, political chief of the Territory, dated the twenty-eighth day of September last past, I proceeded to the place called Demora, within the jurisdiction under my charge, for the purpose of distributing this public land, as is provided in the aforementioned superior decree, and being there, and the settlers interested, amounting to seventy-six citizens, being there also, the lower valley was called "Valle de Santa Gertrudes," and the upper one "Valle de San Antonio," and in the name of the Mexican nation, and of this municipality, the town site was marked out in both valleys, the one at Santa Gertrudes being two hundred varas from north to south, and one hundred and fifty varas from east to west, leaving thirty varas outside for drippage and a common road, and the meadow for the benefit of all, with its entrances and exits free. The site of the town of San Antonio contains two thousand varas from north to south, and one hundred and fifty varas from east to west, leaving the meadow for the benefit of all settlers, with the following entrances and exit: On the north the Cañon of the Comanches, on the south of Casas river, and in the direction of the Cebolla. Thereupon I proceeded to distribute the land suitable to cultivation, and drawing the line from east to west, on the south side of the valley of Santa Gertrudes, there were measured four thousand one hundred varas of land, and on the north, in the direction of Tulquillo, there were measured one thousand seven hundred varas of land, which were distributed among the settlers in the order in which they are arranged on the list. On the subsequent day we proceeded to the valley of San Antonio, and being there, we drew the line from the edge of the Cienega towards the west, another was measured and distributed according to the list aforementioned; two thousand eight hundred varas of land in the valley; five hundred and sixty varas at the Lagunita; and two hundred and fifty varas of land opposite the town, towards the southwest thereof, as will appear by the aforementioned list; the general boundaries of this tract, being for the benefit of the grantees and for common pasturage; on the north, the Ocate river; on the south to where the Sapéyo empties; on the east the Aguage de la Yegua, and on the west, the Estillero, and as having taken possession thereof quietly and peacefully, and without opposition from any person whatsoever, the grantees, in token of joy, pulled up weeds, threw stones, scattered handsfull of earth, and performed other acts of possession, giving thanks to God and to the nation.

As a perpetual and binding evidence in all time to come of what has now been transacted, this title deed of grant was executed, and also the particular deeds to each one, which, together with this act, the petition, and the superior decree thereto attached, are deposited in the archives of the office of the political chief at Santa Fé, and a copy of only what has been done by me is deposited in this office under my charge.

MANUEL ANTONIO SANCHEZ.

Instrumental: TEODOCIO QUINTANA.
               NESTOR ARMIJO.
Attending witnesses: ALBINO CHACON.
                       RAFAEL PAEZ.
  Copied August 12, 1842.

TERRITORY OF NEW MEXICO, *County of Taos:*

I, Manuel Antonio Sanchez, one of the justices of the peace within and for the county of Taos, certify that a document in all respects alike to this (and of which this is a correct copy) was executed by competent authority, at Lo de Mora, on the day, month, and year therein mentioned, and then deposited with the accompanying documents referred to in the archives of the political chief at Santa Fé. And I further certify that the undersigned, now a justice of the peace, was at that time the same alcalde who, by virtue of the authority of the laws of Mexico, executed the said document in all its parts.

Signed and sealed with my hand and private seal, there being no public seal, at No. 7, of El Llano, at my office, this 3d day of February, 1857.

MANUEL ANTONIO SANCHEZ,
Justice of the Peace.

Surveyor General's Office, Translator's Department,
Santa Fé, New Mexico, September 19, 1857.

The foregoing is a correct translation of the original on file in this office.

DAVID V. WHITING,
Translator.

Surveyor General's Office,
Santa Fé, New Mexico, August 20, 1859.

The above is a true copy of the original on file in this office.

WM. PELHAM,
Surveyor General.

RECEIPT FOR DEED—SPANISH.

Recivi del alcalde anterior del año de 1835 una merced constante de cuatro foyas la que existe en poder del C. Miguel Mascareñas residente de este punto de lo Demoro, cuya merced nos entrego el C. Manuel Antonio Sanchez, accompañado con un decreto del sor gefe politico, Don Albino Perez, fecha 10 de Octubre del año anterior, y para su resguardo ledi este delante del Juez territorial del punto de lo Demora, la que firmo yo y dos testigos de asistencia y para su resguardo lo firmamos hoy dia de la fecha.

Valle de lo Demora, 16 de Agosto de 1836.

MIGUEL MASCAREÑAS.

Juez territorial, Juan Lorenzo Alire.
(Testigo) José Miguel Pacheco.
(Testigo) José Estrada.

Trampas, Agosto 19 de 1836, de hecho me hago cargo del anterior recivo lo firme en dicho dia mes yaño.

JUAN DE JESUS CRUZ.

Surveyor General's Office, Translator's Department,
Santa Fé, New Mexico, September 10, 1859.

The above is a true copy of the original on file in this office.

DAVID V. WHITING,
Translator.

RECEIPT FOR DEED—TRANSLATION.

Received of the former justice of the year 1836 a grant, consisting of four pages, which is in the hands of citizen Miguel Mascareñas, resident of this place of De Mora, which grant was delivered to us by citizen Manuel Antonio Sanchez, accompanied by a decree of the political chief, Don Albino Perez, dated on the tenth of October of the previous year, and for his protection I gave him this before the territorial justice of the place of De Mora, which I sign, with two attending witnesses, and for his protection we sign on the day of the date.

VALLEY OF DE LO DE MORA, *August* 16, 1836.

MIGUEL MASCAREÑAS.

Territorial justice, JUAN LORENZO ALIRE.
Attending: JOSÉ MIGUEL PACHECO.
JOSÉ ESTRADA.

TRAMPAS, *August* 19, 1836.

I have taken charge of the foregoing receipt I signed on the date above mentioned.

JUAN DE JESUS CRUZ.

SURVEYOR GENERAL'S OFFICE, TRANSLATOR'S DEPARTMENT,
Santa Fé, New Mexico, June 29, 1859.

The foregoing is a translation of the original on file in this office.

DAVID V. WHITING,
Translator.

SURVEYOR GENERAL'S OFFICE,
Santa Fé, New Mexico, August 25, 1859.

The above is a true copy of the original on file in this office.

WM. PELHAM,
Surveyor General.

TESTIMONY.

MANUEL ANTONIO SANCHEZ sworn:

Question. Have you any interest in this case?
Answer. I have none.
Question. Where do you reside?
Answer. In Santa Barbara, Taos county.
Question. Did you divide out the lands at Mora as stated in the document here presented, purported to have been made by you?
Answer. I did.
Question. When you divided out the land, did you have in your possession the original grant made by Albino Perez?
Answer. I did.
Question. To whom was the original grant made by Albino Perez?
Answer. To the persons referred to in the document made by me, and of which the document previously shown me is a copy.
Question. In what year was this land distributed?
Answer. In 1835.

Question. What did you do with the copy of the original grant which you made?
Answer. It was delivered to Miguel Mascarenas, who was one of the original grantees.
Question. Have the two valleys of Mora been settled and occupied and cultivated from that time up to the present?
Answer. They have been continuously occupied from that period up to this time.
Question. Do you know what became of the copy you gave to Mascarenas?
Answer. I do not know.

MANUEL ANTONIO SANCHEZ.

Sworn and subscribed before me this 1st July, 1859.
WILLIAM PELHAM,
Surveyor General.

VICENTE ROMERO sworn:

Question. Have you at any time seen the copy of the original grant made by Albino Perez to the town of Mora; and if so, when, where, and at what time did you see it last?
Answer. I saw it in the archives of Mora while Thomas Lalande was alcalde. I saw it last in 1846.
Question. What became of the archives of Mora in the alcalde's office?
Answer. The archives of Mora were burned in the beginning of 1847. The United States troops set fire to the house during the revolution of January, 1847.

Cross-examined by United States.

Question. Do you know what became of the copy of the Mora grant which you saw in the archives?
Answer. I know it was burned up, from my own knowledge.
Question. Were you in charge of the archives when they were burned?
Answer. I was not.

VICENTE ROMERO.

Sworn and subscribed before me this 1st July, 1859.
WILLIAM PELHAM,
Surveyor General.

RAFAEL PAEZ sworn:

Question. Have you any interest in this claim, and do you live upon it?
Answer. I have not, and do not reside there.
Question. Were you present in the years 1835 and 1836 as a witness when Manuel Antonio Sanchez placed the parties in possession of the Mora grant?
Answer. I was.

Question. Did you see the original decree made by Albino Perez?
Answer. I did see it, in the hands of Sanchez, who was an alcalde at that time.

Question. What were the contents of that decree?
Answer. That the land of Mora should be divided out between the parties who had asked for it, upon condition that they would break up the land and cultivate it.

Question. Did Sanchez place the parties in possession and distribute the lands among the petitioners in conformity with that decree?
Answer. He did.

Question. When was that possession given?
Answer. In October, 1835. They have occupied it from that time up to this.

Question. How many settlers are there in the two valleys of Mora?
Answer. About one thousand souls.

Question. Were the parties placed in possession by Sanchez the sole grantees under the decree of Perez?
Answer. They were the only ones at that time.

Question. Do you know of any other grant made to the same land besides the one made as above?
Answer. I do not. Other parties have been placed in possession since, under the decree of Perez. I do not know of any documentary evidence of such possession. They were placed in possession by the authorities of Mora and Taos.

RAFAEL PAEZ.

Sworn and subscribed before me this 1st July, 1859.
WILLIAM PELHAM,
Surveyor General.

DAVID V. WHITING sworn:

I hold the office of chief clerk and translator in the office of the surveyor general of New Mexico. I have examined all the papers composing the archives of the former government at Santa Fé, and selected therefrom all the grants, and papers having reference to grants, to lands in this Territory. I did not find the grant to Mora made by Albino Perez in 1835.

DAVID V. WHITING.

Sworn and subscribed before me this 1st July, 1859.
WILLIAM PELHAM,
Surveyor General.

SURVEYOR GENERAL'S OFFICE,
Santa Fé, New Mexico, August 20, 1859.

The above is a true copy of the original on file in this office.
WILLIAM PELHAM,
Surveyor General.

REPORT.

THE TOWN OF MORA vs. THE UNITED STATES.

This case was set for trial on the 1st of July, 1859, and the parties and witnesses being present, the case was taken up and acted upon on the day fixed for the investigation. On the 20th October, 1835, Manuel Antonio Sanchez, constitutional justice of the jurisdiction of San José de Las Trampas, certifies that in compliance with an order issued to him by Albino Perez, political chief of the Territory, dated the 28th of September, 1835, he placed the parties in possession of the vacant and unoccupied lands referred to in said decree, to the petitioners therein mentioned.

The document containing the above purports to be a copy made on the 12th of August, 1842, of the original proceedings had in the premises, which is certified by Sanchez, who became a justice of the peace under the government of the United States on the 3d of February, 1857, to be an exact copy of the original made by him in 1835. The case was argued by Messrs. Jackson & Ashurst on the part of the claimants, and R. H. Tompkins, esq., United States district attorney, on the part of the United States.

The principal objections made by the counsel for the United States, as submitted in his brief, are, that there is no evidence other than the testimony of Sanchez, that a grant was ever made or that it was ever seen at Santa Fé, the place of deposit, and that no evidence is shown that Albino Perez had any authority to make the grant.

That the witness Romero testified to the destruction of the order of Perez when it was not in his possession, nor could he have any certain knowledge that the grant was in the archieves when they were destroyed.

That no evidence has been produced to show that Albino Perez actually executed the order for the distribution of the land, and that the witness testifies that lands were granted by the authorities of Mora and Taos within the limits granted to the original grantees by Perez, showing that the Mexican authorities did not consider the grant to have been made in fee.

That the failure of the petitioners to prove the execution of a grant to said lands by the competent authorities at Santa Fé, with the necessary formalities to sever the land from the public domain, and the failure to prove that any such document ever existed in the archives at Santa Fé, and the evidence that no such document was found among such archives, and the failure to prove the destruction of the archives or any portion of them at Santa Fé, at any time subsequent to 1835, tend strongly to prove that no such grant was ever made, and consequently that the lands in question were never severed from the public domain.

The evidence of Sanchez, a justice of the peace, and one of the constituted authorities under the Mexican government, acting within the scope of his authority, is deemed to be good evidence of the existence of the grant, and it is presumed that he would not arrogate to himself the authority of distributing the public domain without directions from the granting power of the country. Neither would the petitioners, who were going to remove there and expend large sums in improving the lands, be satisfied with the action of a subordinate executive officer alone, unless he was acting by authority and within the scope of his duties, knowing that all their improvements would be forfeited by this action of the justice if illegal and contrary to law.

The fact of the grant never having been seen at Santa Fé is not proven in evidence, and even if it were could have very little weight, as it was not the business of the grantees to look after the preservation and safekeeping of the original after they had received a copy duly certified to by a legal authority. That was a matter intrusted to the executive authorities at the seat of government. The original must have existed or a copy of it could not have been delivered by the alcalde of the previous year to Miguel Mascareñas, as is shown by Mascareñas's receipt.

It has been clearly proven in other cases before this office that authority was vested in the political chief to make grants of land, and the fact of Albino Perez having occupied that position is a matter of history, and it is well known that he was beheaded in one of the many unfortunate insurrections so prevalent in the country at that time.

The witness Romero testifies that he saw the copy of the Mora grant in the archives at Mora, while Thomas Lalande was justice of the peace in 1846. This he knows from his own knowledge; and as the archives of Mora was the proper place for it to be deposited in, and as it was to the interest of the parties interested to keep it, then the presumption is very natural that it was there when the United States troops set fire to the building, and that it was destroyed with the archives.

In granting lands to a number of persons for a town site, the land embraced within the limits of the grant, even under the control of the constituted authorities of the town, who, under the law, had the right to partition out such of the vacant land as might be asked for by other parties desiring to be incorporated in the town. This partition was of course made with the consent of the original grantees, and the granting of lands to others than the original grantees by the authorities of Mora and Taos was proper, and does not prove in any manner that the grant was not made in fee.

The failure to prove that the original grant ever existed at Santa Fé has no bearing on the case whatever, as it was not the business of the grantees to look after the original when it had passed from their hands to that of the justice, who was directed to place them in possession. It was sufficient for them that they were placed in possession under the original grant, as certified by the justice. Again, it is well known that the archives at Santa Fé were not then, neither are they at the present day, under the particular care or custody of any particular officer of the government, especially after the change of sovereignty, and it is believed that important documents have been taken from the archives at Santa Fé on more than one occasion; therefore the fact of the grant not being found in the archives is no evidence that no such grant existed; and it is hardly to be expected that the grantees should be held responsible for it after it had been returned to this place and deposited in the archives under the custody of the proper officer, whose business it was at the time to look after its safe-keeping.

The evidence also shows that the town or towns embraced within the limits granted have been settled upon and occupied by the original grantees and their assigns from the date of the grant up to the present time, and large and well-established settlements are growing up and flourishing there. It is not to be presumed that the government would allow the richest and most fertile portion of its territory to be usurped and taken up by a party of men without the color or shadow of law. Such was not the policy of the Mexican government at the time. There certainly was a grant, or they would not have been allowed to remain unmolested from 1835 to 1846, when the United States took possession of the country.

The grant made to John Scolly and others is acknowledged by the parties before this office to have been made with their consent and approval, given at the time their grant was made. Claimants, in their petition, refer to certain statutes and decisions, a large portion of which are not in the office, neither can they be had here; therefore, no reference is made to them.

The instructions to this office provide that when the existence of a town is proven at the time the United States took possession of the country it is to be considered as *prima facie* evidence of the existence of a grant to said town or to the persons under whom they claim.

This fact also having been established in evidence, the grant is deemed to be a good and valid one, and the land embraced within the metes and bounds set forth in the act of possession severed from the public domain, and is, therefore, approved and ordered to be transmitted to Congress, with the request that it be confirmed to the original grantees and those claiming under, through, or from them, excepting that portion granted to John Scolly *et al.*, and reported from this office on the 30th September, 1857.

WM. PELHAM, *Surveyor General.*

SURVEYOR GENERAL'S OFFICE,
Santa Fé, New Mexico, July 9, 1859.

SURVEYOR GENERAL'S OFFICE,
Santa Fé, New Mexico, August 25, 1859.

The above is a true copy of the original on file in this office.

WM. PELHAM, *Surveyor General.*

CLAIM NO. 33.

HEIRS OF P. ARMENDARIS.

Documents composing claim No. 33.

1. Notice.
2. Additional petition.
3. Grants, testimony, &c., (Spanish.)
4. Grant, translation.
5. Additional grant, translation.
6. Testimony, translation.
7. Testimony, translation.
8. Testimony, English.
9. Report.

NOTICE.

To the honorable William Pelham, surveyor general of the Territory of New Mexico:

Your petitioners, Manuel Armendaris, Henrique Armendaris, Miguel Armendaris, Antonio Armendaris, children of Pedro Armendaris, deceased, and Rodrigo Garcia, father and guardian of the infant children of Beline Armendaris, deceased, being the only surviving heirs and legal representatives of the said Pedro Armendaris, deceased, who died in Chihuahua on the 3d day of May, 1853, would respectfully state that they are residents of the State of Chihuahua, in the republic of Mexico, and that on the —— day of ————, ——, and on the —— day of ————, ——, there was granted to the said Pedro Armendaris two tracts of land known as the Valverde tract and Fray Cristobal tract of land, situate on the east bank of the Rio Grande, and bounded as follows:

Beginning on the Rio Grande, in front of the mountain of San Pascual, and running thence down the Rio Grande until a point three leagues below the Ojo del Muerto; thence southwest to the mountain of Petecas; thence north to the Round mountain; and thence to the mountain of San Pascual. Your petitioners further state that the said Pedro Armendaris took possession of said lands and built houses and corrals upon the same, and had those lands in cultivation, and had pasturing, and raising there large herds of sheep and many cattle and horses, and continued to occupy the said lands until he was forcibly expelled from them by hostile incursions of the Navajo Indians. Your petitioners further state that said lands have never been surveyed, and the number of acres contained within said limits are not known to your petitioners, but the boundaries mentioned in said grants are noted and visible fixed points, universally known and recognized in the vicinity. Your petitioners further state that said lands are now unoccupied, and your petitioners know of no valid claim to said lands except the claim of your petitioners. Your petitioners further state that the said Pedro Armendaris, in his lifetime, left the said title deeds given to him by the governor of the province of New Mexico in the hands of Francisco Chaves, deceased, and said title deeds are now in the possession of the heirs of said Francisco Chaves, who refuse to surrender them to your petitioners, having, in the first place, pretended that said title deeds were in the hands of Francisco Chaves in pledge for money loaned, and now pretending that at Santa Fé, on the 1st day of August, 1823, the said Pedro Armendaris conveyed to the said Francisco Xavier Chaves the lands aforesaid. Your petitioners aver that said Pedro Armendaris never executed any such title or transfer, nor did he owe to Francisco Xavier Chaves any sum of money on any account; and your petitioners ask that José Chavez y Castillo, in whose possession said title deeds now are, and the pretended deed of Don Pedro Armendaris to Francisco Xavier Chaves, be notified to produce the same upon the hearing of this case, if any claim is set up under them to said tracts of land. Your petitioners further state that, for the reason aforesaid, the said grant cannot now be filed with this petition, but the existence of said grant and the occupation of said lands, and the claim of title upon the part of the said Pedro Armendaris, from the date of said grant up to the present time, is well known and susceptible of abundant proof. Your petitioners further state that the said lands are situate in the county of Socorro, in the Territory of New Mexico. Your petitioners ask that such steps may be taken in the premises as will confirm to them their title to said lands under the act of Congress of 22d July, 1854.

All of which is respectfully submitted.

JOHN S. WATTS,
Attorney for Petitioners.

SURVEYOR GENERAL'S OFFICE,
Santa Fé, New Mexico, September 6, 1859.

The above is a true copy of the original on file in this office.

WM. PELHAM,
Surveyor General.

ADDITIONAL PETITION.

To the honorable William Pelham, surveyor general of the Territory of New Mexico:

John S. Watts, attorney for the heirs of Pedro Armendaris, states that in consequence of the absence of the original titles to the Valverde grant, when the petition was heretofore filed in this case, the boundaries of said grants were not correctly set out. The original titles now being on file, he asks that the petition herein be amended so as to set forth the boundaries of said grants as follows:

The grant of December 4, 1819, as follows, to wit: In the first place, the water line of the Rio Grande del Norte; in the second, the peak or knoll that is on the table land of the Contadero, which is the boundary or termination of the aforementioned bottom or valley, and which lies in the direction of the place called Fra Christobal, and drawing a straight line to the little spring called Analla, be included in the possession, and to be the third boundary; and running another straight line from this point over the little hills of San Pascual, a fourth boundary to be the little isolated hill separate from those aforementioned, and which is in the direction of the river and towards the bottom or valley aforesaid, San Pascual, and the Apache woods.

The grant of June 1, 1820, is bounded as follows, to wit: On the table land del Contadero there is a peak or knoll, and from this point, running in a southerly direction, following the water line of the Rio Grande del Norte on the same side of Valverde to a point where the little mountains of Fra Christobal joins the river, being the watering point on said river; and from the aforementioned point of the little mountain over its summit to the spring called del Muerto, which is on one side of the little lake called del Serrito, including the said Muerto spring in the possession; and from its source two leagues in each direction, and from the termination of the distance to the south, the line is to continue to the Analla spring; and from this point two leagues to the south, in order that the line running from the Muerto spring may terminate at the boundary of the said two leagues; and from thence three leagues to the east, and their termination, the line is to continue coming down over the upper point and terminate on the river at the little hills that are isolated from said mountains, and which are near the public road on the side of the Apache woods.

All of which is respectfully submitted.

J. S. WATTS, *Attorney for Claimants.*

SURVEYOR GENERAL'S OFFICE,
Santa Fé, New Mexico.

The above is a true copy of the original on file in this office.

WM. PELHAM, *Surveyor General.*

GRANT, TESTIMONY, &c.—SPANISH.

Balga por el Sello Tercero por el año de mil ochocientos diez y nueva por aucencia de Don José Francisco Ortiz.

YGNACIO ORTIZ.

Sor. Gobor. de la Provincia:

Don Pedro Ascue de Armendaris primer Teniente que fue del Presidio de San Elciario en la provincia de Nueva Viscaya, y actualmente diezmero, por un Quinqueño de esta, siendo el primero del el de la fecha, ante V. S. con el debida respecto, paresco y digo: Que con motivo de tener algunos vienes de campo ahora traidos de aquella provincia, y otros que quisa me puedan resultar sobrantes del diezmo, y que tengo algunos sirvientes destinados al ciudado de ellos, y deben aumentarse estos al ciudado de todo, suplico a V. S. tenga la bondad de mandar se me mercene el terreno siquiente por estar realengo, y es el ancon nombrado de Balverde, para cultivar del, la tierra que pueda, sirviendo de linderos ó guarda rayos, á todo el terreno de la posesion con sus anexos ó sitio para los pasteos, en primer lugar lo que raya el agua del Rio Grande, del Norte, el segundo el picachito sobremesa ó tetilla que queda sobre la mesilla nombrada del contadero, que linda donde acaba el mencionado ancon y que queda á la parte nombrada Fray Cristobal y tirando una linea recta al ojito de agua señalado con el nombre de Analla, seaseme señalado en la misma posesion, y que sirva de tercer lindero, y coniendo desde este punto otra linea recta por sobre los Serritos de San Pascual, sea el cuarto el crestoncito que se halla desprendido de los mencionados Serros rumbo al dicho Rio, y á la parte del Ancon nominado, San Pascual y Bosque del Apache, cuyo terreno Señor, esta enteramente libre, separado de las poblaciones, las que por ningun motivo pueden ser perjudicadas, pues la que se halla mas inmediata á el es la nueva nombrada del Socorrito, quedando opuesta á la otra banda del Rio, y distante Rio arriba, cosa de nueve leguas cuya distancia me parece mas que suficiente para los bienes de dicho pueblo, por lo que atendiendo á dicha circunstancia á la de quedar el mencionado Ancon en el camino Real del Paso, y que les sirva á los caminantes de ancilio por su poblado, la de poblar nuevamente aquel punto con gente, y vienes y la de estar enteramente libres de otro dueño, suplico á V. S. se sirva mandar proveer en los mismos terminos que llevo dicho, y sino como fuese de su agrado.

Villa de Santa Fé, del Nuevo Mejico, 22 *de Noviembre de* 1819.

PEDRO ARMENDARIS.

SANTA FÉ, *Noviembre* 22 *de* 1819.

El Alcalde de Belen informara sobre el particular con circunspeccion del sitio para resolver.

MELGARES.

Señor TENIENTE CORONEL, DON FACUNDO MELGARES.

Sor. Ten'te Coronel y Gov'or:

V. S. me pide informe segun la presentacion hecha por Don Pedro Armendaris asentado el principio de que no es terreno por dueño alguno hasta la presente segun mi local saber y cortos conocimientos que me asisten, el terreno dedemarcado de Norte á Sur graduo de cuatro leguas y de Oriente que es el ojo de Analla pasando la Sierrita de San Pascual á la orilla del Rio puede graduarse de cinco leguas hasta el angostura donde pega el Rio al arroyo que mira al Peñasco que señala dicho Sor. Armendaris y como que no debe estorbarse pasto y abrevadero para los transitantes, queda mucho terreno al punto de Fray Cristobal y del arroyo citado para arriba la estencion bastante hasta el Socorro de una y otra banda, quedando asi mismo libre la parte al Poniente opuesta del Rio de la que V. S. sea servido si lo tiene á bien conceder al indicado Sor. Armendaris, ó como V. S. lo tenga por mas conveniente que es cuanto puedo informar.

BELEN, *Noviembre* 28 *de* 1819.

MANUEL RUVI DE CELIS.

SANTA FÉ, 4 *de Diciembre de* 1819.

Respecto del beneficio que resulta á la provincia por el aumento de la agricultura, consedasele al suplicante lo que solicita bajo la precisa condicion de mantener hombres armados cuantos alli existan, de que ha de ir ubicando casas y poniendo los ganados que corresponden al terreno, y que ha de dar abrevaderos y pastos libres á los transeuntes ya sean arrieros, ya con haciendas, y de que ha de ir sercando en proporcion de loque vaya aumentando su labor.

MELGARES.

Sirva de constancia por esta declaracion, que yo Don Pedro Armendaris, como legitimo dueño del puesto de Balverde, con todas sus pertenencias como consta por la consecion antecedente, que vendi al Sor. Don Francisco Xavier Chavez dicha pertenencia, con todos mis derechos y acciones, y por la mismo le son trasladados asi y para cuando guste enagenarla, sin que ahora ni en ningun tiempo pueda impedirselo persona alguna, por ser asi mi voluntad, y que me lo pago todo á mi satisfaccion, bajo tal virtud y por ser de derecho, suplico á todas las justicias nacionales, le protejan en cualquier evento, á que con la livertad que es consiguiente disfrate de su mencionada finca, y para que consto le di esta escrita, y firmada de mi mismo puño, en la ciudad de Santa Fé del Nuevo Mejico, el dia primero de Agosto del año de mil ochocientos veinte y tres tercero de la independencia Mejicana.

PEDRO ARMENDARIS.

Un Quartillo. [SELLO.] Sello Quarto.

Un quartillo, años de mil ochocientos veinte y veinte y uno. Abilitado jurada por el Rey la Constitucion en 9 de Marzo de 1820.

SOR. GOBOR. DE LA PROVINCIA: Don Pedro Ascue de Armendaris primer teniente que fue de la compania del Presidio de San Elciario, y ahora separado del servicio por enfermo, hace como siete años, haviendo servido antes en las clases de cadete Alfz. y en la dicha de teniente, veinte años y meses, y hallandome en la actualidad á vecindado en esta provincia, y de Diezmero de ella, por un quinqueño trate desde que vine y trato ahora, de fomentar una hacienda mista, de lavorio y cuadrupedo, que he puesto en el paraje de Valverde, que es, de mi pertenencia, y como quiera que el sitio es escaso, no solo para abrevaderos, sino que tambien lo es para pasteaderos, para los mencionados bienes de campo que anualmente con todo empeño aumento, con los que diezmo y introdusco de las provincias confinantes, suplico á V.S. me haga la gracia de aumentarme mi dicho sitio dandome en merced lo siguiente; Sobre la Mesilla del Contadero se alla una tetilla ó Serrito que es mio y desde este quiero que la bondad de V.S. me de para abajo, por toda la Raya del Rio Grande del Norte á la misma banda de Balverde hasta la punta que pega á dicho rio de la Sierrita de Fray Cristobal que es donde quedan abrevaderos á dicho rio, y desde la mencionada punta de la Sierrita por encima de su altura hasta el Ojito llamado del Muerto, que queda aun lado de la Lagunita que llaman del Serrito, incluyendo en la mencionada posesion dicho Ojito del Muerto, y de su nacimiento dos leguas á cada rumbo, y de donde concluyen las dos que miran al mediodia, que siga la linea al Ojito de Analla que es mio, y á este que se le den, dos leguas al mediodia para que en su punto de conclusion sea donde venga á parar la linea que corre del Ojito del Muerto, y de alli tres leguas al oriente, y de donde rematan que continue la linea á bajar por la punta de arriba de la Sierrita de San Pascual, á rematar al Rio en los Crestoncitos que quedan desprendidos de dicha Sierrita, que son mios, y que quedan serca del camino real al lado del Bosque del Apache; todo el centro del mencionado terreno, es seco, sin ningun aguajito, y lo mas de el es mio, y queda en la Jornada del Muerto, y por ser tan seco, le quiero proporcionar con alguna advitrio la agua que pueda, resultando de hay el grandissimo beneficio, que los caminantes que siempre se atrasan en dicha Jornada tengan tan importante aucilio. El susodicho terreno es realengo y esta cuasi en el centro del grandisimo despoblado que hay de esta provincia al Pueblo del Paso, y con ocuparlo yo á nadie le resulta perjuicio, pues la poblacion mas serca á el, es el Socorro que dista como doce leguas, ó algo mas; y si resultan de que yo posea el mencionado terreno muchisimas ventajas resultan á la provincia, siendo entre otras las principales; las siguientes: Primera, que siendo el despoblado que hay del Socorro al Pueblo del Paso, de mas de cien leguas, se encuentran los caminantes con este aucilio, para recurso; segunda, el que tengo formada en Balverde una labor grande de riego, en la que se siembran de todas semillas, y con bastante abundancia, de forma que nunca, ninguna persona la ha hecho igual, en toda la provincia, motivo á que por lo regular se esperimentan, en ella anuales escaseses: Tercera que con los bienes que diezmo, y los mas que introdusco, en mi sitio voy formando una gruesa estancia de ellos, que no solo servira dentro de poco, de recurso para compras sino que viendo los havitantes pudientes el fruto que se saca de reunir sus vienes en un sitio, (cosa desconocida entre ellos,) haran lo mismo que yo ahora, y con esto fomentaran la provincia, y ellos mismos cortaran, los perjudicales abusos de los partidos; cuarta, tambien resultara que sembrando bastante los pudientes, tendran semillas de sobra, y no estaran atenidos entonces, á que los pegujaleros les vendan de las suyas baratas, para mercarselas despues las mismas caras, quedandose á perecer como lo estamos mirando, y que hallandose con ellas en abundancia, podran dedicarse á hacer algunas fabricas regulares, que hoy no se ve ninguna, pues entonces los pobres tendran, (como ahora conmigo) donde ocurrir á ganar con su trabajo con que hecharse un trapo, como se observa en todas partes: Quinta, es claro que para el cultivo de una gruesa labor y el ciudado de bastantes animales, exije mantener ocupada bastante gente, eritando con esto, en mucha parte, el robo para comes, y elque anden tantos de miserables bandios: Y ultimamente Sor. Gobernador S. M. Q. D. G. tiene mandado hace muchos años que se pueble todo el crecido despoblado, rio abajo asta reunir la provincia al pueblo del Paso que es ramo de la misma; y por que yo he sido el primero, que á toda consta, me he sentado en dicho despoblado, y tambien el primero que ha inventado en esta provincia un tan grandisimo fomento, suplico á la bondad de V. S. me haga la gracia de consederme la merced en los terminos que solicito.

Dios nro. Sor. Gue. la vida de V. S. mª. aˢ. Villa de Santa Fé, 15 de Mayo de 1820.

PEDRO ARMENDARIS.

Santa Fé, *Junio* 1° *de* 1810.

Respecto de que no creo inconveniente como lo pide bajo las condiciones del decreto de Balverde.

MELGARES.

Siendo como es anexa esta escritura á la de Balverde, de 22 de Noviembre, de mil ochocientos diez y nueve, y comprenderse a la misma parte en venta de Don Francisco Xavier Chavez, hago saber, que con los mismos derechos, y acciones, es suga como lo es la mencionada que le traspase con fecha primero de Agosto de mil ochocientos veinte y tres, y es mi voluntad que disfrutá con la misma livertad que disfruta de la otra, pues ambas me ha pagado á toda mi satisfaccion con la cantidad de tres mil pesos fuertes, y quince bestias mulares, y para que conste en todo tiempo le di la presente hoy 25 de Agosto de mil ochocientos veinte y tres.

PEDRO ARMENDARIS.

Territorio de Nuevo Mejico, }
Condado de Bernalillo.

Al calse del espediente instruido á peticion del Lo. Manuel Armendaris, ante el H. Francisco Sarracino, prefecto del condado de Bernalillo, esta estampado un auto del tenor siguiente.

Territorio de Nuevo Mejico—Condado de Bernallilo. Haviendosele notificado las antecedentes auctuaciones al peticionario Lo. Manuel Armendaris, dijo: que es conforme y pide se le de ellas copia, testimoniada, y lo firmo por ante mi el H. Francisco Sarracino, prefecto del condado, y por ante el escribano nombrado este dia 14 de Febrero de 1849, en el lugar de Albuquerque—Francisco Sarracino, prefecto—Manuel Armendaris—Ante mi, Jose Armijo y Ortiz, Escribano nombrado—Esta fiel y legalmente sacado de su original á que me remito, lo que certifico y firmo por ante mi escribano nombrado este dia 15 de Febrero de 1849, en el lugar de Albuquerque.

FRANCISCO SARRACINO,
Prefecto.

Ante mi: JOSE ARMIJO Y ORTIZ,
Escribano Nombrado.

Territorio de Nuevo Mejico, }
Condado de Bernalillo.

Como solicita el peticionario Lo. Manuel Armendaris desele por la oficina de la Prefectura del Condado de Bernalillo el testimonio legal que solicita el H. Francisco Sarracino Prefecto del Condado asi lo decreto este dia 15 de Febrero de 1849, en el lugar de Albuquerque.

FRANCISCO SARRACIÑO,
Prefecto.

TESTIMONIO.

Señor Prefecto del Condado de Bernalillo—Manuel Armendaris apoderado de la casa de mi padre Don Pedro Armendaris, ante V. como mas haya lugar en derecho digo que : En los años de diez y nueve y veinte del presente siglo se merceana ron a mi padre los terrenos que componen en hacienda de Balverde, esta hacienda fue inmediatamente poblada, cultivados sus terrenos de labor y embiertos sus terrenos de labor y embiertos sus campos con ganados y caballadas ; asi permanecio hasta el año de veinte y cinco en que los Indios Navajoes destruyeron cuanto habia en ella acabando hasta con el destacamento de tropa que la guarnecia ; llegado este caso y vista la imposibilidad de mantener la hacienda mi padre la abandonó, y al retirarse para Chihuahua dejo en poder de Don Francisco Chavez los titulos de los terrenos situados a la banda izquierda del Rio Bravo cuza terminacion es del modo siguiente—Comensando desde el punto del Rio Bravo en donde desemboca el Arroyo de San Pascual todo el Rio abajo hasta tres leguas Castellanas adelante del nacimiento del Ojo del Muerto, de este punto del Rio distante tres leguas del referido ojo se tira una linea á la cumbre mas elevada de la Sierra de las Petacas, de dicha cumbre se tira otra linea hasta la sima del Serro Redondo, y de aqui se dirije otra linea por la sima de la Sierrita de San Pascual hasta el primer punto que es done junta el arroyo con el Rio—Los titulos que acreditaban esta propiedad y que como dicho antes quedaron en poder de Don Francisco Chavez, se han destraviado segun las contestaciones que Don José Chaves Albacea de la testamentaria de su finado padre, me ha dado en todas las veces que se los he reclamado, por este motivo y siendo notorio en este Territorio que estos terrenos han sido de la propiedad de mi padre, hago uso del articulo 6° titulo registros de tierras de los estatulos vigentes para que conforme á el se sirva V. citar á los Sres. Gral. Don Manuel Armijo, Don Antonio Sandobal, Don Fernando Aragon, Don Antonio Ma. Garcia, Don Francisco Baca y Terrus, y cuantos mas fueren necesarios para que conforme á la ley digan cuanto sepan con relacion á lo contenido en este escrito, por tanto : A V. pido y suplico se sirva proveer conforme á mi solicitud por ser de justicia—Albuquerque, Febrero 13 de 1849—Manuel Armendaris—Territorio de Nuevo Mejico—Condado de Bernalillo—Por presentada y admitido en lo que haya lugar librense por el orden establecido las correspondientes citas á los Señores Armijo, Sandobal, Baca y Terrus, Aragon, y Garcia, para que á las dos de la tarde del miercoles 14 de Febrero de 1849, años se presenten ante la corte especial del H. Francisco Sarracino en la sala del jusgado del H. Alcalde Manuel Armijo, en el lugar de Albuquerque, y notifiquesele este auto al peticionario para su intelligencia, el dicho prefecto asi lo decreto mando y firmo este dia 14 de Febrero de 1849, por ante su Escribano Nombrado—Francisco Sarracino, Prefecto—Ante mi, José Armijo y Ortiz Escribano Nombrado—Se le notifico el antecedente auto al interesado Albuquerque, miercoles 14 de Febrero de 1849—Francisco Sandobal—Territorio de Nuevo Mejico, Condado de Bernalillo—En cumplimiento al interior auto y solicitud del peticionario Lo. Manl.

Armendaris presente que fue el Gral. Manuel Armijo, despues de haber recivido juramento que hizo por Dios de decir verdad nomas la verdad y solo la verdad en lo que supiere y fuere preguntado, digo: que conicio la hacienda de Balverde poblada por Don Pedro Armendaris que en ella vio hacer fabricas caballadas y ganado mayor, que estubo de administrador de dicha hacienda D. Ygnacio Jaramillo por cuenta del espresado Sor. Armendaris, que dura poblada la dicha hacienda algunos años y que es cuanto sabe en lo que se afirma y ratifica bajo el juramento que prestado tiene, y lo firmo este dia 14 de Febrero de 1849—Manuel Armijo, Gral.—Territorio de Nuevo Mejico—Condado de Bernalillo—juramentado y afirmado delante de mi y ante mi escribano nombrado este dia 14 de Febrero, A. D. 1849, en el lugar de Albuquerque lo que certifico—Francisco Sarracino, Prefecto—Ante mi, José Armijo y Ortiz Escribano Nombrado. Territorio de Nuevo Mejico—Condado de Bernalillo—Yncontinente presente que fue el H. Sor. Don Antonio Sandobal despues de haber recivido juramento que hizo por Dios de decir la verdad nomas la verdad y solo la verdad en lo que supiere y fuere preguntado dijo: que conocio la hacienda de Balverde poblada por Don Pedro Armendaris que en ella vio varias veces que por alli que se formo una poblazon, que se abrio labor, que se poblo, con caballada y ganado mayor que conocio en la misma hacienda dos distintos administradores Ygnacio Jaramillo y Julio Telles, que estubo poblada la dicha hacienda algunos años, quo cree de despobló por lo mucho que invadian los Indios barbaros, que es cuanto sabe en lo que se afirma y ratifica bajo el juramento que dado tiene, y lo firmo este dia 14 de Febrero de 1849—Antonio Sandobal—Territoria de Nuevo Mejico—Condado de Bernalillo—Juramentado y afirmado delante de mi y anti mi Escribano Nombrado este dia 14 de Febrero, A. D. 1849, en el lugar de Albuquerque—Francisco Sarracino, Prefecto—Ante mi, José Armijo y Ortiz Escribano Nombrado, —Territorio de Nuevo Mejico—Condado de Bernalillo—Incontinente presente que fue el H. Alcalde Fernando Aragon despues de haber recivido juramento que hizo por Dios de decir verdad nomas la verdad y solo la verdad, en lo que supiere y fuere preguntado dijo: que conocio la hacienda de Balverde poblada por Don Pedro Armendaris que en ella vio varias veces que paso por alli, que se formo una poblazon, que se abrio labor, que se poblo con caballada y ganado mayor que conocio en la misma hacienda hasta un molino y dos distintos administradores, Ygnacio Jaramillo, y Julio Telles, que estubo poblada la dicha hacienda algunos años, que cree se despoblo por lo mucho que invadian los Indios barbaros que es cuanto sabe en lo que se afirma y ratifica bajo el juramento que prestado tiene y lo firmo este dia 14 de Febrero de 1849—Fernando Aragon—Territorio de Nuevo Mejico—Condado de Bernalillo—juramentado y afirmado delante de mi y ante mi Escribano Nombrado este dia 14 de Febrero, A. D. de 1849, en el lugar de Albuquerque lo que certifico—Francisco Sarracino, Prefecto—Ante mi, José Armijo y Ortiz Escribano Nombrado—Territorio de Nuevo Mejico—Condado de Bernalillo—En el espresado presente que fue D. Francisco Baca y Terrus, despues de haber recivido juramento que hizo por Dios de decir verdad nomas la verdad y solo la verdad en lo que supiere y fuere preguntado, dijo: que conocio la hacienda de Balverde poblada por

Don Pedro Armendaris, que en ella vio hacer fabricas, caballadas y ganado mayor que estubo de administrador Ygnacio Jaramillo, por cuenta del espresado Sor. Armendaris, que duro poblada la dicha hacienda algunos años, y que es cuanto sabe en lo que se afirma y ratifica bajo el juramento que prestado tiene, y lo firmo este dia 14 de Febrero de 1849—José Francisco Baca y Terrus—Territorio de Nuevo Mejico—Condado de Bernalillo—Juramento y afirmado delante de mi y ante mi Escribano Nombrado este dia 14 de Febrero, A. D. 1849— en el lugar de Albuquerque, lo que certifico—Francisco Sarracino, Prefecto—Ante mi, José Armijo y Ortiz, Escribano Nombrado—Territorio de Nuevo Mejico—Condado de Bernalillo—En el espresado dia presente que fue Don Antonio Maria Garcia, despues de haber recivido juramento que hizo por Dios de decir verdad, nomas la verdad y solo la verdad en lo que supiere y fuere preguntado, dijo: que conocio la hacienda de Balverde poblada por Don Pedro Armendaris que en ella vio hacer fabricas, caballadas y ganado mayor que estubo de administrador de dicha hacienda Ygnacio Jaramillo por cuenta del espresado Señor Armendaris, que duro poblada la dicha hacienda algunos años y que es cuanto sabe en lo que se afirma y ratifica bajo el juramento que prestado tiene y lo firmo este dia 14 de Febrero de 1849—Antonio Maria Garcia—Territorio de Nuevo Mejico—Condado de Bernalillo— Juramentado y afirmado delante de mi y ante mi escribano nombrado este dia 14 de Febrero, A. D. de 1849, en el lugar de Albuquerque, lo que certifico—Francisco Sarracino, Prefecto—Ante mi, José Armijo y Ortiz Escribano Nombrado—Territorio de Nuevo Mejico—Condado de Bernalillo—Haviendose concluido estas auctuaciones notifiquen sele al Peticionario Lo. Manuel Armendaris el presente Juez H. Francisco Sarracino, Prefecto del Condado por ante su Escribano asi lo decreto mandó y firmo este dia 14 de Febrero, A. D. de 1849, en el lugar de Albuquerque—Francisco Sarracino, Prefecto—Ante mi, José Armijo y Ortiz Escribano Nombrado—Territorio de Nuevo Mejico—Condado de Bernalillo. Haviendosele notificado las antecedentes auctuaciones al peticionario Lo. Manuel Armendaris, dijo: que es conforme y pide se le dé de ellas copia testimoniada y lo firmo por ante mi el Hon. Francisco Sarracino, Prefecto del Condado, y por ante el Escribano Nombrado este dia 14 de Febrero de 1849 en el lugar de Albuquerque.

FRANCISCO SERRACINO,
Prefecto.
MANUEL ARMENDARIS.
Ante mi: JOSÉ ARMIJO Y ORTIZ,
Escribano Nombrado.

Territorio de Nuevo Mejico, }
Condado de Bernalillo. }

Haviendose concluido estas auctuaciones y testimonio que antecede esta fiel y legalmente conforme con el original y por lo mismo entreguese al interesado lo que certifico por ante mi. Escribano nombrado este dia 15 de Febrero de 1849, en el lugar de Albuquerque.

FRANCISCO SARRACINO,
Prefecto.
Ante mi: JOSÉ ARMIJO Y ORTIZ,
Escribado Nombrado.

Sello Tercero. [SELLO.] Cuatro Reales.

Años de mil ochocientos cincuenta y seis y cincuenta y siete.

REPUBLICA MEJICANA,
Estado de Chihuahua, Villa del Paso.

La declaracion del testigo Don Francisco San Juan tomada ante mi, el C. Sisto Yrigoyen Alcalde 1º y Juez 1ª Ynstancia en esta villa del Paso, en el Estado de Chihuahua, Republica Mejicana, para que sea leida como credencial ante el Hon. William Pelham, Agrimensor General del Territorio de Nuevo Mejico, en conocimiento de un reclamo hecho por los herederos de Don Pedro Armendaris, sobre una consecion de terreno, en Balverde y Fray Cristobal, en el Territorio de Nuevo Mejico. Un veras y competente testigo ahora ha comparecido y en mi presencia ha sido legalmente juramentado, y depuso sobre su juramento lo siguiente.

Primera Pregunta : ¿ Conoce V. á los herederos de Don Pedro Armendaris, dijo : que si los conoce.

2ª Pregunta : Diga sus nombres y el lugar de su residencia, dijo : que se llaman Manuel Armendaris, residente en el Paso, Antonia Armendaris, Enrique Armendaris, Miguel Armendaris, y Rodrigo Garcia, como representante y esposo que fue de Belen Armendaris difunta todos estos residentes en la capital de Chihuahua.

3ª Pregunta : Manifieste si sabe cuan do Don Pedro Armendaris, tomo posesion de la consecion del terreno de Balverde, y que tiempo continuo alli poseyendolo, dijo : que en uno de los diversos viages que hizo á Nuevo Mejico, á fines del año de 1819, Don Pedro Armendaris tenia posesion de dicho terreno, y que segun lo mejor que se acuerda, siguio su posesion y continuo en dicha posesion, hasta el año de 1825 ó 1826.

4ª Pregunta : Manifieste que ventajas ó mejoras hizo en dicho terreno, y que numero mas ó menos de ganado, tuvo alli, pastando, dijo: que tenia fincas varias, bastante terreno cultivado, y que no sabe el numero fijo de ganado que tenia, pero que si sabe bien y vio que tenia bastante ganado menor, ganado mayor, y caballada.

5ª Pregunta : Manifieste en que tiempo dejo dicho terreno, y que lo indujo á dejarlo ; dijo que por el año de 1825, ó 1826, dejo dicho terreno despues de haber peraido muchos de sus intereses por las incursiones de los enemigos barbaros, y que esto lo motivo á dejarlo. Sisto Yrigoyen Alcalde 1o. y Juez de 1a. Ynstancia aniva mencionado, por el presente certifico que la antecedente declaracion ha sido tomada por mi y en mi oficina hoy dia 13 de Julio de 1857. Que el referido testigo firmo la antecedente declaracion, en mi presencia y fue legalmente juramentado para la verdad de lo mismo, conmigo el presente juez y los de mi asis tencia, doy fee.

FRANCISCO GARCIA SAN JUAN.
SISTO YRIGOYEN.

Assa : FRANCISCO BARRON.
MAGUINO CASTANEDA.

La declaracion del testigo Don Luis Telles tomada ante mi el C. Sisto Yrigoyen Alcalde 1o. y Juez de 1a. Ynstancia de esta villa del

Paso en el Estado de Chihuahua, Republica Mejicana, para que sea leida como credencial ante el Hon. William Pelham, Agrimensor General del Territorio de Nuevo Mejico, en conocimiento de un reclamo hecho por los herederos de Don Pedro Armendaris sobre una consecion de terreno en Valverde y Fray Cristobal, en el Territorio de Nuevo Mejico. Un veras y competente testigo ahora ha comparecido, y en mi presencia ha sido legalmente juramentado, y depuso sobre su juramente lo siguiente.

1ª Pregunta: ¿Conoce V. á los herederos de Don Pedro Armendaris, dijo: que si los conoce.

2ª Pregunta: Diga sus nombres y el lugar de su residencia, dijo: que se llaman Manuel Armendaris, residente en el Paso, Antonia Armendaris, Enrique Armendaris, Miguel Armendaris, y Rodrigo Garcia, comorepresentante de los hijos de Belen Armendaris, y esposo que fue de esta muerta, todos residentes en la capital de Chihuahu.

3ª Pregunta: Manifieste si sabe cuando Don Pedro Armendaris tomo posesion de la consecion del terreno de Balverde, y que tiempo continuo alli poseyendolo, dijo: que desde el año de 1819, Don Pedro Armendaris tenia ya posesion de dicho terreno, y que segun lo mejor que se acuerda, siguio su posesion y continuo en ella, hasta el año de 1825 ó 1826.

4ª Pregunta: Manifieste que mejoras ó ventajas hizo en dicho terreno, y que numero mas ó menos de ganado tubo alli pastando, dijo: que tenia fincas varias, bastante terreno cultivado, y que no sabe el numero fijo de ganado que tenia, pero que si sabe bien y vio que tenia bastante ganado menor, ganado mayor, y mucha caballada.

5ª Pregunta: Manifieste en que tiempo dejo dicho terreno y que lo indiyo a dejarlo, dijo: que por el año de 1825 ó 1826, dejo dicho terreno despress de haber perdido muchos de sus intereses por las incursiones de los enemigos barbaros, y que esto lo motivo á dejarlo, lo cual le consta al declarante porque alli mismo estubo de estacamento como soldado que era en aquellos tiempos, y peleo con los Indios para impedirles varios robos de los que con frecuencia hacian.

6ª Pregunta: Sirvase manifestar los linderos de las conseciones de Balverde y Fray Cristobal, si acaso se acuerda de ellos, dijo: que recuerda que los linderos son cosa de tres leguas de este lado del ojo del Muerto (esto es) comenzan do desde el Serro de San Pascual por todo el Rio Abajo hasta dicho punto, de alli se tira la linea hasta la sima de la Sierrita de las Petacas, de alli otra asi á la sima de la loma ó Serrito Redondo, y de alli una linea recta á la Sierrita ó Serro de San Pascual ya sitada, que estos en su concepto son los linderos de Balverde y Fray Cristobal. Sisto Yrigoyen, Alcalde 1o. y Juez de 1a. Ynstancia arriba mencionado por el presente certifico que la antecedente declaracion ha sido tomada por mi y en mi oficina hoy dia 13 de Julio de 1857. Que el referido testigo no firmo la antecedente declaracion por no saberlo hacer, pero en mi presencia puso un signo de Cruz y fue legalmente juramentado para verdad de lo mismo, firmando el Juez y testigos de asistencia doy fee.

LUIS TELLES.
SISTO YRIGOYEN.

Assa: FRANCISCO BARRON.
MAGUINO CASTANEDA.

Paso, *Julio* 13 *de* 1857.

Estando tomadas las antecedentes declaraciones entreguensele originales al que las solicito D. Manuel Armendaris, como heredero y Albacea de la testamentaria del defunto Don Pedro Armendaris. El Alcalde 1o. arriba citado asi lo decreto y firmo, con testigos de asistencia segun derecho doy fee.

SISTO YRIGOYEN.

Assa: Francisco Barron.
Maguino Castaneda.

Derechos de las anteriores dilijencias sin el papel, 4 pesos pagados.

No. 10.

Consulate of the United States,
Paso del Norte, Mexico, July 13, 1857.

I, the undersigned, consul of the United States of America, residing at Paso del Norte, republic of Mexico, do hereby certify that the foregoing are the true and genuine signatures of Sisto Yrigoyen, a justice of the peace of this place, and as such are entitled to full faith and credit.

Given under my hand and the seal of this my consulate, at Paso [L. S.] del Norte, this thirteenth day of July, A. D. 1857, and of the independence of the United States the eighty-first.

DAVID R. DIFFENDUFFER,
Consul.

Surveyor General's Office, Translator's Department,
Santa Fé, New Mexico, September 10, 1859.

The above is a true copy of the original on file in this office.

DAVID V. WHITING,
Translator.

GRANT—TRANSLATION.

Equivalent to seal third for the year 1819.

In the absence of Don José Francisco Ortiz,
JOSÉ YGNACIO ORTIZ.

To his Excellency the Governor of the Province:

Don Pedro Ascue de Armendaris, late first lieutenant of the garrison of San Elzeario, in the province of Nuo Vicay, and at present collector of tithes for five years, of which the present year is the first, appears before you with due respect and states: That owning a quantity of stock, which have been recently brought from the aforementioned province, and the probability of obtaining more, the surplus from tithes, and possessing servants, under whose care they are, and as, under proper care, their numbers will increase, pray your excellency to have the goodness to order that the following land, which is vacant, be granted to me, namely: the bottom or valley called Val Verde, for the purpose of cultivating such of the land as is adapted to that purpose. The boundaries or landmarks to all the land, with its appurtenances or lands for pasture, being, in the first place, the water-line of the Rio Grande del Norte; in the (2d) second, the peak or knoll that is on the table land of the Cantaden, which is the boundary or termination of the aforementioned bottom or valley, and which lies in the direction of the place called Fray Cristobal, and drawing a straight line to the little spring called Analla, be included in the possession, and to be third boundary, and running another straight line from this point over the little hills of San Pascual; the fourth boundary to be the little isolated hill separate from those aforementioned, and which is the direction of the river and towards the bottom or valley aforesaid, San Pascual and the Apache woods, (Borque del Apache,) which land, sir, is entirely free, distant from the settlements, which can in no way be injured, the nearest one being the newly formed one called Sacorrito, on the opposite side of the river, and above nine leagues up stream, which space I consider to be more than sufficient for the stock of said town; therefore, taking into consideration the fact that the said bottom is on the public road to El Paso, and the settlement to be formed will be of service to travellers, as well as the settlement of that point with people and stock, and the further consideration of its being free from any other owner, pray your excellency to provide according to the same terms herein mentioned, and if not, according to your pleasure.

City of Santa Fé, New Mexico, November 22, 1819.

PEDRO ARMENDARIS.

Lieut. Col. Don FUCUNDA MELGARES.

SANTA FÉ, *November* 22, 1819.

The justice of Belen will report upon the matter upon an inspection of the premises, in order that action be had thereon.

MELGARES.

To his Excellency the Lieutenant Colonel Governor:

Your excellency requires me to report upon the petition made by Don Pedro Armendaris. Acknowledging the principle that it is land without any known owner up to the present time, according to my knowledge of distance and little intelligence, I consider the land referred to contains, from north to south, four leagues; and from east— that is, from the Analla spring over the little mountain of San Pascual to the banks of the river—I consider the distance to be five leagues to the narrows, where the river joins the arroyo, towards the Penasco, which Mr. Armendaris calls for; and as it does not interfere with the pastures or watering places required by travellers, a great amount of land lying in the direction of Fray Cristobal and a sufficient space above the aforementioned arroyo as far as Sacorro, on both sides of the river, the western side, on the opposite bank of the Rio Grande, being also unoccupied, your excellency will, therefore, be pleased to grant the request of the above-mentioned Armendaris, or as your excellency may deem most convenient ; which is all that I can report in regard to the matter.

MANUEL RUVO DE CELIS.

BELEN, *November* 28, 1819.

SANTA FÉ, *New Mexico, December* 4, 1819.

In consideration of the benefit which will result to the province by the increase of its agriculture, let the request of the petitioner be granted, under the express condition of keeping all the men which may be there armed ; that he shall commence the building of houses and placing upon the land the requisite stock, and that he shall furnish free watering places and pasturage for all travellers, be they with trains or herds of stock, and that he shall continue to enclose his fields as they increase.

MELGARES.

Be it known by this declaration that I, Don Pedro Armendaris, as legitimate owner of the place called Valverde, with all its appurtenances, as appears by the foregoing grant, that I have sold said possession to Don Francisco Havur Chaves, with all my right and title thereto, which are therefore thus conveyed to him in order that he may, when he deems proper, dispose of the same without being prevented from so doing at the present nor any future period by any person whatever. Such being my wish, and having been paid for to my entire satisfaction, by virtue of which and being according to law, I request all the national authorities to protect him, whenever he may so require, in the free and lawful enjoyment of said property; and in order that it may so appear, I have executed this deed and signed with my own hand, in the city of Santa Fé, in New Mexico, on the first day of August, in the year one thousand eight hundred and twenty-three, third of the Mexican independence.

PEDRO ARMENDARIS.

SURVEYOR GENERAL'S OFFICE,
Translator's Department, Santa Fé, N. M., August 10, 1858.

The above is a correct translation of the original on file in this office.

DAVID V. WHITING,
Translator.

SURVEYOR GENERAL'S OFFICE,
Santa Fé, N. M., September 6, 1859.

The above is a true copy of the original on file in this office.

WM. PELHAM,
Surveyor General.

ADDITIONAL GRANT—TRANSLATION.

Seal Fourth. [SEAL.] One Cuartillo.

Years one thousand and eight hundred and twenty and twenty-one. Revalidated: the constitution sworn to by the King on March 9, 1820.

To his Excellency the Governor of the Province:

Don Pedro Ascue de Armendaris, lately first lieutenant of the company of the garrison of San Elizarie, and withdrawn from the service about seven years on account of sickness, having served as a cadet, ensign, and lieutenant for twenty years and some months, and being at the present time a resident of this province, and collector of tithes thereof for five years. I have endeavored from the time I moved here, and am endeavoring now, to improve a stock and agricultural farm which I have established at this point of Balverde, which is my property; and as the site is too contracted, not only for watering places, but also for pasture grounds for the aforementioned stock, which by every effort I endeavor to increase from the tithes as well as from those imported from adjoining provinces, I pray your excellency to do me the benefit of increasing my aforesaid farm, granting to me the following: on the table land (Mesilla) del Contadero there is a peak or knoll which is mine, and from this point I desire you to have the goodness to grant to me in a southwardly direction, following the water-line of the Rio Grande del Norte, on the same side of Valverde, to a point where the little mountain of Fray Cristobal joins the river, being the watering point of said river; and from the aforementioned point of the little mountain over its summit to the spring called del Muerto, which is on one side of the little lake called del Serrito, including the said Muerto spring in the possession, and from its source two leagues in each direction, and from the termination of the distance to the south the line is to continue to the Arroyo spring which is mine, and from this point two leagues to the south, in order that the line running from the Muerto spring may terminate at the boundary of the said two leagues, and from thence three leagues to the east; and from their termination the line is to continue coming down over the upper point of the San Pascual mountain, and terminate on the river at the little hills that are isolated from said mountains which are mine, and which are near the public road on the side of the Apache woods, (Bosque del Apache.)

The entire centre of the aforementioned land is dry, without any water, and the greater portion of it is mine, and is located in the Jornada del Muerto; and as it is exceedingly dry, I desire to adopt some device by which I can supply it with all the water I can, which will result in the great benefit of furnishing important aid to travellers, who are always delayed. The aforementioned land is unoccupied, and is nearly in the centre of the great waste between this province and the town of El Paso; and no one will be injured by my occupation of it, the nearest settlement thereto being that of Socorro, distant about twelve leagues or more; and many benefits will result to the province by my occupation of it, among which the principal are, first, that the deserted waste between Socorro and El Paso, being more than one hundred leagues in extent, travellers will meet with assistance and accomodation; second, that at Valverde I have a large farm under irrigation, whereon all kinds of grain are planted and give an abundant yield, such as has not been equalled before by any person in the entire province, where, on the contrary, yearly failures of the crops are common; third, that the stock I receive from tithes, and with those I introduce, I gradually establish large herds, which in a short time will not only answer the purpose of facilitating purchases, but the inhabitants who have the means will perceive the advantage arising from concentrating their stock at one point, (a circumstance of which they are ignorant,) they will do the same as I am now doing, and by this means will improve the province, and they themselves will do away with the injurious practice of letting out their flocks and herds on shares; fourth, another advantage will be that those having the means will cultivate more extensively and will have grain to spare, and will not rely upon purchasing from the lower classes at a cheap rate, in order that they may sell to the same persons again at a high price, or leave them to starve, as we see every day, and whom, if they have an abundance, will devote their time to ordinary manufactures, of which none are now seen, as the poor would then have (as they now have with me) the means of obtaining with their labor wherewith to clothe themselves, as is seen everywhere; fifth, it is evident that the cultivation of large crops and the care of a large amount of stock will require the services of many persons, avoiding thereby in a great measure the robbery of the means of subsistence, and the vagabond life of many miserable creatures will cease; and lastly, governor, his Majesty, whom may God preserve, has for many years directed the settlement of all the immense waste along the river until the province becomes united with the town of El Paso, which is a branch of the same; and as I have been the first at all hazards to settle upon said waste, and the first to have established in this province so great an enterprise, I pray your excellency to have the goodness to grant my petition in the terms therein expressed.

God our father preserve your excellency's life for many years.

PEDRO ARMENDARIS.

SANTA FÉ, *May* 15, 1820.

SANTA FÉ, *June* 1, 1820.

As it is not deemed inconvenient, as he requests, under the same conditions of the decree of Valverde.

MELGARES.

As this deed is annexed to the one for Valverde of the twenty-second day of November, one thousand eight hundred and nineteen, and included at the same time in the sale made to Don Francisco Xavier Chaves, I hereby make known that it is his with the same right and title as the aforementioned one, which I transferred to him on the first of August, one thousand eight hundred and twenty-three;

and it is my desire that he enjoy it with the same liberty with which he enjoys the other, as he has paid for both to my entire satisfaction, with the sum of three thousand hard dollars and fifteen mules; and in order that it may appear at all times I have executed this document this twenty-fifth day of August, one thousand eight hundred and twenty-three.

PEDRO ARMENDARIS.

SURVEYOR GENERAL'S OFFICE,
Santa Fé, New Mexico, September 6, 1859.

The above is a true copy of the original on file in this office.

WM. PELHAM,
Surveyor General.

TESTIMONY—TRANSLATION.

TERRITORY OF NEW MEXICO, }
County of Bernalillo. }

At the end of the proceedings had at the request of Lecenciate Manuel Armendaris, before the honorable Francisco Sarracino, prefect of the county of Bernalillo, a decree of the following tenor is entered:

TERRITORY OF NEW MEXICO, }
County of Bernalillo. }

The petitioner, Lecenciate Manuel Armendaris, having been informed of the foregoing proceedings, he stated that he was satisfied with them, and asked that a certified copy be given to him, and he signed it before me, the honorable Francisco Sarracino, prefect of the county, and before the clerk appointed on this 14th day of February, 1849, at the town of Albuquerque. Francisco Sarracino, prefect. Manuel Armendaris. Before me, José Armijo y Ortiz, appointed clerk. The above is a true and legal copy taken from the original, to which reference is hereby made, and which I certify and signed before my appointed clerk, on this 15th day of February, 1849, at the town of Albuquerque.

F. SARRACINO, Prefect.

Before me—

JOSÉ ARMIJO Y ORTIZ, Appointed Clerk.

TERRITORY OF NEW MEXICO, }
County of Bernalillo. }

As requested by the petitioner, Lecenciate Manuel Armendaris, let the certified copy he asks for be given to him from the office of the prefect of the county of Bernalillo. The honorable Francisco Sarracino, prefect of the county, so decreed at the town of Albuquerque, on this 15th day of February, 1859.

FRANCISCO SARRACINO, Prefect.

To the honorable prefect of the county of Bernalillo:

Manuel Armendaris, agent for the house of my father, Don Pedro Armendaris, appears before you in the manner provided by law, and states that in the years of nineteen and twenty of the present century there were granted to him the lands which form the Valverde farm. This farm was immediately settled, its tillable lands were placed under cultivation, and horses and cattle were kept upon the pasture lands. It so remained up to the year of twenty-five, in which year the Navajo Indians destroyed all that was there, even to destroying the troop that were stationed there for protection.

This circumstance having taken place, and seeing the impossibility of keeping up the farm, my father abandoned it, and when he withdrew to Chihuahua he left the deeds to the lands situate on the left bank of the Bravo river in the possession of Don Francisco Chaves, the boundaries of which are as follows: Commencing at a point on Bravo river where the Arroyo de San Pascual empties into it, following down the river for three Castilian leagues, opposite the source of the Muerto spring; from this point on the river, distant three leagues from the aforementioned spring, a line is drawn to the highest summit of the Petacas mountain, from which summit another line is drawn to the summit of the Redondo mountain, and from thence another line is drawn over the summit of the little mountain of San Pascual to the place of beginning, which is the junction of the arroyo with the river. The title deeds accrediting this property, which, as I before stated, remained in the hands of Don Francisco Chaves. I have always been told when asking for them by Don José Chaves, administrator of the estate of his father, they have been lost; for this reason, and it being well known in this Territory that these lands were the property of my father, I make use of article 6th of the statutes in force, entitled "Records of Lands," in order that, in conformity therewith, you will be pleased to summon General Don Manuel Armijo, Don Antonio Sandoval, Don Fernando Aragon, Don Antonio Maria Garcia, Don Francisco Baca y Terrus, and as many more as may be necessary, so that, in accordance with the law, they may testify what they know concerning the matter herein referred to. Therefore I pray and request you to be pleased to provide according to my petition, justice requiring it should be done.

MANUEL ARMENDARIS.

ALBUQUERQUE, *February* 13, 1849.

TERRITORY OF NEW MEXICO, }
County of Bernalillo. }

Considered as presented and received, as required by law, according to the established form. Let the summons be issued to Messrs. Armijo, Sandoval, Baca y Terrus, Aragon, and Garcia, requiring them to appear at the special court of the honorable Francisco Sarracino, at the office of the honorable justice, Manuel Armijo, in the town of Albuquerque, on Wednesday, the 14th day of February, at two o'clock p. m.; the petitioner to be notified of this petition for his information.

The said prefect so decreed, ordered, and signed, this 14th day of February, 1849, before his appointed clerk.

FRANCISCO SARRACINO, *Prefect.*

Before me—

JOSÉ ARMIJO Y ORTIZ,
Appointed Clerk.

ALBUQUERQUE, *Wednesday, February* 14, 1849.

The party interested was notified of the foregoing decree.

FRANCISCO SANDOVAL.

TERRITORY OF NEW MEXICO, }
County of Bernalillo. }

In compliance with the foregoing decree and the request of the petitioner, Licentiate Manuel Armendaris, General Don Manuel Armijo being present, and having made oath, which he did by God, to state the truth, the whole truth, and nothing but the truth, in what he knew and might be interrogated, he answered that he knew the Valverde farm, settled by Don Pedro Armendaris; that he there saw buildings erected, and horses and cattle pastured; that Don Ignacio Jaramillo was overseer of said farm, in the employ of the aforesaid Mr. Armendaris; that said farm was settled for a number of years; and that what he has stated is all he knows, which he ratifies and affirms under the oath he has taken, and he signed on this 14th day of February, 1849.

MANUEL ARMIJO, *General.*

TERRITORY OF NEW MEXICO, }
County of Bernalillo. }

Sworn to and affirmed before me, and before my appointed clerk, on this 14th day of February, 1849, at the town of Albuquerque, to which I certify.

FRANCISCO SARRACINO, *Prefect.*

Before me—

JOSÉ ARMIJO Y ORTIZ,
Appointed Clerk.

TERRITORY OF NEW MEXICO, }
County of Bernalillo. }

Incontinently, Don Antonio Sandoval being present, after having made oath, which he did by God, to state the truth, the whole truth, and nothing but the truth, in what he knew and might be interrogated, he stated that he knew the Valverde farm, settled by Don Pedro Armendaris; that he saw buildings erected on several occasions when he passed there, and that horses and cattle were pastured there; that he knew two different overseers on said farm, Ignacio Jaramillo and Julio Telles; that said farm was occupied for several years, and he believes it to have been abandoned on account of the many invasions of the hostile Indians; and that what he has stated is all he knows, which he ratifies and affirms under the oath which he has taken, and he signed on this 14th day of February, 1849.

ANTONIO SANDOVAL.

Territory of New Mexico, }
 County of Bernalillo. }

Sworn to and affirmed before me and my appointed clerk on this 14th day of February, A. D. 1849, at the town of Albuquerque.

FRANCISCO SARRACINO, *Prefect*.

Before me—
JOSÉ ARMIJO Y ORTIZ,
Appointed Clerk.

Territory of New Mexico, }
 County of Bernalillo. }

Incontinently the honorable justice, Fernando Aragon, being present, after having made oath, which he did by God, to state the truth, the whole truth, and nothing but the truth, in whatever he knew and should be interrogated, he stated that he knew the Valverde farm, settled by Don Pedro Armendaris; that having passed by there on several occasions, he saw that a settlement had been formed there; that the land was cultivated; that it was stocked with horses and cattle; that he knew a mill to have been erected there, and that there were two different overseers there, Ignacio Jaramillo and Julio Telles; that said farm was settled for some years, and that he believes it was abandoned on account of the many incursions of the hostile Indians; that what he has stated is all he knows, which he ratifies and affirms under the oath which he has taken, and he signed this on the 14th day of February, A. D. 1849.

FRANCISCO ARAGON.

Territory of New Mexico, }
 County of Bernalillo. }

Sworn to and affirmed before me, and before my appointed clerk, on this 14th day of February, 1849, at the town of Albuquerque, to which I certify.

FRANCISCO SARRACINO, *Prefect*.

Before me—
JOSÉ ARMIJO Y ORTIZ,
Appointed Clerk.

Territory of New Mexico, }
 County of Bernalillo. }

At the same time, Don Francisco Baca y Terres being present, and having made oath, which he did by God, to state the truth, the whole truth, and nothing but the truth, in what he knew and should be interrogated, he stated that he knew the Valverde farm, settled by Don Pedro Armendaris; that he saw buildings there and horses and cattle; that Ignacio Jaramillo was overseer there, employed by the aforesaid Mr. Armendaris; that said farm was settled for some years; that the above is all he knows, which he affirmed and ratified under the oath which he has made, and he signed this on the 14th day of February, A. D. 1849.

JOSÉ FRANCISCO BACA Y TERRES.

TERRITORY OF NEW MEXICO,
County of Bernalillo.

Sworn to and affirmed before me, and before my appointed clerk, on this 14th day of February, A. D. 1849, at the town of Albuquerque, to which I certify.

FRANCISCO SARRACINO, Prefect.

Before me—

JOSÉ ARMIJO Y ORTIZ,
Appointed Clerk.

TERRITORY OF NEW MEXICO,
County of Bernalillo.

On the same day Don Antonio Maria Garcia being present, after having made oath, which he did by God, to state the truth, the whole truth, and nothing but the truth, in what he knew and should be interrogated, he stated that he knew the Valverde farm, settled by Don Pedro Armendaris; that he saw buildings there, and horses and oxen; that Ignacio Jaramillo was the overseer of the farm under the employ of the aforesaid Mr. Armendaris; that the farm was occupied for some years; and that is all he knows, which he ratifies and affirms under the oath which he has taken, and he signed the above on the 14th day of February, A. D. 1849.

ANTONIO MARIA GARCIA.

TERRITORY OF NEW MEXICO,
County of Bernalillo.

Sworn to and affirmed before me, and before my appointed clerk, at the town of Albuquerque, on this 14th day of February, A. D. 1849, to which I certify.

FRANCISCO SARRACINO, Prefect.

Before me—

JOSÉ ARMIJO Y ORTIZ,
Appointed Clerk.

TERRITORY OF NEW MEXICO,
County of Bernalillo.

The foregoing proceedings having been concluded, let the petitioner, Licentiate Manuel Armendaris, be informed thereof. The present judge, the honorable Francisco Sarracino, prefect of the county, before his clerk so decreed, ordered, and signed, on this 14th day of February, A. D. 1849, at the town of Albuquerque.

FRANCISCO SARRACINO, Prefect.

Before me—

JOSÉ ARMIJO Y ORTIZ,
Appointed Clerk.

TERRITORY OF NEW MEXICO, }
County of Bernalillo.

The petitioner, Licentiate Manuel Armendaris, having been informed of the foregoing proceedings, he stated that he was satisfied with them, and asked that a certified copy be given to him, and he signed it before me, the honorable Francisco Sarracino, prefect of the county, and before the clerk appointed, on this 14th day of February, 1849, at the town of Albuquerque.

FRANCISCO SARRACINO, *Prefect.*

Before me—

JOSÉ ARMIJO Y ORTIZ,
Appointed Clerk.

TERRITORY OF NEW MEXICO, }
County of Bernalillo.

These proceedings and foregoing copy being concluded, it agrees truly and legally with the original, and therefore let it be delivered to the party interested, to which I certify before my appointed clerk, on this 15th day of February, 1849, at the town of Albuquerque.

FRANCISCO SARRACINO, *Prefect*

Before me—

JOSÉ ARMIJO Y ORTIZ,
Appointed Clerk.

SURVEYOR GENERAL'S OFFICE, TRANSLATOR'S DEPARTMENT,
Santa Fé, New Mexico, July 18, 1859.

The foregoing is a correct translation of the original on file in this office.

DAVID V. WHITING,
Translator.

SURVEYOR GENERAL'S OFFICE,
Santa Fé, New Mexico, September 6, 1859.

The above is a true copy of the original on file in this office.

WM. PELHAM,
Surveyor General.

TESTIMONY—TRANSLATION.

Seal Third. [SEAL.] Four Reals.

Years one thousand eight hundred and fifty-six and fifty-seven.

MEXICAN REPUBLIC, }
State of Chihuahua, Town of El Paso.

The declaration of the witness Don Francisco San Juan, taken before me, citizen Sisto Irigo Yeu, first justice and judge of first instance of this town of El Paso, in the State of Chihuahua, Mexican republic, to be read in evidence before the Hon. William Pelham, surveyor general of the Territory, concerning a claim made by the heirs of Don Pedro Armendaris, under a grant of land at Valverde and Fray Cristobal, in the Territory of New Mexico, a credible and competent witness, has now appeared, and in my presence has been lawfully sworn, and under oath deposed as follows :

First question. Do you know the heirs of Don Pedro Armendaris? He answered that he did know them.

Second question. State their names and the place of their residence. That their names are Manuel Armendaris, residing at El Paso ; Antonio Armendaris, Eunique Armendaris, Miguel Armendaris, and Rodrigo Garcia, as the representative and husband of Belen Armendaris, deceased ; all of these reside at the capital of Chihuahua.

Third question. State, if you know, when Don Pedro Armendaris took possession of the grant of the land at Valverde, and how long did he remain in possession there? He said that in one of his many journeys to New Mexico, towards the end of the year 1819, Don Pedro Armendaris had possession of said land, and to the best of his recollection he remained in possession and occupied it up to the year 1825 or 1826.

Fourth question. State what improvements he made on said land, and what number of cattle, more or less, did he pasture there? He said that he had several buildings, a large quantity of land under cultivation, and that he does not know the exact number of cattle he had, but he well knows and saw that he had a large number of sheep, cattle, and horses.

Fifth question. State when he left said land, and what induced him to leave it. He said that he left the land about the year 1825 or 1826 ; he left the land after having lost a large amount of property by the incursions of hostile Indians, and that was what compelled him to leave.

Sisto Irigoyen, first justice and judge of first instance aforesaid, hereby certifies that the foregoing declaration was taken by me, and at my office, this 13th day of July, 1857 ; that the aforesaid witness signed the foregoing declaration in my presence, and was legally sworn to the truth of the same with me, the present judge, and those in my attendance, I certify.

      SISTO IRIGOYEN.
      FRANCISCO GARCIA Y SAN JUAN.
Attending :
  Fran'co Barron.
Attending :
  Maguino Castañeda.

The declaration of the witness Don Luis Telles, taken before me, citizen Sisto Irigoyen, first justice and judge of first instance of this town of El Paso, in the State of Chihuahua, Mexican republic, to be read in evidence before the honorable William Pelham, surveyor general of New Mexico, concerning a claim made by the heirs of Don Pedro Armendaris, under a grant of land at Valverde and Fray Cristobal, in the Territory of New Mexico, a credible and competent witness, has now appeared, and in my presence has been legally sworn, and deposed under his oath as follows :

First question. Do you know the heirs of Don Pedro Armendaris? He said that he does know them.

Second question. State their names and the places of their residence. He said their names are Manuel Armendaris, resident of El Paso; Antonio Armendaris, Henry Armendaris, Miguel Armendaris, and Rodrigo Garcia, as the husband and representative of the children of Belen Armendaris, deceased, residents of the capital of Chihuahua.

Third question. State, if you know, when Pedro Armendaris took possession of the grant of land at Valverde, and how long did he continue in possession? He stated that in the year 1819 Don Pedro Armendaris had possession of said land, and to the best of his recollection he continued in possession and remained there until the year 1825 or 1826.

Fourth question. State what improvements he made on the land, and what number of cattle, more or less, he pastured there. He said, that he had several buildings, a large amount of land under cultivation; that he does not know the exact number of cattle he had, but that he well knows and saw that he had a large number of sheep and cattle, and a great many horses.

Fifth question. State when he left that land, and what induced him to abandon it. He stated he left the land about the year 1825 or 1826, after having lost a large amount of his property from the incursions of the hostile Indians, on account of which he was compelled to leave, which the deponent well knows, as he was a soldier at that time, and one of the detachment; that he fought with the Indians to prevent several robberies, which they frequently committed.

Sixth question. Be pleased to state the boundaries of the grants to Valverde and Fray Cristobal, if you remember them. He stated that he remembers the boundaries are about three leagues this side of the Muerto spring; that is, commencing at the San Pascual mountains, and following down the river to said point; from thence drawing a direct line to the summit of the little mountain of Las Petecas; from thence another direct line to the summit of the hill, or little Redondo mountain, and from thence in a direct line to the little mountain, or mountain of San Pascual above mentioned. That, in his opinion, these are the boundaries of Valverde and Fray Cristobal.

Sisto Irigoyen, first justice and judge of first instance above mentioned, certifies that the foregoing declaration was taken by me, and at my office, on this 13th day of July, 1857; that the aforementioned witness did not sign the foregoing declaration, as he did not know how, but that in his presence he made the sign of the cross, and was legally sworn to the truth of the same.

The judge and attending witnesses signing.

LUIS + TELLES.
his mark.

I certify,   SISTO IRIGOYEN.

Attending: FRANCISCO BARRON.
            MAGUINO CASTAÑEDA.

Fees for the foregoing procedure, without the paper, $4, paid.
[Rubric.]

No. 10.

CONSULATE OF THE UNITED STATES,
Paso del Norte, Mexico, July 13, 1857.

I, the undersigned, consul of the United States of America, residing at Paso del Norte, republic of Mexico, do hereby certify that the foregoing are the true and genuine signatures of Sisto Irigoyen, a justice of the peace of this place, and as such are entitled to full faith and credit.

Given under my hand and seal of this my consulate, at Paso del Norte, this 13th day of July, 1857, and of the independence of the United States the eighty-first.

[L. S.]

DAVID R. DIFFENDAFFER, *Consul.*

SURVEYOR GENERAL'S OFFICE, TRANSLATOR'S DEPARTMENT,
Santa Fé, New Mexico, July 21, 1859.

The foregoing, excepting the consular certificate, is a correct translation of the original on file in this office.

DAVID V. WHITING,
Translator.

SURVEYOR GENERAL'S OFFICE,
Santa Fé, New Mexico, August 31, 1859.

The foregoing is a true copy of the original now on file in this office.

WM. PELHAM,
Surveyor General.

TESTIMONY.

Heirs of Pedro Armendaris.

ANTONIO SENA sworn:

Question. Have you any interest in this case?
Answer. None.
Question. Are the signatures of Facundo Melgares genuine on documents A and B?
Answer. They are.
Question. Did you know if Armendaris was placed in possession of the Valverde grant.
Answer. I know that he was placed in possession of the land with all the formalities of the law, and that he built on the land and cultivated it. He had a large amount of sheep and cattle upon it also.
Question. Why did he abandon it?
Answer. I have heard it said that he abandoned it on account of the hostility of the Indians.

ANTONIO SENA.

Sworn and subscribed before me this 8th July, 1859.
WM. PELHAM,
Surveyor General.

AGUSTIN DURAN sworn:

Question. Have you any interest in this case?
Answer. None.
Question. Are the signatures of Facundo Melgares genuine on documents A and B?
Answer. They are. He was military and political governor of New Mexico at the time.
Question. Do you know if Armendaris took possession of the land and made improvements there?
Answer. I do. He built large houses there for his own residence and those of his hands; he also built a house for travellers. He had land under cultivation. He remained there until the escort which had been given him for some years was removed. I believe he was compelled to move away on account of the hostility of the Indians when the troops were removed.

AGUSTIN DURAN.

Sworn and subscribed before me this 8th July, 1859.
WM. PELHAM,
Surveyor General.

SURVEYOR GENERAL'S OFFICE,
Santa Fé, New Mexico, September 6, 1859.

The above is a true copy of the original on file in this office.
WM. PELHAM,
Surveyor General.

REPORT.

THE HEIRS OF PEDRO ARMENDARIS *vs.* THE UNITED STATES.

This case was set for trial the 8th day of July, 1859, and the witnesses being present, their evidence was taken and the case closed on the same day.

On the 22d day of November, 1819, Pedro Arcue de Armendaris, formerly a lieutenant at the garrison of San Elizario, petitioned Facundo Melgares, the civil and military governor of New Mexico, under the Spanish crown, for a tract of land situated at Valverde, in the province of New Mexico, with the boundaries therein stated.

This petition was referred by Governor Melgares to the justice of the town of Belen, requiring him to report on the condition of the land, which report having been made favorably to the petition, possession was ordered to be given to him by the governor aforesaid on the 4th December of the same year.

The documents presented do not show that he was placed in possession as required by the granting decree.

On the 15th May, 1820, the said Pedro Armendaris asked for a further grant adjoining the one previously made, with the boundaries mentioned in the petition, which grant was made to him under the same conditions required under the Valverde grant, which were that all the employés he had then should be well armed. The papers filed for this grant do not show that he was placed in possession by the justice of the peace.

Oral and documentary evidence has been introduced by the claimants to prove that the land was occupied by the said Armendaris for some years, and left it only on account of the hostility of the Indians, which has been clearly shown in evidence. His stock was pastured upon the land, and a large tract of land was placed under successful cultivation, and the promises made in his petition are believed to have been faithfully complied with.

The documents acted upon in this case are the originals filed by the claimants.

The above grant was made according to the well-established usages and customs of the country at the time. The grantee has held possession from the time the grant was made up to the present day, and no one having appeared showing a better title thereto, the original and subsequent additional grant are believed to be good and valid; they are therefore approved to the legal representatives of Pedro Armendaris, and ordered to be transmitted to Congress for its action in the premises.

WILLIAM PELHAM,
Surveyor General.

SURVEYOR GENERAL'S OFFICE,
Santa Fé, New Mexico, July 10, 1859.

SURVEYOR GENERAL'S OFFICE,
Santa Fé, New Mexico, September 6, 1859.

The above is a true copy of the original on file in this office.

WILLIAM PELHAM,
Surveyor General.

CLAIM No. 34.

HEIRS OF PEDRO ARMENDARIS.

Schedule of documents composing claim No. 34.

1. Notice.
2. Grant and testimony—Spanish.
3. Grant—translation.
4. Testimony—translation.
5. Testimony—English.
6. Report.

NOTICE.

To the Hon. Wm. Pelham, surveyor general of the Territory of New Mexico.

Your petitioners, Manuel Armendaris, Henrique Armendaris, Miguel Armendaris, Antonio Armendaris, children of Pedro Armendaris, deceased, and Rodrigo Garcia, the father and guardian of the infant children of Belen Armendaris, deceased, being the only surviving heirs-at-law and legal representatives of the said Pedro Armendaris, deceased, who died in Chihuahua on the 3d day of May, 1853, would respectfully state that they are residents of the State of Chihuahua, in the republic of Mexico, and that on the 1st day of May, A. D. 1820, there was granted to the said Pedro Armendaris a certain tract of land, known as the site opposite Valverde, and bounded as follows: Beginning opposite the ancon of Valverde, on the opposite side of the river, where there is a small ancon which is to serve as a centre, the first boundary being opposite the Mesilla del Contadero, where said little bottom joins the hills; second, the spring of the Cañes Verales, distant about three leagues, and is in the direction of the point of the little hill which runs between Socorro, from the abovementioned spring, that is, from its source one league to the east, two leagues to the north, and three leagues to the west, and returning to the source of said spring, drawing a direct line to the river to the little mountain of San Pascual, the boundary being where the aforesaid Aconcita terminates, where the river again joins the hills on the same side of the river, as will appear by reference to the document herewith filed, marked exhibit No. 1. Your petitioners further state that the said Pedro Armendaris took possession of said lands and built houses and corrals upon the same, and had those lands in cultivation, and had pasturing and raising there large herds of sheep and many cattle and horses, and continued to occupy the said lands until he was forcibly expelled from them by hostile incursions of the Navajo Indians. Your petitioners further state that said lands have never been surveyed, and the number of acres contained within said limits are not known to your petitioners, but the boundaries mentioned in said grant are noted and visible fixed points, universally known and recognized in the vicinity. Your petitioners further state that said lands have been known and recognized as the lands of said Pedro Armendaris since 1820 up to the present time, and there are no claimants to said lands except your petitioners. Your petitioners further state that there are several persons located on said lands, but their title is derived from, and they claim under, the said grant to the said Pedro Armendaris. Your petitioners further state that they wish such steps taken in the premises as will confirm to them said grant under the act of Congress of July 22, 1854, passed for that purpose. All of which is respectfully submitted.

JOHN G. WATTS,
Attorney for Claimants.

Surveyor General's Office,
Santa Fé, New Mexico, August 15, 1859.

The above is a true copy of the original on file in this office.

WILLIAM PELHAM, *Surveyor General.*

GRANT AND TESTIMONY—SPANISH.

Sello quarto. [SEAL.] Un quartillo.

Anos de mil ochocientos veinte y veinte yuno. Havilitado, jurada por el Rey la Constitution en 9 de Marzo, de 1820.

Sor. Governador de la Provincia:

Don Pedro Ascue de Armendariz Teniente que fue de la Compa. de San Elciario, y ahora diezmero por un quingueño en esta Provincia; ante V.S. con el debido respecto paresco y digo; que siendo dueño de Balverde que es labor, y manteniendo en el alguna caballada, y Resés, las que anualmente haumento; suplico á V.S. tenga la vondad de aser me la gracia de darme en merced, para poner mi ganado menor, y tener donde poderlo hayar, el sitio Rialengo que sigue: Enfrente del ancon de Balverde á la otra banda del Rio, se halla un ancon sito el cual ha de servir de sentro, siendo el primer lindero enfrente de la Mesilla del Contadero, en don de pega dicho enconsito á las Lomas, el segunda el ojito de las Cañas Berales, que dista como tres leguas, y queda asia la punta de la Sierrita que corre para abajo del Socorro, del mencionado ojito, esto es de su nasimiento, una legua al Oriente, dos leguas al Norte, y tres leguas al Poniente, y volviendo al nasimiento de dicho ojito, se tira la line para el rio recta, á la Sierrita de San Pascual, y sera el lindera en donde acaba el anconsito subsodicho, en donde pega el Rio otra vez á las Lomas, de la misma banda, bajo la seguridad. Sor que et tal sitio no perjudica á ninguna persona ni reconce ningun dueño, pues la poblacion que tiene mas serca es la del Socorra que dista como nueve liguas, y con consederme V.S. la dicha posesion no Solo fomenta la Provincia, sino que cumple con la voluntad de S M. que tiene mandado se pueble el inmenso despoblado que hay hasta El Paso, por lotanto suplico á V.S. aseda á mi solicitud. Dios Nro. Sor. Gue. la vida de V.S. m⁸. a⁸. Villa de Santa Fé, lo de Mayo, de 1820.

PEDRO ARMENDARIZ.

SANTA FÉ, *3 de Mayo*, 1820.

El suplicante ha acreditado ser libre el terreno que solicita por lo mismo el Alcalde de de Belen le dara posesion real de el y le estendera la correspondiente escritura por su seguridad.

MELGARES.

Este titulo es registrado en el libro A, folios 135, buelta y 136, cara en mi oficiana; lo que certifico firmo y sello para la devida constancia, Santa Fé, Septembre 26, de 1848.

[SELLO.]
DONACIANO VIGIL,
Actual Gobernador del Territorio de Nuevo Mejico.

Sello Tercero. [SEAL.] Cuatro Reales.

Años de mil ochocientos cincuenta y seis y cincuenta y siete.

REPUBLICA MEJICANA,
Estado de Chihuahua, Villa del Paso.

La declaracion del testigo Don Francisco San Juan tomada ante mi el C. Sisto Yrigoyen Alcalde 1º y Juez de 1ª Ynstancia de eta villa del Paso en el Estado de Chihuahua Republica Mejicana, para que sea leida como credencial ante el Hon. William Pelham, Agrimensor General del Territorio de Nuevo Mejico, en conocimiento de un reclamo heco por los herederos de Don Pedro Armendariz sobre una consecion de terreno enfrente de Balverde en lado derecho del Rio Bravo en el Territorio de Nuevo Mejico. A. B. Un veras y competente testigo ahora ha comparecido y en mi presencia ha sido legalmente juramentado, a depuso sobre su juramento lo siguiente.

1ª Pregunta. I Conoce V. á los herederos de Don Pedro Armendariz? dijo: que si los conoce.

2ª Pregunta. Diga sus nombres y el lugar de sus residencias, dijo; Que se llaman Manuel Armendariz, residente en el Paso, Antonia Armendariz, Enrique Armendariz, Miguel Armendariz, y Rodrigo Garcia como representante de los hijos de su Esposa Belen Armendariz difunta, todos estos residentes en la capital de Chihuahua.

3ª Pregunta. Manifieste cuando Don Pedro Amendariz fue ó se le dio posesion de la consecion del terreno frente á Balverde, dijo; que por el ano de 1820, y que lo abandono cuando dejo á Balverde y Fray Cristobal que fue por el año de 1825 ó 1826.

4ª Pregunta. Diga que mejoras hizo á dicho terreno y que numero de granado tenia alli, dijo; que no sabia si hizo alguna mejora pero que si sabe y vio que tenia mucho granado y caballada pastando en dicho terreno.

5ª Pregunta. Diga cuando dejo dicho terreno y porque causa fue compelido á dejarlo, dijo; que por los repetidos robos que le hacian de granado los Indios barbaras y sus incursiones.

Sisto Yrigoyen Alcalde 1º y Juez de 1ª Ynstancia arriva mencionado, por el presente certifico, que la antecedente declaracion ha sido tomada por mi y en mi oficina, hoy dia 13 de Julio de 1857; Que el referido testigo firmo la antecedente declaracion, en mi presencia y fue legalmente juramentado para la verdad de lo mismo conmigo el presente Juez y los de mi asistencia, doy fee.

SISTO YRIGOYEN,
FRANCO. GARCIA Y SAN JUAN.

Asistencias:
MAGUINO CASTAÑEDAS.
FRANCO. BARRON.

La declaracion del testigo D. Luis Telles, tomada ante mi el C. Sisto Yrigoyen Alcalde 1º y Juez de 1ª Ynstancia de esta villa del Paso, en el Estado de Chihuahua Republica Mejicana, para que sea leida como credencial ante el honorable Wm. Pelham, Agrimensor General del

Territorio de Nuevo Mejico en conocimiento de un reclamo hecho por los herederos de Don Pedro Armendariz, sobre una consecion de terreno enfrente de Valverde, en lado derecho del Rio Bravo en el Territorio de Nuevo Mejico. A. B. un veras y competente ustigo ahora ha comparecido y en mi presencia ha sido legalmente juramentado y depuso sobre su juramento lo signiente.

1ª Pregunta. Conoce V. á los herederos de Don Pedro Armendariz, dijo; que si los conoce.

2ª Pregunta. Diga sus nombres y el lugar de sus residencias, dijo; que se llaman Manuel Armendariz, residente en el Paso, Antonia Armendariz, Enrique Armendariz, Miguel Armendariz, y Rodrigo Garcia como representante de los hijos de su Esposa Belen Armendariz difunta todos estos residentes de la capital de Chihuahua.

3ª Pregunta: Manifieste cuando Don Pedro Armendariz fue ó se le dio posesion de la consecion del terreno frente á Valverde, dyo: que por el año de 1820, y que lo abandonó cuando dejo á Balverde y Fray Cristobal, que fue por el año de 1825, ó 1826.

4ª Pregunta: Diga que mejoras hizo á dicho terreno y que numero de ganado tenia alli, dijo: que no sabia si hizo alguna mejora, pero que si sabe y vio que tenia mucho ganado y caballada pastando en dicho terreno.

5ª Diga cuando dejo dicho terreno, y por que causa fue compelido á dejarlo, dijo que por los repetidos rovos que le hacian los indios barbaros y sus frecuentes incursiones. Sisto Yrigoyen alcalde 1o. y Juez de 1a. Ynstancia arriba mencionado por el presente certifico que la antecedente declaracion ha sido tomada por mi, y en mi oficina, hoy dia 13 de Julio de 1857. Que el referido testigo no firmopor no saber la antecedente declaracion, pero en mi presencia hecho una cruz y fue legalmente juramentado para la verdad de lo mismo, firmando yo el Juez y los testigos de mi asistencia segun derecho doy fee.

LUIS + TELLES.
SISTO YRIGOYEN.

Assistencias:
MAGUINO CASTAÑEDA.
FRANCO. BARRON.

Paso, *Julio* 13 *de* 1857.

Estando tomadas las antecedentes declaraciones entreguensele originales al que las solicito Don Manuel Armendariz, para los usos que crea necesarios en defensa de sus derechos y el de sus hermanos. El Señor Juez 1° ya mencionado, asi lo decreto y firmo con testigos de asistencia segun derecho doy fee.

SISTO YRIGOYEN.

Assistencias:
MAGUINO CASTAÑEDA.
FRANCO. BARRON.

Derechos de las antinores dilijencias. Sin el papel 4 pesos pagados.

No. 8.

Consulate of the United States,
Mexico, Paso del Norte, July 13, 1857.

I, the undersigned, consul of the United States of America, residing at Paso del Norte, republic of Mexico, do hereby certify that the foregoing are the true and genuine signatures of Sisto Yrigoyen, justice of the peace of this place, and entitled to full faith and credit.

[L. S.] Given under my hand and the seal of my consulate at Paso del Norte, this the 13th day of July, A. D. 1857, and of the independence of the United States the eighty-first.

DAVID R. DIFFENDERFFER,
Consul.

Surveyor General's Office, Translator's Department,
Santa Fé, New Mexico, August 24, 1859.

The above is a true copy of the original on file in this office.

DAVID V. WHITING,
Translator.

GRANT—TRANSLATION.

Seal Fourth. [seal.] Fourth of a Real.

One fourth of a real for the years one thousand eight hundred and twenty and twenty-one.

Qualified.—The constitution sworn to by the King on the 9th of March, 1820.

To the Governor of the Province, Don Pedro de Armendaris, formerly of the company of San Elizario, and at present collector of tithes in this province for five years:

I appear before your excellency with all proper respect and state, that being the owner of Valverde, which is tillable land, and keeping therein a certain number of horses and cattle, which animals increase, I pray your excellency to have the kindness to grant me, where I can place my sheep and enable them to bring forth their young, the following unoccupied land, to wit: opposite the bend (ancon) of Valverde, on the opposite side of the river, the first boundary being opposite to the Mesilla del Contadero, where said bend (ancon) joins the hills; the second, the little spring of the Cañas Verales, distance about three leagues, and is in the direction of the point of the little mountain which runs below Socorro; from the aforementioned little spring, that is from its source, one league to the east, two leagues to the north, and three leagues to the west; and returning to the source of said little spring, drawing a straight line to the little mountain of San

Pascual, the boundary being the termination of the aforesaid little bend, where the river again joins the hill on the same side of the river; being satisfied, sir, that said tract of land will injure no one, nor is there any recognized owner therefor, the nearest settlement to it being the town of Socorro, which is about nine leagues distant, and by your excellency's granting to me the aforesaid land, your excellency will not only be improving the province, but will also comply with the wishes of his Majesty, who has ordered the immense waste reaching to El Paso to be settled. Therefore I pray your excellency to grant my request. God, our Father, preserve your excellency's life for many years.

PEDRO ARMENDARIS.
TOWN OF SANTA FÉ, *May* 1, 1820.

SANTA FÉ, *May* 3, 1820.

The petitioner having shown that the land he petitions for is unoccupied, therefore the justice (alcalde) of Belew will place him in royal possession thereof, and will execute to him the proper deed therefor for his security.

MELGARES.

SURVEYOR GENERAL'S OFFICE, TRANSLATOR'S DEPARTMENT,
Santa Fé, New Mexico, July 13, 1857.

The foregoing is a correct translation of the original on file in this office.

DAVID V. WHITING,
Translator.

SURVEYOR GENERAL'S OFFICE,
Santa Fé, New Mexico, August 15, 1859.

The above is a true copy of the original on file in this office.

WM. PELHAM,
Surveyor General.

TESTIMONY—TRANSLATION.

Seal Third. [SEAL.] Four Reals.

Years one thousand eight hundred and fifty-six, and one thousand eight hundred and fifty-seven.

MEXICAN REPUBLIC,
State of Chihuahua, Town of El Paso.

The declaration of the witness Don Francisco San Juan, taken before me, citizen Sisto Irigoyen, first justice and judge of first instance of this town of El Paso, in the State of Chihuahua, Mexican republic, to be read in evidence before the honorable William Pelham, surveyor general of the Territory of New Mexico, concerning a claim made by the heirs of Don Pedro Armendaris, under a grant of lands opposite Valverde, on the right bank of the Bravo river, in the Territory of New Mexico. A. B., a credible and competent witness, has now appeared and in my presence has been legally sworn, and under his oath testifies as follows:

1st interrogatory. Do you know the heirs of Don Pedro Armendaris? He answered that he did know them.

2d interrogatory. State their names and places of residence. He said their names are Manuel Armendaris, residing at El Paso; Antonio Armendaris, Enrique Armendaris, Miguel Armendaris, and Rodrigo Garcia as the representative of the children of his wife, Belen Armendaris, all of them residing at the capital of Chihuahua.

3d interrogatory. State when Don Pedro Armendaris was placed in, or received possession of, the grant of land opposite Valverde. He said that about the year 1820, and that he abandoned it when he left Valverde and Fray Cristobal, which was about the year 1825 or 1826.

4th interrogatory. State what improvements he made on the land, and what number of cattle he had there. He said that he did not know that he had made any improvement; but he does know and saw that he had a large number of cattle and horses pastured on said land.

5th interrogatory. State when he left those lands, and the reasons why he was compelled to leave them. He stated the frequent robberies of cattle, and incursions made by the hostile Indians.

FRANCISCO GARCIA Y SAN JUAN.

Sisto Irigoyen, first justice and judge of first instance above mentioned, hereby certifies that the foregoing declaration was taken by me and at my office on this 13th day of July, 1857; that the above witness signed the foregoing declaration in my presence and was legally sworn as to the truth of the same with me, the present judge, and those in my attendance. I certify:

SISTO IRIGOYEN.

Attending:
    FRANCISCO BARRON.
Attending:
    MAGUINO CASTAÑEDA.

The declaration of the witness Don Luis Telles, taken before me, citizen Sisto Irigoyen, first justice and judge of first instance of this town of El Paso, in the State of Chihuahua, Mexican republic, to be read in evidence before the honorable William Pelham, surveyor general of the Territory of New Mexico, concerning a claim made by the heirs of Pedro Armendaris, under a grant of land opposite Valverde, on the right bank of the Bravo river, in the Territory of New Mexico. A. B., a truthful and competent witness, has now appeared and in my presence has been legally sworn, and afterwards under his oath testifies as follows:

1st interrogatory. Do you know the heirs of Don Pedro Armendaris? He stated that he did know them.

2d interrogatory. State their names and places of residence. He stated that their names are Manuel Armendaris, residing at El Paso; Antonio Armendaris, Henry Armendaris, Miguel Armendaris, and Rodrigo Garcia, as the representative of the children of his wife, Belen Armendaris, deceased, all of whom reside at the capital of Chihuahua.

3d interrogatory. State when Don Pedro Armendaris was placed in, or received possession of, the grant of land opposite Valverde. He stated that about the year 1820, and that he abandoned it when he left Valverde and Fray Cristobal, which was about the year 1825 or 1826.

4th interrogatory. State what improvements he made on said land, and what number of cattle he had there. He stated that he did not know if he made any improvements there; but he does know and saw that a large number of cattle and horses were pastured on said land.

5th interrogatory. State when he left the land, and the reasons which compelled him to leave it. He stated that on account of the frequent robberies and incursions of the hostile Indians.

LUIS + TELLES.

Sisto Irigoyen, first justice and judge of first instance above mentioned, hereby certifies that the foregoing declaration was taken by me and at my office on this 13th day of July, 1857; that the aforesaid witness did not sign the foregoing declaration, not knowing how, but in my presence he made a cross and was legally sworn as to the truth of the same, I, the judge, and my attending witnesses, signing according to law. I certify:

SISTO IRIGOYEN.

Attending:
  FRANCISCO BARRON.
Attending:
  MAGUINO CASTAÑEDA.

PASO, *July* 12, 1857.

The foregoing declarations having been taken, let the originals be delivered to Don Manuel Armendaris, who asked for them, for such use as he may deem proper in defence of his rights and those of his brothers. His honor, the first justice, so decreed and signed with his attending witnesses, according to law. I certify:

SISTO IRIGOYEN.

Attending:
  FRANCISCO BARRON.
Attending:
  MAGUINO CASTAÑEDA.

Fees for the foregoing proceedings, without paper, $4. Paid.
[Rubric.]

No. 8.

CONSULATE OF THE UNITED STATES,
Paso del Norte, Mexico, July 13, 1857.

I, the undersigned, consul of the United States of America, residing at Paso del Norte, republic of Mexico, do hereby certify that the foregoing are the true and genuine signatures of Sisto Irigoyen, justice of the peace of this place, and as such are entitled to full faith and credit.

Given under my hand and the seal of my consulate, at Paso del Norte, this the 13th day of July, 1857, and of the independence of the United States the eighty-first.

[L. S.]

DAVID R. DIFFENDERFFER,
Consul.

SURVEYOR GENERAL'S OFFICE, TRANSLATOR'S DEPARTMENT,
Santa Fé, New Mexico, July 14, 1859.

The foregoing, excepting the consular certificate, is a correct translation of the original on file in this office.

DAVID V. WHITING,
Translator.

SURVEYOR GENERAL'S OFFICE,
Santa Fé, New Mexico, August 12, 1859.

The above is a true copy of the original on file in this office.

WILLIAM PELHAM,
Surveyor General.

TESTIMONY.

Heirs of Pedro Armendaris.   Claim opposite Valverde.

M. ASHURST sworn:

Question. Have you any interest in this case?
Answer. None.
Question. How long have you been in this country?
Answer. Since June, 1849.
Question. Are you acquainted with the tract of land opposite Valverde, in Socorro?
Answer. I know a tract of land on the other side of the river, opposite the Valverde ruins, known as the Armendaris grant, and the lands of Smith and Biggs.
Question. By whom has it been occupied and claimed since you have known it?
Answer. Since 1852 I have seen and been upon the land, and have known it to be claimed by the heirs of Armendaris and Smith and Biggs, who claim under the heirs, except old Fort Conrad. I do not

know under whom that is claimed. It is still occupied by the heirs of Armendaris. Fort Conrad has been abandoned since 1853.

M. ASHURST.

Sworn and subscribed before me this 8th July, 1859.
WM. PELHAM, *Surveyor General.*

ANTONIO SENA sworn:

Question. Have you any interest in this case?
Answer. None.
Question. Did you reside at Santa Fé in 1820, and did you know the handwriting of Facundo Melgares?
Answer. I was; I know his handwriting. His signature on document No. 3 is genuine. He was governor of the department at that time.

ANTONIO SENA.

Sworn and subscribed before me this 8th July, 1859.
WM. PELHAM, *Surveyor General.*

AUGUSTIN DURAN sworn:

Question. Have you any interest in this case?
Answer. None.
Question. Did you reside at Santa Fé in 1820, and did you know the handwriting of Melgares, and what office did he hold?
Answer. I was; I know his handwriting; that on document No. 3 is genuine. He was military and political governor at that time.

AUGUSTIN DURAN.

Sworn and subscribed before me this 8th July, 1859.
WM. PELHAM, *Surveyor General.*

SURVEYOR GENERAL'S OFFICE,
Santa Fé, New Mexico, August 15, 1859.

The above is a true copy of the original on file in this office.
WM. PELHAM, *Surveyor General.*

REPORT.

HEIRS OF PEDRO ARMENDARIS *vs.* UNITED STATES.

This case was set for trial on the 8th day of July, 1859.
On the 1st May of 1820, Pedro Armendaris, formerly of the company of San Elizario, petitioned Facundo Melgares, then governor of the province of New Mexico, for a tract of land situated on the Rio Grande, opposite Valverde, with the boundaries set forth in said petition. On the 3d of the same month the governor granted the land petitioned for, and directed the justice of the peace of the town of

Beleu to place him in possession, although there is nothing on the face of the papers to show that possession was given, which is not deemed of sufficient importance to require any further notice.

Testimony has been introduced by the claimants to prove that the land has been in the occupancy of the parties from the time the grant was made up to the present day.

The papers acted upon are the original filed by the claimants.

The above grant appears to have been made and occupied by the parties in good faith. It is, therefore, deemed to be a good and valid grant, and is approved by this office, and ordered to be transmitted to Congress, with the request that it be confirmed to the legal representatives of Pedro Armendaris, the original grantee.

WM. PELHAM, *Surveyor General.*
SANTA FÉ, *New Mexico, July* 20, 1859.

SURVEYOR GENERAL'S OFFICE,
Santa Fé, New Mexico, August 15, 1859.

The above is a true copy of the original on file in this office.

WM. PELHAM, *Surveyor General.*

CLAIM No. 35.

ANTONIO SANDOVAL.

Schedule of documents composing claim No. 35.

1. Notice.
2. Grant—original.
3. Grant—translation.
4. Testimony.
5. Report.

NOTICE.

UNITED STATES OF AMERICA *vs.* TERRITORY OF NEW MEXICO.

To William Pelham, surveyor general of New Mexico:

Antonio Sandoval, a citizen of the United States, resident in the county of Bernalillo, Territory of New Mexico, respectfully represents to you that he is the claimant and legal owner in fee of a certain tract of land lying and being situate in the county of Socorro, Territory of New Mexico, and known as the Bosque de los Apaches, and bounded on the north by the rancho known as the rancho de los Bacas, on the south by the grant of Valverde, and on the east and west extending two leagues on each side of the river Del Norte, all of which points and boundaries are well-known landmarks, or easily to be ascertained, in the said county of Socorro; and the said Antonio Sandoval, the present claimant, claims a perfect title to said lands by virtue of a perfect and unconditional grant made to him on the 28th day of November, A. D. 1845, by Manuel Armijo, the then acting and actual governor of New Mexico; which said grant was made, as expressed upon the grant, for meritorious services rendered the republic of Mexico, and in conformity to the laws, usages, and customs of the republic of Mexico in force at the time said grant was made, for which power and authority see the decrees of Mexico of June 4 and September 18, 1823, pages 123 and 180 of 2d volume of Galvan's Decrees; see also the colonization laws of the republic of Mexico; see also decision of the Supreme Court of the United States in Frémont's case, 19th Howard's Reports, page 542.

The said Antonio Sandoval, the present claimant, further states that he cannot show the quantity of land claimed by him except as the same is set forth in the grant, nor can he furnish a plat of survey, as no survey has ever been executed; claimant further states that he knows of no adverse claim to said land, and that by virtue of said grant he was legally put in possession of said lands and has retained the same down to the present time; claimant files this his claim before you under the 8th section of the act of Congress approved 22d of July 1854, entitled "An act to establish the offices of surveyor general of New Mexico, Kansas, and Nebraska, to grant donations to actual settlers therein, and for other purposes," and respectfully asks confirmation by you of this his said claim.

M. ASHURST,
Attorney for Claimants.

SURVEYOR GENERAL'S OFFICE,
Santa Fé, New Mexico, August 26, 1859.

The above is a true copy of the original on file in this office.

WM. PELHAM,
Surveyor General.

GRANT—ORIGINAL.

Sello Tercero. [SEAL.] Un Peso.

Años de mil ochocientos cuarenta y cuatro y mil ochocientos cuarenta y cinco.

EXMO. SOR. GOBOR.

El C. Anto. Sandobal, vecino de la villa de Albuquerque ante la recta justificacion de V. E. como mas en derecho haya lugar y al mio convenir pueda salvo las protestas utiles y necesarias conparesco y digo: Sor. que á virtud de haberme incontrado en los margenes del Rio del Norte en el punto que llaman el Bosque del Apache, un terreno baldio, yerto, y despoblado y sin perjuicio de tercero, y siendo como lo es en mi concepto el referido terreno muy ameno, abundante de aguas, pastos y demas, y para el aumento de la agricultura paso á inpetrar la venebolencia de V. E. para que en nombre de ntros. soberanos poderes de la nacion Mejicana, se sirva el hacerme la gracia de concederme por posesion dicho terreno para lavorias y poner crias de ganados menores y mallores, sirviendose igualmente concederme los limites siguientes; que son desde el Rancho de Las Bacas que le llaman para abajo una y otra banda del Rio hasta Balverde, esto es por los margenes del Rio, y por ejidos del lado del veste y el Sudeste dos leguas por cada rumbo si lo tubiere á bien V. E. segun las leyes. Por todo lo cual: A V. E. rendidamente pido y suplico sea bien servido acceder á esta mi solicitud en lo que recivire merced y gracia que impetro, Juro no proceder de malicia protesto la buena fe, constas y lo necesario, &a.

ANTONIO SANDOBAL.

Albuquerque, *Noviembre 24, de* 1845.

Santa Fé, *Noviembre 28, de* 1845.

A consecuencia de los servicios analogos y meritorios que Don Antonio Sandobal ha hecho á la patria, tanto con su persona como con sus bienes, en prestamos forzosos y demas sutencilios he unido á bien consederle el terreno que solicita en nombre del Supremo Gobierno de la nacion Mejicana, y haciendo merito este gobierno de lo benefico que dicho Sandobal ha sido á la patria, y segun las faculta des se me confieren por las leyes, le hago esta concepcion, *integrum* con los limites y ejidos que pide libre de todo y franco de pencion, por lo cual pase el postulante al Juez de Paz del Socorro para que ponga en posesion al suplicante y haga la escritura correspondiente.

MANUEL ARMIJO.

En este puesto y demarcacion de Sn. Miguel del Socorro perteneciente al 3er Disto. del Departamento del Nuevo Mejico á los siete del mes ae Marzo del presente año de mil ochocientos cuarenta y sies: Yo Don Vicente Pino Juez de Paz de dicha demarcacion autuando con testigos instrumentales, y de asistencia, con quienes auto por receptoria á falta de Escribano publico y nacional que no lo hay segun derecho en Justo obedecimiento al decreto del E. S. Gobernador fecha 28 de Noviembre ultimo pase al terreno que se solicita en la anterior instancia que ase Don Anto. Sandobal vecino de la Villa de Albuquerque y haviendolo inspecionado con bastante esaminucion y delica deza lo incuentro baldio yerto y despoblado y sin perjuicio de tercero, como lo relaciona la referida instancia á lo que haviendo dado estos pasos, le hice al presentante saber, en presencia de los testigos la peticion que hacia, y que respecto á lo arresgado y frontericio del terreno habia de mantenerse la gente que lo havitara bien proveido de armas de fuego, ó flechas, para defensa de sus personas é intereses, como igualmente que se guarden todas las reglas y estitutos que los demas colones guardan, á lo cual estando entendido de todo lo que se le arvieste lo tome por la mano, lo pasie por dichas tierras, tiro piedras arranco sacates, y dio voces de alegria diciendo viva el Soverano Congreso de la nacion Mejicana, tomando posesion quieta y pacificamente y por lo mismo yo el referido Juez de paz dije; en claras y inteligibles voces, que en nombre del Soberano Congreso de la nacion y sin perjuicio de sin nacional haver, ni el de tersero le hacia la concepcion del mencionado terreno, libre de todo y franco de pencion señalandole por linderos que son por el Norte una mojonera de piedra y lodo que se pusa cuando se dono el Socorro quedande contiguas una y otra posesion siendo la linia debisoria dicha mojonera, y por el sur siguiendo el curso del Rio para abajo hasta toparse con los limites de Balverde quedando tambien contiqua, por el oriente las dos leguas que se citan en la instancia referida, y por el Poniente otras dos leguas segun queda citado, y por lo tanto compliendo con lo prevenido por el E. S. Govor. y que incuentro el terreno sin perjuicio de tercero, como que da referido, pongo al citado Sandobal en legitima posesion para que con libre franca y general administracion pueda usar de ella, como propriedad legitima, y para su constancia y que el presente documento de dona tenga la fuerza y validacion que en derecho se requiere é interpuse y interponge la autoridad que por derecho me es conferida, firmandolo con los testigos referidos en dicho dia mes y año de que doy fee.

VICENTE PINO.

Asistencia:
  JOSÉ ANTO BACA Y PINO.
Asistencia:
  PEDRO BEJIL.
Ynsl. JOSÉ ANASTACIO TORRES.
Ynsl. JOSÉ DIONICIO SILVA.
Ynsl. JUAN BERTA.
Derechos del jusgado 26 lo Juro.

Este titulo es registrado en el libro letra "B" folios 18 y 19 en mi oficina. Loque certifico firmo y sello para constancia, Santa Fé, Diciembre 30, de 1848.

[SELLO.]   DONACIANO VIGIL, *Registrador de titulos de tierras del Territorio de Nuevo Méjico.*

SURVEYOR GENERAL'S OFFICE, TRANSLATOR'S DEPARTMENT,
Santa Fé, New Mexico, August 24, 1859.

The above is a true copy of the original on file in this office.

DAVID V. WHITING,
Translator.

GRANT—TRANSLATION.

Seal Third. [SEAL.] One Dollar.

Years one thousand eight hundred and forty-four and eight hundred and forty-five.

Citizen Antonio Sandoval, resident of the town of Albuquerque, appealing to the upright justice of your excellency in the most approved manner prescribed by law and convenient to me, saving such protests as may be useful and necessary, appears and states that, by virtue of having found, on the banks of the Del Norte river, at the point called Bosque del Apache, a tract of uncultivated, waste, and unoccupied land, and without injury to any third party, and as I believe said land to be extremely fertile, with an abundance of water and other requisites necessary for the advancement of agriculture, I proceed to impetrate the benevolence of your excellency that, in the name of our sovereign power of the Mexican nation, you be pleased to grant me possession of said land for cultivation, and the raising of cattle and sheep, being pleased to grant me also the following boundaries, which are from what is called El rancho de los Vacos (the cow herd) down the river, on both sides, to Valverde, that is to say, following the river, and for pasture on the west and southeast, two leagues in each direction, if your excellency, under the laws, sees proper to do so. In view of all which I humbly pray and request your excellency to be well pleased to comply with my request, by which I will receive that grace and favor which I sue for. I swear that I am not acting through malice. I protest good faith, costs, and whatever may be necessary, &c.

ANTONIO SANDOVAL.

ALBUQUERQUE, *November* 24, 1845.

SANTA FÉ, *November* 28, 1845.

In consequence of the analogous and meritorious services rendered to the country by Don Antonio Sandoval, not only personally, but also with his property, in forced loans and in other ways, I have seen proper to grant him the lands he solicits in the name of the supreme government of the Mexican nation; and as this government takes into consideration the benefit the said Sandoval has been to the country, and by virtue of the power conferred upon me by law, I invest him with the grant *integrum*, (unconditionally,) with the boundaries and commons for pasture he asks for, free from all and exempt from tax. Therefore the petitioner will present himself to the justice of the peace of Socorro, who will place the petitioner in possession, and execute the proper deed.

MAN'L ARMIJO.

At this place and demarcation of San Miguel del Socorro, belonging to the third district of the department of New Mexico, the seventh day of the month of March of the present year, one thousand eight hundred and forty-six, I, Don Vicente Pino, justice of the peace of said demarcation, acting with instrumental and attending witnesses, with whom I act in the well-known absence of public or national notaries, there being none, according to law, in strict compliance with the decree of his excellency, the governor, bearing date the 28th of November last, I proceeded to the land referred to in the foregoing petition made by Don Antonio Sandoval, resident of the town of Albuquerque, and having inspected it with a great amount of care and delicacy, I find it vacant, waste, and unoccupied, and without injury to third parties, as stated in the foregoing petition. Having taken these steps, I proceeded to make known to the petitioner, in the presence of witnesses, the request he made ; and in regard to the land being in a dangerous locality and on the frontier, he should provide the people he would keep there with a sufficiency of fire-arms, or bows and arrows, in order to defend their persons and property, and also that he should comply with all the rules and regulations provided for other colonists. Having acknowledged that he was duly informed of the above conditions, I took him by the hand and walked with him over said lands. He threw stones, pulled up grass, and cried aloud with great joy, saying "Long life to the sovereign congress of the Mexican nation," taking possession quietly and peaceably. And therefore, I, the aforesaid justice of the peace, stated, in a clear and audible voice, that, in the name of the sovereign congress of the nation, and without injury to its national reverence nor to third parties, the aforesaid grant was made to him, free of everything and exempt from taxation, specifying as boundaries : On the north, a monument of stone and mud, which was erected when Socorro was granted, the two possessions being adjoining, the said monument being the dividing line ; and on the south, following down the course of the river to where it is intersected by the boundaries of Valverde, being also adjoining ; on the east, the two leagues mentioned in the foregoing petition ; and on the west two leagues more, as therein mentioned ; and therefore, in compliance with the instructions of his excellency, the governor, and finding the land will not injure any third party, as aforementioned, I place the said Sandoval in legitimate possession, fully empowered to use it with free, unencumbered, and general administration, as his legitimate property. And in order that this granting deed may have the force and validity required by law, I did and do interpose the authority conferred upon me by law, signing, with my aforesaid witnesses, on the said day, month, and year. To which I certify.

VICENTE PINO.

Attending :
   José Antonio Baca y Pino.
   Pedro Vigil.

Instrumental :
   José Anastacio Torres.
   José Dionisio Silva.
   Juan Beyta.

Justice's fees, 26 dollars.
I swear it.   [Rubric |

SURVEYOR GENERAL'S OFFICE,
Translator's Department, Santa Fé, N. M., July 2, 1859.

The foregoing is a correct translation of the original on file in this office.

DAVID V. WHITING,
Translator.

SURVEYOR GENERAL'S OFFICE,
Santa Fé, New Mexico, August 25, 1859.

The above is a true copy of the original on file in this office.
WM. PELHAM,
Surveyor General.

TESTIMONY.

Antonio Sandoval's Claim.—Bosque del Apache.

SERAFIN RAMIREZ sworn:

Question. Have you any interest in this case?
Answer. None.
Question. Did you know General Armijo?
Answer. I did. He was governor and commander-in-chief in 1845. The signature on the grant to Antonio Sandoval is genuine.
Question. Did you know Vicente Pino?
Answer. I do. The signature on the document is his.
Question. Do you know the rancho of the Bosque del Apache?
Answer. I do. It is between Valverde and Socorro, on Rio del Norte. I have been there many times since 1845. It has been in possession of Antonio Sandoval since the year 1845, up to this time, and has been settled upon by persons under him. The houses belong to Sandoval, and there is land under cultivation.
JOSÉ SERAFIN RAMIREZ.

Sworn and subscribed before me this 13th day of July, 1859.
WM. PELHAM,
Surveyor General.

SURVEYOR GENERAL'S OFFICE,
Santa Fé, New Mexico, August 25, 1859.

The above is a true copy of the original on file in this office.
WM. PELHAM,
Surveyor General.

REPORT.

ANTONIO SANDOVAL *vs.* THE UNITED STATES.

This case was set for trial on the 13th day of July, 1859.

On the 24th November, 1845, Antonio Sandoval petitioned Manuel Armijo, civil and military governor of New Mexico, for a tract of land situated in what is now the county of Socorro, in the Territory of New Mexico.

On the 28th November of the same year the governor, in consideration of the valuable services rendered to the government by Sandoval, not only in his person, but also with his fortune, granted the land unconditionally, with the boundaries set forth in the petition, and directed the justice of the peace of Socorro to place him in possession of the land, which was done on the 7th day of March, 1846.

The land is proven in evidence to have been occupied and cultivated by Sandoval from the date of the grant to the present day.

The papers acted upon in the case are the originals filed by the claimants.

The grant having been made by the proper authority of the county, for services rendered to the government, and being absolute and unconditional, it is approved to the said Antonio Sandoval, and ordered to be transmitted to Congress for its action in the premises.

WM. PELHAM,
Surveyor General.

SURVEYOR GENERAL'S OFFICE,
Santa Fé, N. M., July 20, 1859.

SURVEYOR GENERAL'S OFFICE,
Santa Fé, N. M., August 26, 1859.

The above is a true copy of the original on file in this office.

WM. PELHAM,
Surveyor General.

CLAIM No. 36.

TOWN OF CHAMITA.

Documents composing claim No. 36.

1. Notice.
2. Grant—Spanish.
3. Grant—translation.
4. Testimony.
5. Report.

NOTICE.

UNITED STATES OF AMERICA, }
Territory of New Mexico. }

To the surveyor general of New Mexico:

Manuel Trujillo, a citizen of the United States, on behalf of himself and other citizens of the United States, residents of and settlers in the town of Chamita, county of Rio Arriba, represent that they are the claimants and legal owners in fee of a certain tract of land lying and being situate in the county of Rio Arriba in said Territory, and known as the town of Chamita, and bounded on the east by a hill which joins the Rio del Norte, on the west an angostura or narrow, which forms a table land with the Chama river, on the north the said table land, and on the south the Chama river, which points and boundaries are well-known landmarks. And the said Manuel Trujillo, and the other settlers and inhabitants of said town of Chamita, claim a perfect title to said lands by virtue of being purchasers, and heirs and descendants of Antonio Trujillo, to whom the original grant was made on the eighth day of June, A. D. 1724, by Juan Domingo de Bustamente, the then acting governor and captain general of the Spanish province of New Mexico; which said grant was made, as aforesaid, by authority of the laws, usages, and customs of the government of Spain, to which government the province of New Mexico at that time belonged. The said claimants cannot show the quantity of land claimed by them except as set forth in said grant as within the above-described well-known metes and boundaries, nor can they furnish a plat of survey, as no survey has ever been executed. They further state that they know of no other claimant or claimants of said lands.

For the power and authority of making the grant, see collection of the decrees and orders of the cortes of Spain, published in Mexico by Mariano Galvan, in 1829, page 56, and from pages 91 to 101. The claimants file this their said claim before you, under the eighth section of the act of Congress approved 22d of July, 1854, entitled "An act to establish the offices of surveyor general of New Mexico, Kansas, and Nebraska, to grant donations to actual settlers therein, and for other purposes," and respectfully ask confirmation by you of their said claim.

M. ASHURST,
Attorney for Claimants.

SURVEYOR GENERAL'S OFFICE,
Santa Fé, New Mexico, August 15, 1859.

The above is a true copy of the original on file in this office.

WM. PELHAM,
Surveyor General.

GRANT—SPANISH.

Sor. Gobernador y Capitan General:

Antonio Trujillo vecino de la villa nueva de Santa Cruz ante V.S. paresco en la mas bastante forma que en derecho haya lugar y al mio convenga, y digo que registre un sitio de tierras yermo y despoblado que esta de la otra banda del Rio del Norte el cual tube por merced en nombre de Su Magestad, la cual me hizo el General Don Juan Flores Mogollon y de ellas me dio posesion el Capitan Sebastian Martin Alcalde Mayor entonces de dicha villa en las cuales saque sequia y sembre una milpa cuyo reconocimiento hiso el dia ocho del corriente, el General Don Juan Paes Hurtado Theniente General de este Reyno, y son sus linderos por el oriente una loma que se junta con el Rio del Norte, y por el Poniente con una angostura que hace una mesa con el Rio de Chama y por el Norte con dicha mesa y por el Sur con el mismo Rio de Chama y dichas tierras se ha de servir V.S. de concedermelas de nueva en nombre de Su Magestad; yo mis hijos herederos y susesores con entradas y salidas pastos aguas, abrevaderos usos y costumbres derechos y servidumbres mandando se me de la real posesion obligandome á poblarlas dentro del termino de la ley por todo lo cual y lo demas que alegar puedo y à mi favor haga que aqui day por espresado.

A V.S. pido y suplico con las veras de mi mayor rendimiento sea muy servido de hacer y determinar como llebo pedido, que en hacerlo asi recibire bien y merced, con justicia, juro este mi escrito en forma no ser de malicia, el real ancilio imploro y en lo necesario &a.

ANTONIO TRUJILLO.

Y vista por Don Juan Domingo de Bustamante Gobernador y Capitan General de este reino la hube por presentada y le concedo al contenido en ella la merced de tierras que me pide en nombre de Su Magestad para el sus hijos y herederos sin perjuicio de tercero que mejor derecho tenga, y mando al Alcalde Mayor de la villa nueva de Santa Cruz pase á darle posesion de las referidas tierras que menciona, y para que asi conste lo firme en esta villa de Santa Fé en ocho dias del mes de Junio de mil setecientos y veinte y cuatro años.

JUAN DOMINGO DE BUSTAMANTE.

En este puesto de Yunque en veinte dias del mes de Junio de milsetecientos y veinte y cuatro años yo el Alferes reformado Crisptobal Torres alcalde mayor y Capitan á Guerra de la villa nueva de Santa Cruz y su jurisdicion, pase á darle la posesion real á Antonio Trugillo, como Su Señoria me manda y habiendo llegado y reconocido el sitio de tierras que menciona en su pedimento le tome de la mano y le pasee por el, tiro piedras arranco sacate, y dio voces como suyo propio, y en señal de posesion la cual le di en nombre del Rey muestro Señor que Dios Guarde la cual aprendio quieta y pacificamente, y fueron testigos instrumentales Domingo Montes Vigil, y Diego Martin, y son sus linderos los espresados en su pedimento, y dicha posesion se la di con la circunstancia de que las pueblo dentro del termino de la ley y para que conste lofirme como Juez Receptor con los infrascritos de mi asistencia en dicho dia ut supra.

CRISPTOBAL TORRES,
Ante mi como Juez Receptor.

De asistencia:
MIGUEL DE QUINTANA.

SURVEYOR GENERAL'S OFFICE,
Santa Fé, New Mexico, September 16, 1859.

The above is a true copy of the original on file in this office.

DAVID V. WHITING,
Translator.

GRANT.—TRANSLATION.

To the Governor and Captain General:

Antonio Trujillo, resident of the new town of Santa Cruz, appears before your excellency in the manner most approved in law and convenient to me, and states that: I register a tract of land, which is wild and unsettled, on the opposite side of the Del Norte river, which I received as a grant in the name of his Majesty, from General Don Juan Flores Mogollon, and was placed in possession thereof by Captain Sebastian Martin, at that time senior justice of said town, and upon which I made a ditch and plowed up a field, an examination of which was made on the 8th instant by Don Juan Paez Hurtado, lieutenant general of this kingdom; and its boundaries are, on the east a hill which joins the Del Norte river; on the west an augostura or narrow, which forms a table-land, with the Chama river; and on the north said table-land, and on the south the Chama river. Said lands your excellency will be pleased to regrant to me anew, in the name of his Majesty, for myself, my children, heirs, and successors, together with entrances and outlets, pastures, water and watering-places, rights, interests, customs, and appurtenances, thereunto belonging; directing royal possession to be given to me, compelling me to settle them within the time prescribed by law, in view of all which and whatever more I may set forth and may do in my own favor, and which I here express.

I pray and request your excellency, with the most sincere expression of submission, to be pleased to do and determine as I have requested; and by so doing I will receive grace and favor with justice. I swear that this my petition is not made through malice. I implore royal aid and whatever may be necessary, &c.

ANTONIO TRUJILLO.

And seen by Don Juan Domingo de Bustamente, governor and captain general of this kingdom. He considered it as presented, and I grant to the person therein mentioned the grant of land he asks me for, in the name of his Majesty, for himself, his children and heirs, without injury to any third parties who may show a better title; and I direct the senior justice of the new town of Santa Cruz to proceed to place him in possession of the aforesaid lands, and in order that it may be a matter of record I have signed it at this city of Santa Fé, on the 8th day of the month of June, one thousand seven hundred and twenty-four.

JUAN DOMINGO DE BUSTAMENTE.

At this place of Tunque, on the 20th day of the month of June, in the year one thousand seven hundred and twenty, I, the reformed, Ensign Cristobal Torres, chief justice and war captain of the new city of Santa Cruz and its jurisdiction, proceeded to give royal possession to Antonio Trujillo, as I am directed to do by his excellency; and having arrived and examined the tract of land referred to in his petition, I took him by the hand and walked with him over the land. He threw stones, pulled up grass, and cried out in a loud voice, as if the land was his, and in proof of possession which I gave him in the name of the king, our sovereign, (whom may God preserve,) and which he received quietly and peaceably, Domingo Montes Vigil and Diego Martin being instrumental witnesses, and with the boundaries mentioned in his petition; and possession was given to him with the condition that he should settle it within the term prescribed by law. And in order that it may so appear, I signed as acting judge, with the undersigned as attending witnesses, on said day *ut supra*.

Before me as acting judge,

CRISTOBAL TORRES.

Attending:
MIGUEL A. QUINTANA.

SURVEYOR GENERAL'S OFFICE,
Santa Fé, New Mexico, August 15, 1859.

The above is a true copy of the original on file in this office.

WM. PELHAM,
Surveyor General.

TESTIMONY.

Town of Chamita, Rio Arriba county.

SEVERO TRUJILLO and PABLO TRUJILLO, sworn:

Question. Have you any interest in this case?
Answer. None.
Question. Where do you reside, and what opportunity have you had of knowing the town of Chamita?
Answer. We are both natives and residents of Los Luceros, distant about twelve miles from Chamita; have resided there all our lives.
Question. Was the town of Chamita in existence when the United States took possession of the country?
Answer. It was, and was in existence many years before.
Question. How many inhabitants are there in the town?
Answer. It is a large town; contains at least three hundred souls.

SEVERO D. TRUJILLO.
PABLO TRUJILLO.

Sworn and subscribed before me this 9th day of June, 1859.

WM. PELHAM,
Surveyor General.

SURVEYOR GENERAL'S OFFICE,
Santa Fé, New Mexico, August 15, 1859.

The above is a true copy of the original on file in this office.

WM. PELHAM,
Surveyor General.

REPORT.

Town of Chamita *vs.* The United States.

This case was set for trial on the 9th day of June, 1859.

The present claimants claim the land embraced within the limits of the town by virtue of a grant made to Antonio Trujillo, on the 8th June, 1724, by Juan Domingo Bustamente, governor and captain general of the province of New Mexico, and possession given by due course of law.

The grant is so old as to be beyond the period of being proven, and, as no contest has been made in the case, it is considered to be a good and valid grant; and, as the present claimants show no claim of title from the original grantee to themselves, it is approved to the legal representatives of Antonio Trujillo, and ordered to be transmitted to Congress for its action in the premises.

WILLIAM PELHAM,
Surveyor General.

Surveyor General's Office,
Sant Fé, New Mexico, July 2, 1859.

Surveyor General's Office,
Santa Fé, New Mexico, September 6, 1859.

The above is a true copy of the original on file in this office.

WILLIAM PELHAM,
Surveyor General.

CLAIM No. 37.

TOWN OF EL TEJON.

Documents composing claim No. 37.

1. Notice—Spanish.
2. Notice—translation.
3. Certificate of possession—Spanish.
4. Certificate of possession—translation.
5. Testimony.
6. Report.

NOTICE—SPANISH.

Aviso.—Al Agrimensor Grat. del Nuevo Mejico.

Se le aviso por el presente que bajo las prebenciones de la 8ª secion del decreto del Congreso aprobado el dia 22d de Julio, de 1854, titulado " Un acto pard crear los Destinos de Agrimensor Grat. del Nuevo

Mejico, Kansas y Nebraska para consedar Donaciones á las Pobla dorras actuales y para otros fines."

Yo Salbador Barreras por si (y en coman con otras personas) vecino del condado de Santa Ana en el Territorio de Nuevo Mejico reclamo la donacion de una Sitio pa. plaza y labor pues el dho. reclamante original al tiempo de tomar posesion el Gob'no de los E. V. él se hallard en actual posesion de dho. citio y el cual hasta la fha. se alla poblado des de el tiempo de sa consecion, el titulo adjunto al presente abiso no es completo en razon del estrabio de la peticion y otros docum'tos al tiempo de haverse tomado la dho. posesion en que la mayor parte de los archibos publicos padecieron estrabios y en ellos se encontraban tales docum'tos y solo existe hoy en poder del reclam'te él que se presenta que es la posesion judicial que por las LL. de España y Mejico se requina para completan el titulo, el tal titulo ó posesion fui concedido bajo la autorisacion que las LL. concedian à los Ineces de Paz y Ayuntam'tos de las respectivas jurisdicciones como esta esprado en la ley de 4 de Enero, de 1813, y 20 de Marzo, de 1837, y otras sobre la materia —la referida concesion fue concedida y dada al reclam'te el dia 7 de N'bre, de 1840, la cantidad reclamada séra una y media leguas cuadradas segun los linderos espresados en el titulo de posesion que se acompaña á este abiso dho. Sitio está dentro del condado de Santa Ana y en el 4ª Precinto Judicial y conocido el dicho Sitio con el nombre de la Plaza del Tejon.

SALBADOR BARRERAS.

SURVEYOR GENERAL'S OFFICE,
Santa Fé, New Mexico, August 31, 1859.

The foregoing is a correct copy from the original, now on file in this office.

DAVID V. WHITING,
Translator.

NOTICE—TRANSLATION.

The surveyor general of New Mexico is hereby informed that under the provisions of the eighth section of the act of Congress, approved July 22, 1854, entitled an act to establish the offices of surveyor general of New Mexico, Kansas, and Nebraska, to grant donations to actual settlers therein, and for other purposes:

I, Salvador Barreras, for myself and in common with other persons, residents of the county of Santa Ana, in the Territory of New Mexico, claim the donation of a site for a town and for cultivation, said original claimant having been in actual possession of said site from the time the United States took possession of the country, and it has been occupied from the date of the grant up to the present day. The title accompanying this notice is inchoate, the petition and other documents having been lost at the time that a large portion of the public archives were lost when said possession was taken, among which the above mentioned documents were filed. The only paper existing in the hands of the claimant, and which is herewith presented, is the judicial possession required by the laws of Spain and Mexico to complete title; said grant or possession was given by virtue of the authority vested by the laws of Spain and Mexico in justices of the peace and corporations, within their respective jurisdictions, as expressed in the law of January 13, 1813, and March 20, 1837, and others in regard to the matter; said possession was given to the claimant on the seventh of November, 1840. The quantity claimed is one and one-half league, more or less, as will appear by the boundaries set forth in the deed of possession herewith accompanying; said grant is situated in the county of Santa Ana and fourth judicial precinct, and said grant is known as the town of Tejon.

SALVADOR BARRERAS.

Surveyor General's Office,
Santa Fé, New Mexico, June 14, 1859.

The above is a correct translation of the original on file in this office.

DAVID V. WHITING,
Translator.

Surveyor General's Office,
Santa Fé, New Mexico, August 30, 1859.

The above is a true copy of the original on file in this office.

WILLIAM PELHAM,
Surveyor General.

CERTIFICATE OF POSSESSION—SPANISH.

En el punto de la Angostura jurisdiccion de Sandia á los diez y siete dias del mes de Noviembre de 1840 años, ante mi el C. Antonio Montaya juez de Paz Constitucionel de la referida jurisdiccion y sus partidos comparecieron presento por sus propias personas, Salvador Barreras por si y á nombre de sus agregados á quienes conosco y doy fe y dijo, Barreras ante mi jusgado y el de mi asistencia que en virtud del reparto de terrenos que constan en la lista nominal de todos sus comprendidos en el punto de Tyon y Tunque, que por orden superior se les dio de posesion y fue repartido por mi jusgado me sirviera estenderle y hacer constar judicial mente la hijuela de la posesion que el recivio en el Tejon y Tunque, y en efecto de lo estipulado que consta en este archivo de mi cargo se le dieron á reconocer por linderos del terreno que á dicho Barreras se le entrego, desde la agua del collole, que comunmente le llaman, y por abajo por el propia arrollo que le nombran Tunque hasta conlindar con terreno del Pueblo de San Telipe, y por el Poniente hasta la Cuchia de San Francisco, por el Sur hasta donde comunmente llaman la aguo del Bernado, y por el oriente hasta la linea de la Uña de Gato, que dieron á reconocer los mismos interesados quedandole á dicho Barreras el derecho mismo de montes y pastos comunes lo mismo que á los demas comprendidos, y por se justo su pedido asi se lo concedi estendiendole su presente hijuela del terreno señalado para que lo gosen por si sus hijos herederos y susesores como propias suyas que son, y que á nombre de la Nacion se les dono por este jusgado estendiendoselles la presente hijuela en favor de dicho Barreras, en el presente papel por no haber del Sellado obligandose el interesado á copiarlo cuando necesario sea, autorizandola yo el enunciado juez de paz con los de mi asistencia, á notoria falta de escribano Nacional y publico que de ninguna clase lo hay en este Territorio, ni en muchas leguas en contorno autuando por receptoria con las facultades que por derecho me son conferidas en el mismo dia mes y año de que doy fe

ANTONIO MONTOYA,
Juez de Paz.

Dhros. 3 p.

Asistencia: JOSÈ YGNACIO MESTAS.
Asistencia: JOSÈ MA. GUTIERRAS.

SURVEYOR GENERAL'S OFFICE, TRANSLATOR'S DEPARTMENT,
Santa Fé, New Mexico, September 10, 1859.
The above is a true copy of the original on file in this office.
DAVID V. WHITING,
Translator.

CERTIFICATE OF POSSESSION—TRANSLATION.

At the place of Angostura, jurisdiction of Sandia, on the seventeenth day of the month of November, in the year 1840, before me, citizen Antonio Montoya, constitutional justice of the peace of the aforementioned jurisdiction and its dependencies, personally appeared in their own proper persons Salvador Barreras, for himself and in the name of his associates, whom I certify are known to me, and stated before my court and those in my attendance, that by virtue of the distribution of the lands contained in the list of his associates at the place called Tejon and Tunque, which was given to them by superior orders, and was distributed by my predecessor, he requested that I should be pleased to judicially execute and place upon record a certificate of the possession he received of Tejon and Tunque; and in view of what he stated, which is recorded in this office, the following boundaries are recognized as those given to said Barreras: From the Aqua del Coyote, commonly called, and below to the arroyo called Tunque until it joins the lands of the Indians of the pueblo of Sandia, and on the west to the sharp ridge of San Francisco; on the south to the place commonly called El Aqua del Berrendo, and on the east to the line of Una de Gato, which were acknowledged as such by the parties interested. The said Barreras being entitled to wood and common pasture, the same as his other associates, and their request being just, it was granted to them by executing this certificate of the land referred to, in order that they may enjoy it for themselves, their children, heirs, and successors in fee, and which was given to them by this court in the name of the nation. This certificate is given to said Barreras on this common paper, there being none of the stamped, the parties interested binding themselves to copy it whenever it may be necessary to do so, and the aforesaid justice of the peace, authorizing the same, with my attending witnesses, in the absence of a national or public notary, there being none of any description in this Territory nor within many miles around, acting by appointment with the authority conferred upon me by law, on the same day, month, and year to which I certify.

Fees, three dollars.

ANTONIO MONTOLLA,
Justice of the Peace.

Attending:
  JOSÉ IGNACIO MESTUS,
  JOSÉ MARIA GUTIERRAS.

SURVEYOR GENERAL'S OFFICE,
Santa Fé, New Mexico, June 14, 1859.

The above is a correct translation of the original on file in this office.

DAVID V. WHITING,
Translator.

SURVEYOR GENERAL'S OFFICE,
Santa Fé, New Mexico, August 30, 1859.

The above is a true copy of the original on file in this office.

WILLIAM PELHAM,
Surveyor General.

TESTIMONY.

Town of Tejon.

SERAFIN RAMIREZ and YNES ARMENTA sworn:

Question. Have you any interest in this case?
Answer. No.
Question. How many years have you resided in the Territory, and what have been your opportunities of knowing the town of Tejon?
Answer. I (Ramirez) have lived in the Territory for twenty years, and I (Armenta) over forty; we both live at a short distance from the place
Question. Was the town of Tejon in existence in the year 1846, when the United States troops took possession of the Territory?
Answer. It was in existence then, and was settled before that time.
Question. What is the present population of the town?
Answer. About 130.

SERAFIN RAMIREZ,
YNES ARMENTA.

Sworn and subscribed before me this 6th day of May, 1859.
WILLIAM PELHAM,
Surveyor General.

SURVEYOR GENERAL'S OFFICE,
Santa Fé, New Mexico, August 30, 1859.
The above is a true copy of the original on file in this office.
WILLIAM PELHAM,
Surveyor General.

REPORT.

TOWN OF TEJON *vs.* THE UNITED STATES.

This case was set for trial on the 6th day of May, 1859.
The parties claim the land embraced within the limits of the town by virtue of an order issued for its distribution, as will appear by the certificate of the justice of the peace of the town of Angostura, dated November 17, 1840, which certificate was filed by the claimants as the basis of their claim.

It is also proven in evidence that the town was in existence in 1846, showing that it was recognized as a town by the former governments of the country.

The claim is deemed to be a good and valid one, and the land embraced within the limits set forth severed from the public domain. It is therefore approved and ordered to be transmitted to Congress for its action in the premises.
WILLIAM PELHAM,
Surveyor General.
SURVEYOR GENERAL'S OFFICE,
Santa Fé, New Mexico, May 7, 1859.

SURVEYOR GENERAL'S OFFICE,
Santa Fé, New Mexico, August 30, 1859.
The above is a true copy of the original on file in this office.
WILLIAM PELHAM,
Surveyor General.

CLAIM NO. 38.

RAMON VIGIL.

Schedule of documents composing claim No. 38.

1. Notice.
2. Grant—Spanish.
3. Grant—translation.
4. Report.

NOTICE.

TERRITORY OF NEW MEXICO, *County of Santa Fé:*

To the Hon. William Pelham, Surveyor General of the Territory of New Mexico, under the act of Congress approved July 22, 1854:

Your petitioner, Ramon Vigil, of the county of Rio Arriba, in the Territory of New Mexico, would respectfully state, that on the 20th day of March, 1742, Don Gaspar Domingo de Mendoza, lieutenant colonel, governor, and captain general of this kingdom of New Mexico, upon the petition of one Pedro Sanchez, granted to him a piece of land situated in Rio Arriba county, bounded on the north by the lands of the Indian pueblo of San Ildefonso, on the south by the lands of captain Andres Montoya, on the east by the Del Norte river, and on the west by the Rocky mountains; and the said Pedro Sanchez, on the 28th day of March, 1742, was duly put into possession of the lands so granted to him, as will more fully appear by reference to said petition, grant, and possession, on file in the office of the surveyor general, a copy of which is hereby made a part of this petition, marked as paper No. 1.

Your petitioner further states that on the 15th day of August, 1749, Francisco Sanchez became the owner of said land by purchase, as will appear by reference to a deed on file in the office of the surveyor general, a copy of which is hereby made a part of this petition, marked as paper No. 2 herein.

Your petitioner further states that on the 8th day of August, 1851, he purchased of one Antonio Sanchez, the interest he held in eight pieces of the land contained in the grant aforesaid, as will appear by said deed on file in the surveyor general's office, a copy of which is hereby made a part of this petition, marked as paper No. 3 herein.

Your petitioner further states that he has continued to possess and occupy said land since the execution of said deed, in peace and quietude, and does not know of any adverse claim or right to the same; that the boundaries of said land are well known and easily found, but the quantity of land situated within said grant is not known to him, as it has never been surveyed; and he makes this application in order that such steps may be taken as will secure to him a good title to his interest in the lands aforesaid.

All of which is respectfully submitted.

RAMON VIGIL,
By J. S. WATTS, *his Attorney.*

SURVEYOR GENERAL'S OFFICE,
Santa Fé, N. M., September 20, 1859.

The foregoing is a correct copy of the original petition now on file in this office.

WM. PELHAM,
Surveyor General.

GRANT—SPANISH.

Señor Gobernador y Capitan Generale:

Pedro Sanches, Natural de este Reino y vecino de la Villa de Santa Cruz en la mejor forma que por derecho haya lugar y al mio convenga; ante V.S. paresco y digo que por que me hallo cargado con doce hijos y tres huerfanos de Padre y madre sobrinos mios tres mosas despersa mi exposa é todo que hara el numero completo de veinte personas y hallarme en un pedaso de tierra que compre ran corto que es necesario pedir prestado á otros vecinos inmediatos en que poderme alargar todos los años en la siembra y no poder aun con esta diligencia mantenerme como asi mismo mantener en dicho pedaso unas obejitas y cuatro Bacas y unas lleguas y caballos necessario todo para el peso de tanta familia sobre que se esqullma por falta de pastos y padecemos muchas necesedades y para poderlas remediar he tenido por conveniente registrar como registro un sitio de tierras que estra de la otra banda del Rio del Norte yermo y despoblado y como tal realenga seri haber quien á el derecho tenga, siendo sus linderos por la parte del Norte las tierras que por derecho gosan los Indios del Pueblo de San Yldefonso por el Sur las del Capitan Andres Montoya, por el Oriente el Rio del Norte, y por el Poniente la Sierra Madre, é imploranda el Real ancilio de V.S. como leal vasallo de Su Mgd. devajo de todo lo que llebo espresado pido y suplico sea muy servido de hacerme la merced del en nombre de S. M. que Dios guarde para luego que el alcalde mismo de la dicha villa de Santa Cruz me de la posesion real poblado, como lo espero de la caridad y justificacion de V.S. y juro por Dios Nuestro Señor y la sénal de la Santa Cruz no ser mi pedimento de malicia sino justa necesidad y en lo necesario.

PEDRO SANCHES.

En la villa de Santa Fé en viente dias del mes de Marzo del ano de mil seticientos cuarenta y dos yo el Theniente Coronel D. Gaspar Domingo de Mendoza, Governador y Captain General de este Reino del Nuevo Mejico, visto el presente escrito del firmado á la vuelta le hube por presentado y en la inteligencia de su peticion debia mandar y mando en nombre del Rey Nuestro Señor se le de la merced de tierras, que pide para que la pueble cultive y beneficie para si sus hijos herederos y subsesores en lo que mas dericho tengan y esta dicha merced sera sin perjuicio de tercero la que debera poblarse en el trempo que mandan las reales leyes y mando á el Alcalde mayor de la jurisdiccion dela Canada lo ponga en posesion observando en su data las circunstancias, que en tales casos se practican asi lo provei mande y firme con los testigos de mi asistencia por la notoria falta de escribano real y publico, en esta parte en el presente papel por no correr el Sellado.

DON GASPAR DOMINGO MENDOZA.

José de Terrus.
José Trujillo.

En viente y acho dias del mes de Marzo de mil setecientos y cuarenta y dos anos: Yo Theniente Juan Joseph Lovato, Alcalde mayor, yo capitan á Guerra interino de esta jurisdiccion de la villa Nueva de Santa Cruz, &c., en atencion á el auto de arriba espedido por el Señor Gobernador y Capitan General Don Gaspar Domingo de Mendoza pase el sitio que otorgo su Señoria al Capitan Pedro Sanches por merced real y para darle la posesion sin perjuicio de tercero acorde que devia mandar y mande comparecieran los indios, principales de el Pueblo de San Yldefonso y otros que no tienen instrumentos de la tierra, que gosaro por la parte que cita su lindero dicho Capitan Pedro Sanches sin embargo para que en ningun tiempo haya obstaculo ni contradicion por dichos indios les alargue á mas de latierra que tienen de labor hasta donde les parecio lo mejor para poder alargare sus cementeras y por comun consentimiento de los dichos se puso alli una Santa Cruz, que les sirviese á ellos de parte de el Sur de lindero y a dicho Capitan Pedro Sanches para el Norte y habiendo testigos á dichos indios y los demi asistencia le di la posesion real de dicho sitio á dicho Don Pedro Sanches con lo solemnidad acostumbrada dentro de los mismos linderos que en su peticion senala á la que me remito y para, que conste lo firmo con los de asistencia actuando por receptoria por la notoria falta de escribano publico ó real y en el presente papel por mo correr del Sellado en estras partes que de todo doy fee. Y es fecho en dicho dia mes yano ut supra.

JUAN JOSEPH LOVATO,
Juez Receptor.

De asistencia:
    Juan Garcia de Mora.
De asistencia:
    Joseph Quintana.

Surveyor General's Office, Translator's Department,
Santa Fé, New Mexico, September 10, 1859.

The above is a true copy of the original on file in this office.
DAVID V. WHITING
Translator.

GRANT—TRANSLATION.

To his Excellency the Governor and Captain General:

  Pedro Sanchez, a native of this kingdom, and a resident of the town of Santa Cruz, in the most approved manner prescribed by law, and most convenient to myself, appear before your excellency, representing that, whereas I have to support twelve children and three orphan nephews, who are without father or mother, three female servants, and, with my wife, will make, in all, the number of twenty persons, and having a piece of land acquired by purchase, which is so small that I am compelled to borrow lands from my other immediate neighbors in order to extend my crops every year, and even in this manner I cannot support myself, nor can I maintain on said land a few sheep and four cows and some mares and horses, all of which are necessary to the

support of so large a family, and which are poor for the want of pasture, and suffer a great many wants, and, in order to supply them, I have deemed proper to register, and do register, a piece of land on the other side of the river Del Norte, uncultivated and abandoned, and as such unoccupied, there being no one having any claim thereto; the boundaries being on the north the lands enjoyed by right by the Indians of the pueblo of San Ildefonso, on the south the lands of Captain Andres Montoya, on the east the Del Norte river, and on the west the Rocky mountains; and, imploring the royal aid of your excellency, as a loyal subject of his Majesty, in view of all that I have stated, I pray and request that you be pleased to grant me said land in the name of his Majesty, (whom may God preserve,) in order that I may settle upon it so soon as the alcalde himself of Santa Cruz places me in possession, all of which I expect from the charity and justice of your excellency, and I swear by God, our Father, and the sign of the most holy cross, that my petition is not made in malice, but of absolute necessity, and whatever may be necessary, &c.
PEDRO SANCHEZ. [Rubric.]

In the city of Santa Fé, on the twentieth day of the month of March, in the year one thousand seven hundred and forty-two, I, Don Gaspar Domingo de Mendoza, lieutenant colonel, governor and captain general of this kingdom of New Mexico, having seen the present petition of the person whose name is signed on the reversed side, considered it as presented, and in view thereof, I should order, and did order, that the lands asked for be granted to him, in the name of the King, our sovereign, in order that he may settle upon, cultivate, and improve it, for himself, his children, heirs, and successors, according to right, and this grant is understood to be made without injury to any other third party, and which he will settle within the period prescribed by the royal laws, and I direct the senior justice of the jurisdiction of Cañada to give him possession, observing in his proceedings the forms used in similar cases. I have so ordered, directed, and signed, with my attending witnesses, in the well-known absence of a royal or public notary in this vicinity, and on the present paper, in the absence of stamped.
DON GASPAR DOMINGO DE MENDOZA. [Rubric.]
JOSÉ DE TERRUS. [Rubric.]
JOSÉ TRUJILLO. [Rubric.]

POSSESSION.

On the twenty-eighth day of the month of March, in the year one thousand seven hundred and forty-two, I, Lieutenant Juan Joseph Lovato, senior justice and acting war captain of this jurisdiction of the new town of Santa Cruz, &c., by virtue of the above order, issued by his excellency Don Gaspar Domingo de Mendoza, governor and captain general, I proceeded to the land granted by his excellency to Captain Pedro Sanchez by royal grant, and, in order to give him possession without injury to any third party, I considered that I should order, and did order, the principal Indians of the pueblo of San Ildefonso, and, having no deeds to the lands they hold on the side called for by the boundary of Captain Pedro Sanchez, however, in order that no obstacle or dispute should arise in the future with these Indians, I extended their lands beyond those which they cultivate, so as to include that which they considered to be the best, in order that they might increase their crops, and, by the common consent of the aforenamed, a holy cross was erected, to serve as the southern boundary of said Indians and the northern boundary of said Captain Pedro Sanchez, and, taking said Indians and those in my attendance as witnesses, I gave Captain Pedro Sanchez royal possession of said land, with the customary solemnities, within the boundaries set forth in his petition, to which reference is made, and in order that it may so appear, I signed, with those in my attendance, acting by appointment, in the well-known absence of a public or royal notary, and on the present paper, there being none of the stamped in this vicinity, to all which I certify, and done in the month and year first above mentioned.

JUAN JOSEPH LOVATO, [Rubric.]
Acting Judge.

Attending:
JOSEPH QUINTANA, [Rubric.]
JUAN GARCIA DE MORA. [Rubric.]

SURVEYOR GENERAL'S OFFICE, TRANSLATOR'S DEPARTMENT,
Santa Fé, New Mexico, September 20, 1859.

The foregoing is a correct translation of the original on file in this office.

DAVID V. WHITING, *Translator.*

SURVEYOR GENERAL'S OFFICE,
Santa Fé, New Mexico, August 25, 1859.

The foregoing is a true copy of the original on file in this office.

WILLIAM PELHAM,
Surveyor General.

REPORT.

RAMON VIGIL *vs.* THE UNITED STATES.

This case was set for trial on the 13th of July, 1859.

Pedro Sanchez, a resident of Santa Cruz de la Cañada, made application to Don Gaspar Domingo de Mendoza for a tract of land in what is now the county of Rio Arriba, and contained within the boundaries therein mentioned. On the 20th day of March, 1742, Governor Mendoza granted him the land asked for, and ordered the chief justice of the jurisdiction of Cañada to place him in possession, which was done on the 28th day of the same month.

The claimant, although he refers to other documents in his petition, [i]s never filed them, and consequently can show no transfer of title [fr]om the original grantee to himself.

The grant referred to above, and acted upon by this office, is the [or]iginal filed by the claimants, and is believed to be genuine.

The case has been advertised. The parties are and have been in [qu]iet and peaceable possession of the land from time immemorial. It [is] therefore deemed to be a good and valid one, and is approved to the [leg]al representatives of Pedro Sanchez, and is ordered to be trans[mi]tted to Congress for its action in the premises.

WM. PELHAM,
Surveyor General.

SURVEYOR GENERAL'S OFFICE,
    Santa Fé, New Mexico, July 15, 1859.

SURVEYOR GENERAL'S OFFICE,
Santa Fé, New Mexico, September 10, 1859.

The foregoing is a true copy of the original on file in this office.

WM. PELHAM,
Surveyor General.

www.ingramcontent.com/pod-product-compliance
Lightning Source LLC
Chambersburg PA
CBHW070731160426
43192CB00009B/1393